THE UNION GAME

A RUGBY HISTORY

THE UNION

GAME
A RUGBY HISTORY

SEAN SMITH

This book is published to accompany the BBC Television series *The Union Game,* which was first broadcast in 1999.

Producer and Director: Dafydd Llŷr James
Series Writer: Dai Smith
Series Consultant: Gareth Williams

Published by
BBC Worldwide Ltd,
Woodlands,
80 Wood Lane,
London W12 0TT

First published 1999
© Sean Smith 1999
The moral right of the author has been asserted.

ISBN 0 563 55118 6

Commissioning Editor: Ben Dunn
Project Editor: Sally Potter
Art Director: John Calvert
Designer: Norma Martin
Picture Researchers: Matt Corrall and David Cottingham

Text set in Bell Gothic
Printed and bound in France by
Imprimerie Pollina s.a.
Colour origination by Imprimerie Pollina s.a.
Jacket printed in France by Imprimerie Pollina s.a.

CONTENTS

ACKNOWLEDGEMENTS

This book could not have been written without the enthusiasm and expertise of everyone at BBC Wales who put together the excellent and thought-provoking television series *The Union Game*. Thanks are due to Dafydd Llŷr James, Marc Evans, Phil George, Tom Adams and Dai Smith. I must give a special mention to Derwena Thomas for her tireless work and good humour acting as liaison between author and programme.

At BBC Books Ben Dunn and Sally Potter gave me great encouragement and support. I am also grateful to Gareth Williams for his work on the original television scripts, to Garth Gibbs for his research in London and to Zoë Lawrence for her help with the manuscript.

Finally I would like to thank the many players and devotees of rugby who gave their time to talk about the game they love.

INTRODUCTION

Early autumn in 1963. The air at Oxford University's Iffley Road ground was still and cold, chilling the crowd of duffel-coated undergraduates. We waited behind the ropes until they ran on, their black jerseys sombre rectangles against the pale English sky. God, they were big! These were the All Blacks – Wilson Whineray's New Zealanders. In this first match of their tour they were relentlessly, powerfully unforgiving, just as my grandfather had often told me they were over the years. Three months later, on a much colder late December day, they would become the first All Blacks ever to beat Wales in an official international at Cardiff Arms Park. On the ground where the very first All Blacks had lost to Wales by 3–0 points in the only match they conceded during their magnificent 1905 tour, their successors now won by a margin of 6–0. My grandfather had witnessed the first encounter when he was 18 years old. Now I, at the same age, saw the sides meet again in 1963. It was the Union game at its best.

As a young collier in the booming Rhondda Valley, my grandfather had been part of the generation who remade their country as modern Wales. Rugby football, a sport in which these new Welsh could be judged in an international arena, would, from 1905 onwards, be a touchstone of their national identity. For another small country on the opposite of the globe, with a comparable population but with an economy and culture based on agriculture rather than industry, 1905 was just as much a test of national worth. That sole defeat by Wales on December 16 made 1905 an unforgettable year for New Zealand too.

In retrospect it is clear that the cultural significance of rugby in a place such as the post-war Wales of my youth was bred in the population by some form of communal osmosis. You just knew, somehow, who the defining rivals really were. The 'Invincibles', the wondrous All Blacks of 1924, had avenged the 1905 defeat with a 19–0-point spanking at Swansea, but that was at St Helens, not the sacred Arms Park, where we overturned them by 13–12 points in 1935 and 13–8 in 1953. My grandfather knew all the players' names, all the moves and exactly who stood next to him in the crowd; and in 1953, Gareth Griffiths, one of the red-jerseyed heroes was even a teacher of mine in primary school. I knew then what I was waiting to see in October 1963 and why I was filled with awe and admiration for the sinuous power of Waka Nathan, the indomitable force of Colin Meads in the forwards and the darting grace of Mac Herewini in the backs.

The subsequent string of Welsh defeats at All Black hands since that date has acted not only as a complete deflater of overweening sporting egos, but also as an utter, maybe salutary, dampener on the memories and traditions of a nation which has changed so much since 1980. Wales is not alone in that respect. The truth is that, win or lose, there are some countries and some people whose overall social history cannot be fully told without recounting their relationship with rugby. That is why I believe the four films BBC Wales has made for BBC2 and this accompanying book possess a worldwide resonance.

Standing with me on that Iffley Road touch-line in 1963 was my old schoolfriend Gareth Williams. For the third match of the same All Blacks tour on a wet October day, we huddled together around a crackling radio in Balliol College, Oxford, to listen to the commentary from Wales as Whineray's team went down to their only defeat, 3–0 to the black-and-ambers of Newport. The shared experience of many matches was what enabled us in 1980 to write the official history of Welsh rugby, *Fields of Praise*, an early attempt to stitch social history and sporting activity into a whole. A proposal to do something similar on world rugby for BBC2 was first put forward by BBC Wales in 1994. After various revisions, the project was given the go-ahead in 1996.

The first name on the team sheet, as historical consultant and contributor, was Gareth Williams. Our executive producer was Phil George, head of arts, music and features at BBC Wales, and John Geraint was head of production. We quickly resolved the crucial task of finding a producer with the qualities of long-term commitment to the subject and lyrical engagement with the game sufficient to sustain the film-maker on his global odyssey and return to the prison of Norman Gettings' editing suite in Cardiff. He would also have the little task of briefing, supervising and then reining in the scriptwriter, yours truly. The man who met all these requirements was Dafydd Llŷr James: in the most essential sense the films are his.

Dafydd, armed with concepts and arguments that were fiercely detailed but still in development, flew out of Wales, clutching his research files and shooting scripts, to film the contemporary locations where our story unfolded and where our interviewees waited in South Africa, New Zealand, Australia and France, then home to the British Isles itself. These countries, the giants of world rugby for most of this century, were the key components of the game plan. We decided, after much discussion, that it would be impossible in four 50-minute films to include every rugby-playing country or deal with all aspects of the game's social history. We had to be selective to be convincing. The burden of proof would lie in the brilliant analysis provided by an array of respected sports historians. Theirs would be the incisive reflections based on hard research already done. They were the ones who could place rugby within its formative context. These witnesses proved to be the enlightening chorus to our four-act drama. Rugby football is indeed fortunate that in the past ten years it has been in the forefront of an intellectual revolution in the field of sports history. It has enabled us to demystify the enigma of sporting glory and national identification.

Around the world rugby has had certain desirable qualities that particular societies, or segments of them, have wished to possess as their own, and often on an exclusive basis. These qualities began on the field of play, where the variety of the game attracted all shapes and sizes, degrees of skill, elements of strength, moments of static struggle, passages of pure release, tension and joy, physicality and athleticism. It already embodied all these things by the 1890s when its ragbag origins in pre-industrial folk football and in the esoteric confines of public schools had given way to the recognizable modern game of winning possession and running in tries. How it was developed and utilized, who seized it for their own, and why amateurism was not a passing piece of idealism but a core value in Rugby Union became our story.

Each film, like each chapter in this book, examines a key aspect of rugby's history. The first, *The Class Game*, looks at the battle for ownership of the game between the middle classes, who saw it as peculiarly their own in origin and tradition, and the working classes who regarded it as an expression of their own solidarity. We go on to examine the breakaway of the Northern Union (later Rugby League); the Scottish divide between the public-school educated and the farmers of the rugged border country; the unique position of rugby in Ireland, where it is the only major sport that unites the troubled North and South; and finally Wales, where late industrial expansion enabled an invigorated working class to claim the game for a nation reborn.

As in Wales, rugby in New Zealand provided a blossoming nation with a voice on the international stage. In the second film, *The Empire Game*, we monitor the development of the game in both New Zealand and South Africa and reveal how politics became inextricably involved, allowing the spectre of racism to wield unwelcome influence in both countries. When President Mandela wore the Springbok jersey for the 1995 World Cup Final, played between his new South Africa and the first official world champions, New Zealand, a picture really did say more than words.

For our third film, *The Adopted Game*, we looked to France to show how rugby was a game that could take root away from its British Imperial heritage. France provided a fascinating story of conflict and pride, an often turbulent ride from international ostracism because of violent play through the domestic civil war of the Vichy period to its position as national standard-bearer under the astute General de Gaulle. The adopted had become the native son, unchallenged as France's team game until the wonderful multi-ethnic French soccer team took their own World Cup in Paris in 1998.

In the last of our four films, *The New Game*, this time led by directors Marc Evans and Dave Simmonds, we posed the questions brought to mind by the inevitable changes in the sport during the last decade, particularly the roles of amateurism and professionalism in rugby's future. We travelled to Australia to discover how changes set in motion there – historically a most unlikely venue – led unswervingly to media involvement in big-time sport worldwide. With player power bellowing in their ears, the northern hemisphere unions have followed their southern counterpart's lead. We peek inside Pandora's box.

Rugby is not alone in its social significance: cricket in the West Indies, soccer in Italy and baseball in the USA are also examples of where a particular sport can, over time, be not only popular but also representative of people's (there is no other word for it) soul. We set out, therefore, to dissect the bodies of our chosen countries to see if we could release a spirit. It has to be said that some of the blind identification we encountered to this great sport reveals that the soul can indeed be bartered and show a spirit malign. On the other hand, we can also assert that the use of the sport for narrow ends is ultimately self-defeating. The game invariably measures its meaner users by values and passions greater and grander than the iniquities and compromises of life. It is, after all, an art.

Early autumn 2016. The air is cold and still, and thousands of us are standing at the Merlin end of the Sardis Road ground, waiting for our beloved club, Pontypridd, to appear for the quarter-final of the European Cup against the French champions, Dax. My grandson, aged 18, is proud as I introduce him to his father's contemporary and hero, Wales's record points scorer, the 45-year-old Neil Jenkins. Jenkins is long retired from the golden summer of his career with Auckland, where he had accompanied coach Graham Henry after they had together won the 2003 World Cup for Wales. But as Jenks smiles his crooked grin and the crowd shyly parts to let him through, I see again a splay-legged, ginger-haired youngster back from the upright ball, wipe his right boot on his left calf, stand preternaturally still, jerkily swipe a left hand down his number 10 jersey, loosen the digits of his right by shaking them, turn his palm forwards to usher an imaginary ball between the uprights, and then, running up, boot it unerringly between the sticks. A grandfather smiles to himself at a remembered ritual and whispers in his grandson's ear. A new Union game.

Dai Smith

Head of Broadcast (English Language), BBC Wales and scriptwriter of the BBC Television series The Union Game

THE CLASS GAME

THE BATTLE FOR OWNERSHIP
OF BRITISH RUGBY

Rugby is a sport bedevilled through its history by class conflict. No other game has been claimed as such a valuable possession by a middle class who saw it as an emblem of their status. To the controllers of the game in England it was as important a symbol of their class as an old school tie or a glass of vintage port. In a brilliant piece of public relations the middle class claimed ownership of the game by inventing the myth of William Webb Ellis picking up the ball at Rugby School and running with it as if he had been Archimedes in the bath shouting 'Eureka'.

The threat of professionalism was perceived as a working-class plot to take over the game and its defeat led to a breakaway in the north of England and eventually to Rugby League. Arthur Budd, one-time president of the Rugby Football Union (1888–89), once declared that the troubles of Rugby Union began when the working man took up the game. Desperately the game's rulers have clung to the ideals of Victorian gentlemen, condemning the game in England to a century as an élite pursuit. Only Wales stood up to this exclusivity and managed to turn rugby into its national game – but not without a struggle.

EARLY POSSESSION
AND THE BIG BANG THEORY

Claiming the William Webb Ellis trophy is now the pinnacle of achievement in the rugby world. Three captains – David Kirk of New Zealand, Nick Farr-Jones of Australia and South Africa's François Pienaar – have kissed and embraced the cup named after the pupil at Rugby School who, in the best traditions of comic strip heroism, caught the ball and ran with it in 1823. At least, that is what the public-school influences controlling Rugby Union wanted everyone to believe when they literally etched the name of Webb Ellis in stone in 1900. The Webb Ellis myth was assured when they set a commemorative plaque in the Headmaster's Wall in the Close at Rugby School.

It was a master stroke by a public-school élite anxious to confirm possession of a game which, during the 1890s, had been split in two in England by the breakaway of northern clubs seeking payments for players. By creating the myth of Webb Ellis, the controllers of the game were in effect saying that this is our game, we invented it and you can't have it. It was a classic case of invented tradition, described by rugby historian Gareth Williams as displaying a 'fine disregard for the rules of evidence'. It reinforced a class structure in the game in England that has been challenged only in recent times through the all-powerful influence of money and professionalism. There is precious little room now for Will Carling's 'old farts', as he so memorably described rugby's administrators, in a world where big business has seized control of much of the sport.

On 20 September 1893 the old farts of their day successfully defeated a motion to permit payment for broken time – lost working hours – by 282 votes to 136, thus leading directly to the breakaway in the North. By so doing, they sentenced 'their' game to a century in a class jail. Seven years later Webb Ellis became the 'great man' of rugby. In truth credit should probably go to some anonymous Roman centurion, creator of the ancient game of *harpastum*. Then again, the Romans almost certainly stole the idea from the Greeks, as *harpastum* is derived from a Greek word meaning 'to snatch'. *Harpastum* was a sort of organized mêlée in which two sets of players endeavoured to catch a ball and to be the first to carry it over goal-lines marked at either end of the playing surface. It was encouraged by Roman commanders as a way of keeping their men fit and primed for fighting.

A host of exuberant ball games around Britain, all of a violent and anarchic nature, can also lay claim to possessing at least some of the characteristics of the game that emerged in Victorian England. There were many regional variations of this 'folk football' but most of them involved a combination of kicking and handling. In Cornwall, for instance, they played a game known as 'hurling over country', where village would take on village and some form of ball was transported by literally any means and by an unlimited number of players between goals that were miles apart. It bore more resemblance to a battle than a sport. In ancient Wales they played *cnapan*, a game of great danger to life and limb. It was a holiday or feast-day free-for-all in which a small ball was carried or thrown by hand, with sometimes 2000 or more people taking part. Woe betide anyone caught in possession. He was obliged to throw it when others demanded it. If he failed to do so by the third time of asking, he was set upon by the mob and beaten senseless with sticks and bare knuckles – not too dissimilar from a latter day full-back being caught by the opposition's front-row forwards.

Even in Victorian times, rugby was a physical game – not for the faint-hearted

Springbok captain François Pienaar joyfully lifts the Rugby World Cup – the William Webb Ellis trophy – after South Africa's triumph in 1995

In the early decades of the 19th century pupils at public schools in England played their own variation of the ball game. Far from inventing, they were merely adapting the traditional forms of folk football played at fairs and festivals into games they could play within the confines of their school. The form these games took was often dependent on what area of ground they had at their disposal for recreation. Games were being adopted in public schools as a relatively safe way of allowing the boys to let off steam and to make men of them. The Eton Wall Game was played on a long strip of land adjoining a high wall. At Rugby there was a 'wide-open grass playground of ample proportions' ideal for the game that would bear the school's name. Victorian author Sir Montague Shearman wrote, 'No school but Rugby played the old style of game where every player was allowed to pick up the ball and run with it, and every adversary could stop him by collaring, hacking over and charging or any other means he pleased.' Hacking, an important part of the early game, is best defined as 'using the toe either in kicking the shins of an opposing player or tripping him up'.

Far more deserving of credit in the growth of rugby than William Webb Ellis is the school's most famous headmaster, Dr Thomas Arnold (1828–42), whose advanced ideas about education set an example that the rest of Victorian England followed. He was perceived as some sort of saviour of the English public-school system, which was having huge problems dealing with the rowdy, undisciplined children of the upper-middle class, who resented being taught by schoolmasters of a lower class. In fact, many contemporaries of Webb Ellis were expelled from Rugby in 1821 after a rebellion at the school. Arnold set about making religion the centre of the school, and having all other activities revolve around it. He displayed no great interest in rugby himself, but he allowed the boys to indulge in it. The chapel and sport together gave rise to 'muscular Christianity'. Rugby School under Arnold's leadership became the successful role model for other schools of the age. Author Tim Chandler explains the ingredients: 'Arnold's Rugby had a headmaster who was the senior chaplain, a chapel and a wonderful game called Rugby football, which was a good way of keeping boys amused.'

Rugby football was a manly game, a muscular activity of guts and glory that captured the expectations of upper-middle-class men of the age. The game around this time was nothing short of licensed thuggery, with the appalling practice of hacking at its core. Boys even wore steel tips to their boots as they hacked at opponents trying to run through their

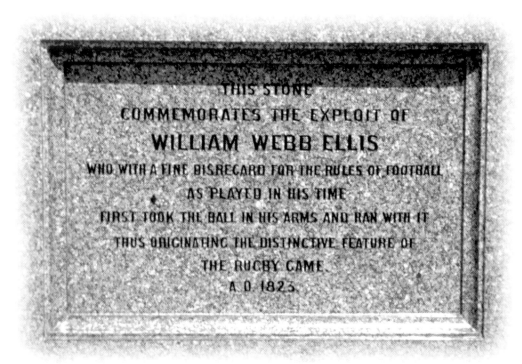

The famous plaque at Rugby School, which assured William Webb Ellis a place in history

lines. The violence was so bad that a pupil at Rugby died as a result of his injuries. It is rather ironic that Matthew Arnold, son of the famous headmaster and one of the most famous poets of his age, abhorred physical violence and any form of sport. Certainly, Arnold senior's attitude to his school's game was toleration rather than enthusiasm.

Old boys of Rugby School were proud of their game and of their school's success, and when they left to become respected members of Victorian society – many as headmasters – they took their game with them. Members of their own class adopted rugby with enthusiasm. New schools mushroomed to meet the growing demand from the new factory owners, manufacturers and managers of industrial England, who harboured middle-class aspirations and wanted a public-school education for their children. They recognized that handling the ball separated their game from the sport of the streets. Rugby was similar to a Masonic handshake, an unspoken device for networking. It was also famously publicized by Thomas Hughes in *Tom Brown's Schooldays*, one of the most popular books of the age. Published in 1858, the book is a classic account of Hughes' own schooldays at Rugby in the 1830s. Although he attended the school just nine years after William Webb Ellis is supposed to have transformed the game at a stroke, there is no mention of Webb Ellis in the book. There is, however, a thrilling account of a rugby match.

Author and historian, Tony Collins, explains the influence of the book: 'It was a runaway bestseller. Not only was it a good read, but it gave an ideology to middle-class leisure. It was about having a healthy mind in a healthy body. When you played the game, it meant that you were getting not only physical exercise but also some of the culture of Rugby School itself. Some of the muscular Christianity rubbed off – even if you did not have the status of actually being an Old Rugbeian.'

A WEBB OF INTRIGUE

William Webb Ellis knew nothing about his rise to fame. His canonization as the inventor of rugby came after his death in 1872. It wasn't his fault that he was unable to say in person whether he had been responsible for a change in the playing practices at his old school. Rugby football certainly played little or no part in his life after he left. He might have run with the ball against the acknowledged rules of the time. He might have been the only boy who did this, or one of several. It's often the case that a schoolboy who cheats or bends the rules of a particular game does so because he is either useless at playing it or considers it stupid. However Webb Ellis chose to play his school's game, it was probably little more than bravado. As a senior boy he was bigger and older than most of the opposition, so why not take advantage of that? He was, according to a contemporary, 'an admirable cricketer'.

Ellis is first mentioned as the pioneer of the handling game in 1876, four years after his death, by a former pupil of Rugby called Matthew Bloxam, an

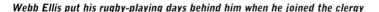

Webb Ellis put his rugby-playing days behind him when he joined the clergy

antiquarian and solicitor who still lived close to the school. He wrote to the *Meteor*, the Rugby School magazine, that he had ascertained that the change from a kicking game to a handling game was 'originated with a Town boy or foundationer of the name of Ellis, William Webb Ellis'. Bloxam had left the school in 1821 when the game was still exclusively a kicking game, but his assertion that Webb Ellis was the boy who changed it is only second-hand. He was not an eyewitness – none ever came forward. Three years later, Bloxam was expanding his theory about Webb Ellis in the same magazine. The agreed rule at the time was that when you caught the ball it was similar to a modern-day mark. You could go back as far as you liked and either punt the ball or place it for someone else to kick. 'Ellis,' wrote Bloxam, 'disregarded this rule and, on catching the ball, instead of retiring backwards, rushed forwards with the ball in his hands towards the opposite goal with what result as to the game I know not.' Bloxam actually knew very little, and yet from this acorn of evidence a legendary oak was born.

In 1895 the Northern Union was formed, effectively splitting rugby down the middle.

The playing fields of Rugby School, where pioneers learnt the Union game before introducing it to outposts of the Empire

The same year the Old Rugbeian Society set up a committee to investigate the origins of the game at the school and began canvassing old boys to see if they could substantiate Bloxam's account of the birth of Rugby football. Only one former pupil, a Thomas Harris, could remember Webb Ellis at all: 'He was an admirable cricketer but was generally regarded as inclined to take unfair advantages at football.' And that is really all there is to justify Webb Ellis as the great man of rugby. If handling the ball had been a criminal offence and Webb Ellis had been on trial, he would have been acquitted. In fact, so weak was the evidence that the matter would never have come to court. Instead, the men of the Old Rugbeian Society chose to believe the Webb Ellis story and erected the nonsensical plaque commemorating his exploit. Author and Rugby School archivist Jennifer Macrory commented, 'The popular history of Rugby football was written in 1900 quite literally in a tablet of stone. The report of the committee carefully noting the *gradual* acceptance of the carrying game was forgotten and the "big bang" story was born.'

Webb Ellis left Rugby in 1825 bound for Brasenose College, Oxford. He took Holy Orders before becoming the incumbent of St Clement's Dane Church in the Strand. He died in France on 24 January 1872, never having, so far as we know, picked up a rugby ball from the time he left school to the day he died. It is ironic that while so many pupils of Rugby School had so much to do with the growth and administration of the game, the 'founder', by most accounts an unpopular boy, contributed very little. The beauty of Webb Ellis as an historical tool for the élitist controllers of rugby was that, while it is nearly impossible to prove that he invented rugby in its modern form, it is absolutely impossible to prove that he didn't. Webb Ellis served a purpose well.

A QUESTION OF CLASS

The paraphernalia of rugby knows no bounds as its participants over the years have tried to perpetuate the idea that it is some sort of all-embracing gentleman's club. This is a nonsense, of course, but one that the middle-class public-school boys of Victorian England were anxious to cling on to. They promoted this notion by the wearing of ties, scarves, caps or blazers in club colours. And don't forget badges – there's always a badge to confer some imagined status on the wearer. 'Club' members didn't mind showing their game to the

BARBARIANS 23 – NEW ZEALAND 11
CARDIFF ARMS PARK
27 JANUARY 1973

If William Webb Ellis had done what Phil Bennett audaciously achieved after two minutes of this most glorious of games, he might have justified his status of the 'great man' of rugby. Bennett fielded a long, probing kick from All Black Bryan Williams deep in his own half. He had time to gather himself and loop one of his distance-eating punts safely into touch, but he chose not to. Instead, he chose to run with the ball. With All Black forward Alistair Scown bearing down on him, the dapper Welshman feinted to his right and

with the grace of a ballet dancer swerved to his left. Another mesmerizing dummy and the All Blacks attackers were left clutching at thin air as Bennett forged towards the left-hand touch-line. The rampaging J.P.R. Williams was at his shoulder and powered forward before passing to English hooker John Pullin, who galloped on to half-way. The immaculate, unruffled John Dawes took the ball and still the All Blacks were in disarray. Tom David, the swashbuckling Welsh flanker, received the ball and, with

Tom David (left) about to take the pass from Barbarian's skipper John Dawes. John Pullin is in support but, lurking a few yards behind is the great Gareth Edwards, poised to score one of the finest of tries

a one-handed pass, moved it on to Derek Quinnell. Surely now the mighty All Blacks would bring the move shudderingly to a halt, but no, 40 yards out, sprinting outside Quinnell came the legendary Gareth Edwards, ears pinned back like a cavalry horse charging towards enemy lines. A thousand men would not have prevented Edwards diving over in the corner for rugby's most famous try.

The celebrity of this wonderful try, and the 80 minutes of champagne rugby that followed, owes much to the power of television. As author T.P. McLean described it, 'Whether the try was the greatest ever, as is still contended, is unimportant. Simply, it was perfection.' Here was a rugby moment that deserved to be set in stone. It was a triumphant vindication of Barbarian matches, a that had begun in 1890 when the club was formed by Percy Carpmael, who rejoiced in the nickname of 'Tottie'. He had been part of a London invitation team enjoying a tour of the North. After a late and agreeable dinner in Bradford, he decided that these end-of-season jaunts should become a regular fixture, and the Barbarians were born.

An overseas team's last match against the Barbarians, or Baa-Baas, as they were nicknamed, while keenly fought, was traditionally a joyous occasion – the dancing after the formalities of

internationals were completed. The 1970s were not a golden age for the All Blacks. Barry John, Gareth Edwards and David Duckham were among the heroes of the 1971 series-winning British Lions. The All Blacks tour of 1972/3 was a public-relations disaster and the tourists were possibly the least popular team from New Zealand ever to visit Britain.

The most famous story of the tour was the expulsion of Keith Murdoch, a massive front-row forward and a popular player with his team-mates. He was sent home – the ultimate indignity for an international sportsman – for punching a Welsh security guard after a row in his hotel. The full circumstances of his humiliating dismissal from the tour are still shrouded in mystery all these years later. Many New Zealanders believe that the four home unions might have played a part in demanding his departure. The All Black captain, Ian Kirkpatrick, said at the time, 'The home unions wanted Keith out. It was a bad business. The fellers all liked Keith.' Murdoch has become one of rugby's tragic figures. On his way back home, he left his plane at Darwin in Australia and disappeared from view for 16 years, until a television crew found him driving a bulldozer on a north Queensland banana farm.

Despite the volatile off-field situation, Kirkpatrick's men had proved *themselves formidable opponents, beating Wales 19–16, Scotland 14–9 and England 9–0 before drawing a titanic Grand Slam match against Ireland 10 points all. Without the tenacious and talented contribution from the All Blacks, the game against the Barbarians would never have achieved such legendary status that still sees it plucked from the shelves of video stores by nostalgia-filled rugby fans. Although the Baa-Baas cut across national boundaries in their famous black-and-white hooped jerseys, this was very much a Welsh occasion, marking the swan-song of John Dawes, masterful captain of his country and the British Lions. The flair and majesty of the great Welsh players of the time was so much in evidence that Englishman David Duckham, the most thrilling runner in world rugby, was re-christened Dai for the day by the jubilant crowd who chanted 'Wales! Wales!' at half-time.*

By the interval, the Baa-Baas led 17–0 against a team hampered by playing an unfit Sid Going, who was clearly carrying a leg injury that would eventually lead to his early departure. Fergus Slattery and John Bevan added to Edwards' try with Bennett managing a conversion and a penalty. The Baa-Baas appeared to have at least 20 players on the pitch as they swept the ball imperiously from one side of the field to the other. Duckham, his

blond hair flowing behind him like a Nordic warrior, sped past flailing All Blacks as if they were rabbits transfixed by a car's headlights. Somehow, after the interval, the visitors clawed their way back into the game, first with a penalty from full-back Joe Karam, and then with a blistering try from Grant Batty after his opposite wing, Bryan Williams, had left the great Mike Gibson for dead with a blind-side break. Then the wild-haired Batty, looking like a refugee from a rock band, chipped a little kick over the head of J.P.R. Williams and touched down for the simplest of tries. At 17–11 the match was, to say the least, getting interesting.

Once more Duckham raced through All Black ranks to find Mike Gibson popping up for the pass. And there was J.P.R. Williams hauling himself up from full-back for one final breath-sucking attack. The pass was scored, J.P.R. sold the All Black defence an outrageous dummy and the try was scored. This was not an epic match but a classic game and the result, 23–11, was irrelevant, although don't tell that to the Welsh crowd, who undoubtedly saw it as a home win.

Boys at Rugby School run on to the pitch to take part in the 1991 World Cup Opening Ceremony

working classes, or even instructing them on its finer points. Rather like those who colonized the Empire overseas, they were keen to show the natives a British game that they could imitate and thereby improve themselves. There is only one golden rule in such an arrangement. The pupils must never beat the master.

In the 1830s and 1840s the working classes had little time for rugby or, indeed, for leisure of any kind. The growing demands of industrialization consigned the working classes to working 12-hour days, six days a week. Urbanization was taking up the old green spaces, and it would not be until rugby had gained a firm footing throughout the country as a middle-class activity that working men discovered it. The middle classes had a free reign at developing the game along the lines they wanted and were jolly pleased with themselves for doing so. In the late 1830s Arthur Pell, a former pupil of Rugby School, introduced the game to Cambridge. Along with other Old Rugbeians, he founded the first club at King's College. There were problems initially because it became clear that different

The early game: a painting of the first Yorkshire Cup Final in 1877 (Halifax v York)

schools were playing to different rules. Sides would gather at Cambridge and have little clue as to the rules of engagement. When Pell's Old Rugbeians played a team of Old Etonians in 1840, all hell broke loose when the Rugby men started handling the ball, a totally alien concept on the playing fields of Berkshire.

Clearly, an agreed, universal set of rules would need to be devised – universal, that is, if your world began and ended at Rugby and Cambridge. Over the following 20 years a set of laws did, indeed, evolve, culminating in the Cambridge rules of 1848. There were four main rules: 1. A player may be hacked on the front of the leg below the knee while running with the ball. 2. A player may run with the ball in his hands if he makes a fair catch or catches the ball on the first bound. 3. Tripping shall not be allowed except when running with the ball. 4. A player may be held while running with the ball.

Another set of rules published in 1863 by the Blackheath Football Club in London, one of the earliest and most influential London clubs, included the priceless direction: 'Though it is lawful to hold a player in a scrummage, this does not include attempts to throttle or strangle, which are totally opposed to the principles of the game.'

These principles seemed designed to take much of the violence out of rugby, particularly the practice of hacking. The idea was allowed to develop that the middle classes had a code of ethics in which they played the game purely for enjoyment. Tony Collins believes, 'It is one of the big myths of sport in the 19th century. It is one of the great lies of all sport. When the middle classes played rugby they played it violently.' After the Rugby Football Union (RFU) was formed in 1871 to bring some sort of order to the nation-wide chaos, there were renegade teams of former public-school boys who arranged games between themselves that would allow hacking. The players would come off with their shins battered and bleeding. Middle-class players were also argumentative. There were no neutral referees at this early stage, so the two captains had to sort out disputes themselves. These arguments were generally won by the most bolshy of the two because the game would not continue until someone gave in. The idea that gentlemen were not interested in the result was also far from the truth, as these early games were often spoilt by blatant gamesmanship. The team that took the lead would often do everything it could to keep the ball out of play and thus prevent the opposition from getting possession. It would be kick after kick into touch – a practice many teams of the modern era have followed.

There was no great geographical divide in the development of rugby. It did not become working class just because it spread north of the River Trent. Clubs formed in the North of England were developing along the lines of those in the South, such as Blackheath and Richmond. Old boys of Rugby, Marlborough and lesser public schools were endorsing their social identity by playing a sport that was their property. They were maintaining a design for living, a Thomas Arnold blend of the physical and the spiritual – rugby as a game of body and soul. When these young men left school and went home to run the family business or enter a profession, the rugby club became one way of mixing with like-minded people of the same background. The early clubs in the North of England had a very high social standing. The first clubs were formed in the large conurbations of Liverpool and Manchester in 1857, but within ten years major towns, such as Hull, Leeds and Bradford, had followed suit.

In the early days in Liverpool, Old Rugbeians would organize games based on the alphabet: A to M would play N to Z. The early composition of Manchester FC was like a public schools' conference. Old boys of Rugby, Uppingham, Edinburgh Academy, Fettes and Manchester Grammar School, as well as those who had attended Oxford and Cambridge, ensured there was nothing cloth cap about their side. In the London area great clubs such as Blackheath and Richmond were very much a suburban phenomenon. But in the North the rugby team became a matter of civic pride, and towns such as Halifax, Huddersfield, Rochdale and Wakefield soon boasted their own clubs. This was a time in the third quarter of the century when a greater degree of prosperity was creeping into society. The middle classes had more leisure time and this was something that would soon permeate down to the working classes. Town halls were built, public parks opened and rugby clubs formed.

Hand in hand with this civic pride came publicity, a sense of showing off, and it was this inability to keep their game a secret that led to the middle classes giving the working men a look-in. At first the working classes didn't take to the game. On a public common in York, for example, the working-class people who gathered to indulge in a spot of rabbit coursing would stay on to watch the York Football Club train and play because it was an endless source of amusement to them. Here was a bunch of toffs – solicitors, doctors, bankers and the like – falling over in the mud and losing their front teeth.

Gradually, interest in the game spread as town took on town and county played county. Posters advertised fixtures and newspapers carried reports, so rugby matches became a focal point of conversation, much as any sport does today. A combination of three main factors accelerated the boom: the church, the workplace and, last but not least, the pub, which was then, as it has always been, the epicentre of working-class social life. The church, following on from the ideals of Arnold and his disciples, believed that rugby was a good pastime for their flock, so many teams were formed by church social clubs. The famous Wakefield Trinity Club is one that began in this way in 1873 and still exists today. Self-made men who owned the factories would see rugby as a way of encouraging a corporate identity for the workers – a team that plays hard together works hard together. Pubs also formed their own teams to take on other pubs, just as happens today with darts or quiz leagues. The game was beginning to slip from the grasp of the public-school élite.

Cup competitions made an enormous difference to the image of rugby. Nothing can thrill the public or capture its imagination like a high-octane cup competition, which is why the

World Cup in soccer, cricket and now rugby are so successful. Attendances in the North soared when the Yorkshire Challenge Cup began in 1871. Crowds that were normally no more than 1000 or so strong swelled to more than 10,000 to watch these cup matches. In 1891 a crowd of 23,000 watched the Roses match between Yorkshire and Lancashire. Supporting a team did wonders for community spirit. Cup-winners might not have had an open-topped double-decker from which to wave to their adoring fans, but they would be greeted by fireworks, torchlight processions and, of course, the local brass band.

While leaders of the South's newly formed Rugby Football Union were immersed in sorting out the rules and a coherent structure for the game – reducing the number of play-ers in a team from 20 to 15 in 1875, for instance – the men of the North were sweeping all before them. The physical strength gained from spending days down the mines or in fac-tories was giving working-class players an unpalatable edge. Yorkshire dominated the early County Championship competition, which began in 1888, winning seven of the first eight tournaments. Eleven of the English team that beat Wales in 1892 hailed from the North. A will to win, skills improved by the vigour of cup competition and sheer physical presence were an unbeatable combination. These Yorkshire sides in many ways conjured up the same formidable presence personified for so many years by the All Blacks of New Zealand.

Success in these cup competitions bred yet more success and greater public interest. It is a well-worn formula, just as true of Bath Rugby Club or Manchester United Football Club today as it was more than a century ago in Yorkshire. The popularity of the game was snowballing and more people wanted to watch or play. As Tony Collins observes, 'It took the cork out of the bottle and the working-class participation in rugby exploded.' In fact, at the time, rugby games were attracting far greater crowds than the FA Cup.

In the early days, a 'football club' such as Blackheath would be one that played rugby and not soccer

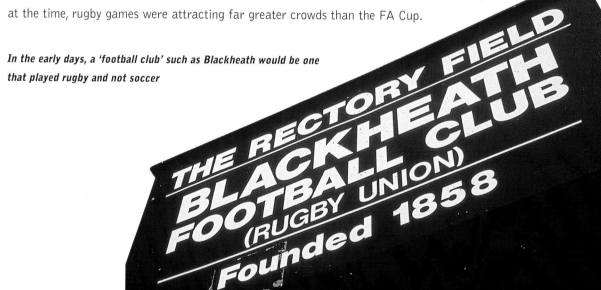

THE RUGBY INQUISITION

If the Reverend Frank Marshall were alive today, he would be a television star. Here was a minor figure but a major showman who saw himself at the centre of the rugby universe and set himself up as a one-man Spanish Inquisition, aiming to purge the game of those who sought to tarnish it by accepting rewards. A stocky, bearded figure, he refereed games

Rugby's first historian, Frank Marshall, was a stern Victorian whose vigorous defence of the amateur game made him deeply unpopular in the North

while smoking his customary cigar. He was a man of the grand gesture, who handed out cigars to all the players at the end of the England–Scotland match in 1892. Yet he was a man who loved rugby tradition as he perceived it. His rugby was the educational rugby, the Christian, muscular rugby that he practised at Almondsbury Grammar School, near Huddersfield, where he had become headmaster in 1878. His ability to organize and his enthusiasm for the game saw him rise up the official ranks until, in 1888, he became treasurer of the Yorkshire Rugby Union and then its president two years later. As the Yorkshire representative on the Rugby Football Union (RFU), he was at the forefront of opposition to broken-time payments (money to compensate for time off work) and actively investigated clubs thought to be abusing their amateur status.

Marshall was very unpopular in the North and local youths stoned his carriage after he investigated the neighbouring club of Elland. If Marshall and his cohorts heard gossip that a player was being paid, receiving gifts or a cushy job, they would haul him up before a special court of the committee to answer the charge of professionalism. The court consisted of Marshall and various prosperous and social-climbing industrialists who wanted to keep the workers in their place. The result was something akin to the communist witch-hunts of Senator McCarthy in the 1950s, except that these were no Hollywood figures. They were simple miners and labourers. One can easily imagine the self-important Marshall treating these working-class sportsmen as he did the naughty schoolboys sent to his study to be birched for impudence. Kangaroo courts continue to exist in all forms of sport, so-called governing bodies doing just as they please.

More and more money was creeping into the game in the North. Bumper crowds were boosting gate receipts and the players who provided the entertainment wanted payment for their services, especially when they were taking time off work to train or play matches. It was not a ground-breaking idea. Payments in working-class recreation were commonplace, especially if an event had been organized by the local pub, whether it was rugby, rabbit coursing or a game of quoits. The victors would receive a jug of ale or a leg of mutton. If the game was a Yorkshire Cup match, the winners might expect a new suit. Gradually, the market forces that apply in sport today turned the screw on rugby in late Victorian times. If a team wanted to stay at the top, it had to pay its best players, so the professional teams of the North were simply the best. The rugby chiefs were fearful that the new profession-alism of the 1880s might force rugby along the same path as soccer, which had consigned public schools and amateurs to obscurity. While the working man took over soccer, the dictators of rugby were desperately trying to maintain a middle-class grip on their game.

The idea of broken-time payments was a compromise, a half-way house to paper over the cracks in the sport. Those cracks were getting worse. When Frank Marshall took his place in the stand for a game at Manchester's Fallowfield ground, he was heckled by a spectator who shouted, 'If the Reverend Marshall sets foot in Oldham, he'll be shot.' To this the splendidly pompous Torquemada replied, 'I do not care twopence what my assailants say of me. I do not feel offended or hurt. The offence is rather to those persons who have the lawlessness and imbecility to utter such remarks.'

And so to the most crucial vote in the history of Rugby Union. On 20 September 1893 the motion by the Yorkshire Union to allow broken-time payments was defeated by 282 votes to 136 and was greeted with delirium by those who, like Marshall, wanted to preserve the gentlemanly status of the game. It would take two years for the northern clubs to offi-cially break away, but the deed was effectively done that afternoon at the Westminster Palace Hotel in London, a suitably middle-class location. The defeat came during a period of working-class unrest throughout the North of England. Two years earlier striking miners had set fire to the Pilkington Glass Factory in St Helens; in 1892 there was a five-month lock-out in the Lancashire cotton industry, and a year later a six-week strike at Hull Docks had even led to gunboats being stationed in the River Humber. Troops were called to Featherstone Colliery to deal with strikers, leaving two dead and several more wounded. Now it was the turn of rugby to enter this battle. Administrators referred to spectators in

The Northern Union proved very popular. A crowd of 29,569 saw Batley beat Warrington 6–0 in the Challenge Cup Final of 1901

Yorkshire as 'howling mobs' threatening the social harmony of their precious game.

Marshall continued his campaign. Huddersfield, Leeds, Wigan and Salford were all suspended in 1894. The following year the RFU threatened to introduce a rule whereby any club accused of being professional would be suspended, in other words guilty until proven innocent. Faced with that ultimatum, officials from 20 clubs met at the George Hotel, Huddersfield, on 29 August 1895 and formed the breakaway Northern Union. A broken-time payment of 6 shillings a day was fixed. It had been inevitable. Within three years the 20 had grown to 98. And as the popularity of what would become Rugby League grew, so Rugby Union and the triumphant middle class entered a slump. Yorkshire did not win the County Championship for 30 years, Lancashire for more than 40. England suffered too, not winning the International Championship for nearly 20 years. In 1893 there were 481 member clubs of the RFU, but by 1902 that had fallen to 244. Here was a classic case of a triumph at any cost incurring awful wounds and losses on the victors. It enabled Wales, who had kept out of the fight, to become the most powerful rugby nation.

The war that had divided Rugby Union in England was not about North against South or an issue involving payments. In 1895, the same year as the final break, W.G. Grace, the most famous cricketer in the land, received a second testimonial worth, in those days, a king's ransom of £9000. Yet the good doctor was an amateur. The issue in rugby was about payments to working-class players and was used as a means of driving them out of the game. Arthur Budd, a former president of the RFU, once said that its troubles began when the working man took up the game. Tony Collins confirms, 'The middle classes wanted total control over the football, nothing more and nothing less.'

During this period of spiralling misfortune, the William Webb Ellis myth was born, resulting in the plaque at Rugby School. In the context of what had happened to rugby in the past decade, it is almost a war memorial. For his part, Marshall is now best remembered as rugby's first historian. His love of the game resulted in *Football – the Rugby Game,* a history of Rugby Union up until 1892. He does not mention Webb Ellis once.

BORDERLINES:
THE SCOTTISH GAME

Within two months of the Rugby Football Union being formed in 1871, England took the field in the first international match against Scotland. The most pressing decision for this fledgling game was what to wear. The English chose all-white jerseys with a red rose insignia, still the basis for the strip today. The white shorts were so long, reaching well below the knee, that the players were able to tuck them into their dark brown stockings. They looked rather like cricketers playing a round of golf who, not wanting to get their kit dirty, tucked their whites into their socks. The Scottish team, in blue jerseys, actually wore cricket flannels tucked into their socks. Rugby has never had high sartorial standards.

The game had already been enthusiastically embraced north of the border and this mirrored the growth of the game in England (and Ireland) by gaining popularity in colleges, with sides such as Edinburgh University, Glasgow Academicals and St Andrews University leading the way. In fact, the Scottish side gave England a lesson in team-work and fitness, winning comfortably – in the days before the points system was established – by a goal and a try against a single try. The Scottish forwards were much faster on their feet than ponderous England, a state of affairs that has barely changed for over a century since. It was a match, 20 a side, full of controversy and incident, feeding the desire for more fixtures. A Scottish try was hotly contested by England but the referee, or the umpire, as he was then known, a headmaster called H.H. Almond, followed a rule that should find its way into all referees' instruction manuals. He declared afterwards, 'When an umpire is in doubt, I think he is justified in deciding against the side that makes the most noise. They are probably in the wrong.'

Scotland proved formidable opponents for England in these early years. The country also had a north-south divide of a sort. The former pupils of establishments such as Edinburgh Academy, Merchiston and Loretto – where the formidable Mr Almond was head and rugby was compulsory for all boys – dominated the Scottish Rugby Union when it was formed in 1873 and shunned the lower-class players from the Borders. Famous and prestigious clubs such as Hawick, Gala, Jedforest and Melrose were then second class and looked upon with a certain mistrust. In the rugged Border country the men who played were weavers, masons and farmers who, instead of using studs, would bar their boots with strips of leather from the local tweed mills. Despite their vigour and prowess at rugby, it would be 20 years before a Border player, Adam Dalgleish of Gala, was capped, and 30 years before one, T.M. Scott of Hawick, was made captain. In 1903 a Scottish referee of note, Crawford Findlay, encapsulated Scottish middle-class distrust for working-class involvement in the game when he expressed surprise that the Welsh selected miners, steelworkers and policemen for their international teams when such players belonged in the Northern Union. Clearly, the Northern Union was perceived as a dustbin for the undesirable lower elements of the game – the Rhondda miner, the Border farmer, the Yorkshire factory worker.

Broadcaster Bill McLaren, born and bred in Hawick in the 1920s and 1930s, remembers that Border players regarded the city gents as 'kind of soft'. The first-ever Edinburgh referee who went to the Borders to take charge of a match was asked on his return how it went: 'These people don't need a referee,' he declared. 'They need a missionary.' In the Borders rugby was part of the community to a far greater extent than in England. It was intrinsic to everyday life, just as it was in Welsh mining towns or remote districts of New Zealand. McLaren explains, 'There was never any class distinction down here. I remember the managing director of one of Hawick's leading firms used to play alongside his frame-maker. There was a kinship and you never thought that the other fellow might be your boss.

Bill McLaren, the voice of rugby for half a century, sets the scene for BBC Television

'If a Border player plays badly, he has to run the gauntlet on the Saturday night with everybody in the pub telling him how badly he did and then on the Monday morning the same thing happens at his workplace. The city gent plays badly, leaves the clubhouse and disappears into anonymity. Rugby was and is a religion up here.' In many ways the Borders mirrored the plight of Yorkshire in the English game. And just like the North, they loved the rivalry and spirit of cup competitions. The game in the Borders did not follow the North of England into rebellion and professionalism. Perhaps it might have done if in those days there had been more people than sheep to watch the games.

Perversely, considering how much the middle-class establishment of both England and Scotland abhorred cups, the most famous cup competition in Rugby Union was founded in 1878. 'Competition' is something of a misnomer because the Calcutta Cup has only ever been contested by England and Scotland. But it has always been fiercely fought and Bill McLaren, the great man of rugby broadcasting, rates the 1990 renewal as the most emotional game he has seen in more than 50 years of watching and commentating on rugby. Needless to say, the Calcutta Cup owed much of its existence to the enthusiasm of a group of old boys from Rugby School. They were stationed in India and started agitating for the formation of a rugby club in Calcutta. Although the Indian climate is not one that would normally catch the eye as suitable for rugby, the determination of the Old Rugbeians to get things moving resulted in a match on Christmas Day 1872 between the English ex-pats on one hand and the Scottish, Irish and Welsh on the other. Unfortunately, interest waned, and in 1877 the club folded. Members, however, were determined to mark its demise and it was decided to offer the Calcutta Cup to the Rugby Football Union back home. The suggestion beat off opposition from members who thought a gymkhana a more attractive prospect. The silver cup – made from actual silver rupees – is one of sport's most magnificent trophies, a fine example of Indian workmanship. Standing some 18 inches high, it has snake-shaped handles and a carefully modelled elephant on top of the lid. It speaks volumes for the traditions of class prejudice in England and Scotland that the two countries play every year for a trophy made in the Raj.

HUGH McLEOD:
BORDER GUARD

If ever a man personified the heart and soul of Border country, it was Hughie McLeod. Born and bred in Hawick, like his great friend Bill McLaren, he won a record 40 consecutive caps for Scotland. He was a straightforward, no-nonsense prop who served club and country well and who, you felt, would have little time for the niceties of public-school life. Although by today's standards not a particularly big front-row forward, weighing in at under 14 stone, he was as hard as a bag of nails. He took his sport very seriously indeed.

Unusually, McLeod did not play the game as a schoolboy, but came to it as a 17-year-old when he had already started work as an apprentice plasterer. He was a natural for the game, surprisingly mobile, uncompromising and brutally frank. He made his international début against France in 1954 and was never dropped over the next eight years, retiring at the premature age of 29 because 40 caps was a 'nice round figure'. Twice he was a British Lion – to South Africa in 1955 and to New Zealand in 1959. This was no golden age for Scottish rugby – no Grand Slam, no Triple Crown, not even a championship – but every time he took the field in his dark blue jersey, Hughie McLeod never gave less than 110 per cent for his country. His team-mates held him in the highest regard, and when he broke John Bannerman's record for Scottish caps, he was carried off the pitch shoulder high. It didn't hurt that he had just been part of a Scottish team recording a rare victory over Wales in Cardiff.

Bill McLaren recalls the story of when McLeod was made pack leader, a job he did not particularly want. At the Friday training session before the game he called his men round him for a pep talk: 'Now, ah want tae tell ee that ah've been asked ti lead this pack tomorrow, that ah'm no very keen on the job and if any of you lot want to be pack leader, just let me know and ah'll put in a word for you at the right place. Meanwhile, the next one who opens his trap will get my boot bloody hard at his arse.'

Typically for a Border man, Hugh McLeod, Scotland's record-breaking prop, never gave less than one hundred per cent for his beloved country

According to McLaren, an Anglo-Scottish player failed to pick up McLeod's Hawick tones. He told a team-mate, 'I didn't understand a word of it but it all sounded so damned impressive.' No wonder the pack played like demons the next day.

After his retirement, McLeod took his place as a much-respected member of the town of Hawick, rather in the way All Blacks became esteemed citizens in their own remote rural areas of New Zealand. Down Hawick High Street on a Monday morning old ladies of 75 or 80 will always be able to tell you how Hawick got on the previous Saturday. Everyone in Hawick loved their rugby.

Perhaps McLeod would have made a great All Black. A favourite story about him is told by author Keith Quinn. One day McLeod turned out for Hawick in a local game in which the opposition included a young upstart who was heard to declare boldly during the match,

SCOTLAND 13 – ENGLAND 7
MURRAYFIELD
17 MARCH 1990

This was a marvellous day to be Scottish. Some 53,000 Scots packing the Murrayfield stadium stood to join their 15 champions on the pitch to sing 'Flower of Scotland' and challenged England to take their pride away. It was rousing enough to have inspired Don

Quixote to pick up his lance and tilt at windmills. That is a fair description of the giant England pack the home team faced. Behind the scrum a back division that included Rob Andrew, Rory Underwood, Will Carling and Jeremy Guscott were on hand to rattle up the

Scottish full-back Gavin Hastings holds the ball for Craig Chalmers, whose immaculate kicking helped Scotland to an unlikely Grand Slam

was able to build up a crescendo of excitement. England, drilled and powerful, charged on to the pitch like the invincible gladiators many onlookers feared them to be. Next came the Scots led by prop David Sole. They marched on methodically and menacingly to a fanfare of cheers. The two teams were like heavyweight contenders vying for the best entrance to the ring. Scotland won hands down and Carling admitted afterwards that it was a masterstroke, giving the Scottish team a psychological edge they were not going to relinquish.

At the very first scrum the English front row conceded a silly penalty which set the tone for an afternoon of mistakes and petty infringements which cost the auld enemy dear. The dependable and calm Craig Chalmers had slotted home two penalties before England had threatened the Scottish line. But when the famed English backs changed gear, it was awe-inspiring and threatened gloom on the home support. Mike Teague, always industrious, picked up at a scrummage and moved the ball to the battling Richard Hill, an unflamboyant English scrum-half of indomitable spirit. His beautifully weighted pass caught Scott Hastings slightly out of position in the Scottish midfield and Carling had half a yard and was away. He gave the ball to the dazzling Guscott, who sold the defence a cavalier dummy and England had scored.

Gradually, the English pack were coming back into things, although another

points like clockwork after the windmills of the pack had blown the opposition away. They had raced past France, Wales and Ireland and started the match hot favourites, even though Scotland too was undefeated (although nothing like as impressively). Here for the first time the Grand Slam, Triple Crown, the Championship and the Calcutta Cup were all resting on one match. Carling, England's dashing captain, thought it might have been 'the most eagerly anticipated international ever played on British soil'. Certainly, television unnecessary penalty for foul play gave Chalmers the opportunity to stretch the lead to five points. It was gratefully received and Scotland turned around at 9–4. Their game plan was working like a dream, especially in the line-out where their forwards swapped positions in a successful bid to prevent the key England jumpers, Paul Ackford and Wade Dooley, from finding a rhythm. England's line-out had been invincible earlier that season, but when it really mattered, it was found wanting. England didn't help their cause by running some kickable penalties or opting for a scrummage. Many later argued that they should have been leading at half-time and not chasing the game.

Still, after the interval, the English pack would have the wind and the boot of Andrew to help get up a head of steam. An early score and they would be right back in it. Instead, almost immediately it was Scottish wing Tony Stanger who went over for a try. The tireless John Jeffrey picked up and set Gary Armstrong off on the narrow side. Gavin Hastings was up from full-back to take a clever little pass from his scrum-half before kicking ahead to the English line with Stanger in pursuit. With all of Scotland holding their breath, Stanger stretched up to gather the kick and touch the ball down. As Bill McLaren

remarked, 'The move will be etched on the minds of Scottish rugby folk for a long time.' It is a tribute to McLaren's professionalism that he could stop himself from shouting from the top of the commentary box roof for, like himself, Stanger was born and bred in Hawick.

From that moment, on with Scotland leading 13–7, the Scottish team fought as though defending Thermopylae. The English would not pass. All they managed was one penalty goal to bring themselves within six points. Scotland tackled like men possessed, led by their passionate back row with Finlay Calder outstanding as usual. Rory Underwood looked odds-on to score until Hastings brought him down close to the line. Then Will Carling, captain courageous, found himself just 10 yards out travelling at full speed towards a try. Suddenly he was engulfed by a sea of blue shirts, who not only stopped him in his tracks but swept him back almost as fast in the opposite direction.

This day belonged to Scotland. It was the greatest day in Scottish rugby history.

'I wonder what lesson we'll learn from the great McLeod today?' At the very next scrum the young player put his hand out on the ground, whereupon it felt the full force of McLeod's boot when Scotland's most capped player stood on it. The young man was left in agony. McLeod moved off muttering, 'There endeth the first lesson, sonny boy.'

IRELAND UNITED

Éamon de Valera, fervent republican and Irish president, whose career spanned 50 years in politics, loved his rugby. As a promising young centre and full-back, he had been a trial-ist for Munster and throughout his life he took his place in the crowd at Lansdowne Road,

Dublin, to cheer on the Ireland team. When doing so, he set his politics aside. The team he supported was an all-Ireland XV and has remained so through thick and thin. It is incredible that this most volatile of nations has remained united through rugby and yet divided so bloodily elsewhere. Established loyalties, however, still applied. De Valera saw only interna-tional matches in Dublin. Between 1922 and 1954 they were played alternately with the Ravenhill ground in Belfast. De Valera never ventured north of the border to watch.

The excitement of Gaelic football would prove a serious threat to the popularity of Rugby Union in Ireland

Since 1954 Dublin has hosted all Irish internationals because the players and officials of southern Ireland were unhap-py about acknowledging the Union Flag and 'God Save the Queen' when their own Irish flag and anthem were illegal in the North. Fortunately, that has not prevented great Ulstermen, such as Mike Gibson and Willie John McBride, making the reverse journey from Belfast to Dublin to play arm in arm with their southern compatriots, such as Ray McLoughlin and Fergus Slattery. The question of which anthem to play has always been a problem. When the Irish national anthem was 'The Soldier's Song', and played at Lansdowne Road, you could, as historian John Sugden observes, 'put your rent on it that the players of the North would be just looking at their boots'.

Part of the reason why rugby has not been used as a sectarian tool can be identified in de Valera himself. Here was an educated man – he attended Rockwell College in Dublin – who learned to love his rugby in an academic world. Rugby spread in Ireland, as it had in England, through schools and universities. It did not spring up in mining communities or cotton mills. This was a middle- and upper-class game, and class was able to cross the ideological boundaries of North and South and the 1922 division of the country. Over the generations Ireland has struggled to lay claim to the traditions and origins of Rugby football just as the public-school boys of England did with William Webb Ellis. Indeed, many claim that Ellis was, in fact, an Irishman from Tipperary. There is also the suggestion that rugby is derived from the old Gaelic game of *cad*, another version of folk football widely played in the county of Kerry. However, given that the word *cad* means the scrotum of a bull, rugby seems a splendid name for the handling game.

Éamon de Valera, whose support of rugby helped Ireland to keep a united team, addresses an election rally in 1948

One of the main battles faced by rugby in Ireland has nothing to do with overcoming geographical, political or even religious division. The conflict has been with Gaelic sports and groups who saw rugby as an English game. Fortunately for Irish rugby, by the time the Gaelic Athletic Association was formed in Thurles County, Tipperary, in 1882, the game was established among the middle classes, with Trinity College, Dublin, at its heart. The Trinity

Club was founded in 1854, making it one of the oldest in the world. Opponents were scarce, so games were arranged within the student body. Old boys of Rugby School (naturally) and Cheltenham would take on the Rest. Rugby School was very influential in the spread of the game in Ireland, and the key figure in early Trinity rugby, Charles Barrington, was an old boy. He was also instrumental in writing a set of rules for the game at the college.

By the late 1860s the game was spreading around the schools and colleges of Leinster and Ulster. Trinity, however, had a firm grip on possession of the game. No team could play their first XV without having first proved their worth by defeating the second Trinity XV. A rugby section of the North of Ireland Cricket Club was formed in 1868. Officially called the North of Ireland Football Club (NIFC), it was more commonly known as North. They played and lost their first game against Trinity in 1871, the same year as the first international between Scotland and England. Both clubs undertook tours to England and Scotland, and it was only a matter of time before efforts were made to include Ireland in

Below: The grand Trinity College, Dublin, the heart of Irish rugby for more than a century
Following pages: The legendary Willie John McBride fearlessly jumping for the British Lions on the victorious 1994 tour of South Africa

the international scene. The Irish Football Union was formed in 1875 and the first international team took to the field on 15 February of that year. It is an indication of the game's exclusivity in Ireland that the first meeting of club representatives to discuss forming a union took place in the rooms at Trinity of George Hall Stack, later to be Ireland's first captain. He was rich, intellectual and a born organizer, decidedly a middle-class gentleman. Of the 20 players who proudly took the field in their emerald green jerseys, nine were from Trinity and six from North.

The Irish would have to wait six years for their first international win, against Scotland in Belfast. Scotland scored a classic try that day, described by contemporary journalist Jacques McCarthy: 'McMullen of Cork, making a mis-catch at a long kick, placed the whole of the Scottish team on side, and Graham, who was leaning against the Irish goalpost, rubbing his shin after a recent hack, leisurely limped over the line and touched the ball down.' Scotland lost because Ireland scored a drop-goal, which in those days counted for one point more than a try. The Irish Rugby Football Union (IRFU), as the governing body was now called, was plunged into financial crisis after the game. The cost of the dinner for the Scottish team at the Imperial Hotel, Belfast, was £24 5s. Unfortunately, the IRFU had only £23 4s 7d in the kitty. Even worse, there was still a balance owing to the Shelbourne Hotel, Dublin, of £8 5s 6d for a previous dinner to a visiting England team. The IRFU found the perfect solution and a bill was sent to every hero of the victorious Irish team requesting the payment of one guinea. This was taking amateurism to the extreme.

Against this background of gradual international success, Irish rugby was facing a threat at home for the sporting heart of its countrymen. Battle lines were being drawn up between the Anglicized games, such as hockey, cricket and particularly rugby, and the traditional Irish games of hurling and Gaelic football. In this respect, Ireland was very different from countries such as Wales and New Zealand, who discovered that rugby was a way of creating and confirming a national identity for their people. In Ireland rugby was perceived by those wanting independence for Ireland as a symbol of English culture and colonial rule. This was at a time when, towards the end of the 19th century, the struggle for Irish independence was gathering momentum.

Ironically, the man behind the Gaelic Athletic Association (GAA), Father Mike Cusack, was a Trinity man and a rugby player of no mean ability, who would later coach the game at student level. His feelings of nationalism far outweighed his interest in rugby. He represented the view that at this point in Ireland's history, rugby, so clearly associated with England, was not something Irish people wanted to play. Cusack gave Irishmen a choice, and one that still exists today. As historian John Sugden observes, 'Which sport you choose today to play makes a statement about who you are and what you stand for. It says something about the notion of Irishness that you adopt.' Rugby in Ireland was saved because it was middle class, and those who played embraced the culture from across the Irish Sea. 'They lived in Dublin,' says Sugden, 'but their hearts and minds were in London.'

Gaelic sports were a lifeline to the Irish people who wanted to reject imperial games. And they rejected them fiercely — so much so that members of the GAA caught watching a rugby match would be banned from Gaelic games in future. Foreign games were also forbidden on hallowed Gaelic turf. Rugby, an English game, is decidedly foreign, so Gaelic football and rugby cannot be played on the same ground. One of the saving graces of rugby in the 1880s and 1890s was that it represented an area of combat where the English could be beaten. The struggle for independence would take far longer than an afternoon in the Dublin drizzle. But on 5 February 1887, England were beaten for the first time

Right: Slattery, the superb Irish wing forward, tries out Willie John McBride's pipe, during the Lions' 1974 South African tour
Opposite: Willie John McBride was an Ulsterman who proudly led the united Irish rugby team

Many critics rate Michael Gibson of Ireland and the Lions the most complete rugby player of modern times

at Lansdowne Road. It was a start, and the 1890s went on to be a very successful decade for the Irish, with the Triple Crown captured on two occasions, in 1894 and 1899.

A lasting problem for rugby in Ireland is that it has never been a working-man's game, unlike Gaelic football, which boasts many working men who are among Ireland's finest sportsmen. Just as England has never had the opportunity to pick many of the great players for their international team because the players had only ever performed in Rugby League, so Ireland has missed out on the great ball-playing stars of Gaelic football. In the North rugby is the game of the Protestant middle classes, who can afford to send their children to Protestant grammar schools. In the South it is the game of the Catholic middle classes, who have the money for Catholic grammar schools. Class, then, is the glue that has bound rugby in Ireland together and helped it to survive the country's split in 1922. The men who played it, professional people such as doctors, teachers and businessmen, kept ties across the border and rugby remained one of them. After 1922 there were a maximum of three days every year – matches against England, Scotland and Wales – when the Protestant men from Belfast would travel to Dublin to shout their support for an all-Ireland team. Historian Paul O'Leary observes, 'For 90 minutes they can lose themselves in the excitement of the crowd and that pervading spirit of rugby. What Ireland needs is more rugby and not less of it, if that kind of unity can be sustained if only for a short period.'

It would be naive to suggest that rugby is a sectarian-free zone in Ireland. But the middle classes in Ireland are more adept at separating sport and politics – as de Valera himself could do. If Mo Mowlam, secretary of state for Northern Ireland, and Gerry Adams, leader of Sinn Fein, were ever to go to a sporting occasion together, it would undoutably be a rugby match. Their shared love of the game makes not a jot of difference to their political views or agendas. As historian John Sugden says, 'Just because everyone is wearing a green jersey with a shamrock on the front doesn't mean that there is a united Ireland around the corner.'

At least violence and the threat of violence have not ruined rugby in Ireland. There have, however, been some terrible incidents. On the first day of the Easter Rising in 1916 a detachment of de Valera's republican volunteers spotted a group of veteran soldiers returning from a route march and mistakenly thought they were combat soldiers. They opened fire and Frederick Browning, president of the IRFU, was shot dead.

DIFFERENT CLASS:
THE NATIONAL GAME OF WALES

In the first decade of the 20th century Wales became the dominant force in British rugby. Only Scotland could rival them. In the same way that Scotland owed much of their battling qualities to the introduction of working men from the Borders, so Wales owed much to the miners. This first golden age of Welsh rugby coincided with a great boom period in South Wales, where miners earned good money. While England effectively banished its working-class players to their own rugby world of the Northern Union, Wales embraced the working men who had flooded into the coalfields. Between 1871 and 1911 the population of Wales increased by nearly a million, and a third of all working men were miners. Historian Dai Smith has described Wales at that time as one of the 'hot spots of the British Empire' with a dynamic economy. Perhaps it is no coincidence that the next golden age of Welsh rugby coincided with the increased wealth of Britain in the late 1960s and 1970s, while the industrial policies of the Thatcher years, which fractured the old mining and steel communities, sent the Welsh national game into a decline from which it has yet to recover.

Although Old Rugbeians had much to do with founding the game in Llanelli, one cannot imagine that they have since provided many members of that famous team. Rugby was seized upon as a means of giving a focus to the new immigrant population of South Wales. Migrants came into the coalfields from the west of England,

The hard-working mining communities of South Wales took the physical game of rugby to their hearts

Scotland and Ireland, as well as from the Welsh-speaking areas of north and west of Wales. Just as in northern England, rugby filled a need for vigorous sport and compelling entertainment away from the relentless hard graft at the coalface. And similarly, it was the pub that provided a base for the rugby-playing community. When they started up, many clubs had their headquarters at a local inn; Pontypridd was based at the White Hart, Rhymney at the Tredegar Arms, and Penygraig at the Butcher's. Historian Gareth Williams, co-author of the official history of the Welsh RFU, *Fields of Praise*, explains, 'This was a new society. It was bustling and energetic. It was a society that took sport and drink and physical exertion in large quantities. Rugby provided an opportunity for self-expression and collective expression. An aggressive, self-confident working class were increasingly creating their own institutions, whether they were trade unions, choirs or rugby football clubs. They had a growing sense of Welsh nationality.'

Lloyd George realized the importance of sport in winning votes

The brand of rugby enjoyed in the mining communities was not for the faint-hearted. Fighting among spectators carried away by the intensity of the match was commonplace, as was fighting on the pitch, where injuries were frequent. If that wasn't bad enough, a victorious away team would afterwards have to confront angry home spectators who might hurl stones and abuse at them. Between 1895 and 1900 many famous clubs, including Cardiff, Llanelli, Neath, Aberavon and Abertillary, were suspended because of rioting spectators. At the time a newspaper in Merthyr Tydfil carried an article with some helpful hints for rugby players: 'Hint 1 – Make your will.'

The introduction of rugby into Wales was lucky in its timing because it beat soccer into the hearts and minds of the principality by some 20 years. Nor did its players need to possess the skill and finesse of that game. Dai Smith explains, 'Just as in New Zealand, they discovered that the tall, the fat, the short and the thin could all take part in rugby.' Wales also mirrors the experience of New Zealand in the way that politicians recognized rugby as a way of improving national identity and political strength. The Welsh politician, and future prime minister, David Lloyd George cashed in by kicking off a rugby match between Cardiff and Blackheath in 1907.

Think of a Welshman abroad and you think of rugby players in scarlet jerseys and male choirs with glorious voices. Rugby gave the nation a character that was exportable. Two events of great significance led more than anything else to rugby becoming the national game of Wales: the Gould Affair of 1896/7 and the 1905 victory over the All Blacks.

KING ARTHUR:
FIRST SUPERSTAR OF RUGBY

Arthur Gould was the first rugby superstar. Around the streets of Newport, where he lived and played his rugby, a group of awed schoolboys would always trail their hero. Even the Reverend Frank Marshall, scourge of the working man, was moved to write in 1893 that Gould was the 'central figure in the football world' and 'the greatest centre three-quarter that has ever played'. He was a player at the height of his rugby powers, an athlete who could run 100 yards in 10.2 seconds, and the man who had inspired Wales to their first-ever Triple Crown that same season. He would also be the central figure in a dispute that, a few years later, would change the face of Welsh rugby for ever. Frank Marshall would not have approved of that.

Although more famous than Lloyd George in his local community, 'Monkey' Gould was always a man of the people. Nicknamed for his childhood prowess at climbing trees, he was handsome, with dark curly hair and a black moustache, but his head was never turned by public adulation or the attentions of newspapers. He was, says Dai Smith, 'the Omar Sharif of his day'. He had great charisma and the camera loved him. His father, Joseph, worked in a local brass foundry and was a keen supporter of the town's rugby club. He also started a small dynasty of great Welsh sportsmen. Monkey's brothers Bob and Bert won Welsh

WALES 3 – NEW ZEALAND 0
CARDIFF ARMS PARK
16 DECEMBER 1905

Welsh by birth, by heart and by voice, they came from the length and breadth of the country. Fifty special trains were laid on to bring the Welsh support into Cardiff. The city docks closed early to give the wharfmen, the coal trimmers and tippers and the shipping clerks time to make their way to the ground. At 1.30 the gates closed on a crowd of 47,000 excitedly waiting for their first glimpse of the awesome colonials who had beaten and demoralized every team they had competed against on this their first official visit to the British Isles. Only the

The New Zealand tourists of 1905 (the 'Originals') were among the greatest ever, yet Wales beat them in this historic encounter

801 points and conceding just 22. The Welsh heroes ran on, resplendent in scarlet jerseys, the cheers of their countrymen ringing in their ears. The All Blacks gathered at the half-way line and, as the South Wales Daily News *later* wrote, 'Amidst a silence that could almost be felt, the Colonials stood in the centre of the field and sang...their weird war cry.' It was the first time the All Black haka had been witnessed on Welsh soil and the crowd seemed strangely cowed, maintaining a reverential hush as the visitors promised to 'be strong and fight to the death'.

Quietly at first, almost apologetically, the men in scarlet began to sing 'Hen Wlad fy Nhadau' ('The Land of My Fathers'). It was a pre-arranged decision of the Welsh RFU, who hoped the spectators would join in the chorus. The 47,000-strong crowd responded magnificently and the strains of that most elegiac of melodies sought out every nook and cranny of the Arms Park until the stadium was of one voice. From that moment on this would be the anthem of Welsh rugby. All Black captain Dave Gallaher remarked afterwards that he had never heard such an impressive sound. The two teams assembled, each with very different calls to arms, but both with the same purpose – to give their all for victory.

tiny principality of Wales, holders of the Triple Crown, stood in their way. It would be an epic struggle. It would be the first World Championship of rugby.

All morning from lark rise, the sound of Welsh singing voices reached the ears of the 'Originals' whose hotel stood adjacent to the Arms Park. Ten minutes to kick-off and the men in black appeared, taking to the field with the jaunty confidence of a team that had won all of its previous 27 matches, scoring

The Welsh began like men possessed, the speed of their forwards making the much bigger All Blacks seem lumbering by comparison. They swarmed all over the field and for the first 15 minutes the tourists struggled to launch a meaningful attack on the Welsh line. Behind the scrum the incomparable will-o'-the-wisp R.M. (Dickie) Owen, the 'Pocket Oracle' as he was known, teased and tormented the All Blacks with his guile and ever-present grin. A speeding pass to his partner Percy Bush saw the fly-half fall just short with an attempted drop-goal. Willie Llewellyn on the right wing just failed to gather a pass behind him with his route to line and glory clear.

Despite their industry, Wales still had nothing to show for it after 25 minutes. It took the genius of Owen to unlock the powerful New Zealand defence. It was a planned move. Wales won a scrum 15 yards in from the right touch-line and a little over 35 yards out. Owen attacked down the blind side, supported by Bush, Llewellyn and by his captain and centre Gwyn Nicholls. The New Zealand defence flooded across, leaving left wing Teddy Morgan unmarked, but not unseen. Owen had spotted him. In the blink of an eye he changed direction, hurled a long pass to roving back Cliff Pritchard, a Pontypool undertaker; he passed to centre Rhys Gabe, who sent Morgan away with

20 yards to make. He accelerated to the line and pandemonium broke out in the stands. The great Arthur Gould danced on the press tables, proclaiming, 'The fastest rugby sprinter in the world! Teddy Morgan has scored!'

It was a narrow, precarious lead. Bert Winfield missed a difficult conversion, so surely Wales would need at least one more score to see themselves home. Morgan, the hero of one moment, was villain when he dropped a scoring pass from Bush, who himself then narrowly missed with another drop-goal attempt. Gradually, the All Black forwards pressed the home team back on to the defence. Time and again Winfield's precise kicking to touch cleared their lines. Ten minutes were left when a controversy occurred which has raged ever since and has established legendary status for this majestic match. It is the most notorious non-score in the history of rugby.

Burly All Black centre Bob Deans took a pass on the Welsh 25 and set off for the line, clear and inviting in front of him. He cut back inside, aiming to score closer to the posts, and was caught right on the chalk by left wing Morgan, who had sprinted across and by centre Rhys Gabe, who brought him down. Was he over the line or a few agonizing inches short? Deans claimed afterwards that it was a fair try. He sent a telegram to the Daily

Mail *which read: 'Grounded ball 6 inches over line. Some of Welsh players admit try. Hunter and Glasgow can confirm was pulled back by Welshmen before referee arrived. Deans.'*

The New Zealand vice captain Billy Stead was not playing that day, but instead was acting as 'line umpire'. He was sure the try had been scored and told the referee who, in the fashion of the day, was wearing street clothes, that Deans' had been pulled back. Morgan also always believed that Deans had scored, but Gabe was adamant that the All Black was brought down short and tried to struggle over the line. His view was endorsed by captain Gwyn Nicholls, who thought Deans should have been penalized for trying to wriggle over. The last word in those pre-action-replay days went to the Scottish referee, John Dallas, who strenuously denied that he 'disallowed' the try. 'When Deans was tackled, he grounded the ball 6 to 12 inches short of the goal-line. At that moment he could neither pass nor play the ball, and as I passed between the Welsh goalposts, my whistle went shrill and loud. It is true that when I got to the spot to order a scrum, the ball was over the line but without hesitation I ordered a scrum at the place where Deans was grounded. I never blew my whistle at the spot. It had gone before.

No try was scored by Deans.'

Discussions and debates about the try have raged over the intervening years, but nothing can change the final score of 3–0 to the heroes of Wales. The controversy helps to keep the match alive in the memory. Fifty years later Rhys Gabe was still sticking to his version of events, but not one All Black has ever believed it.

Not in doubt, however, is that the Welsh deserved to win. After the game, the two opposing captains exchanged jerseys. Gallaher, a giant among sportsmen, told the reporter from the South Wales Daily News, *'It was a rattling good game, played out to the bitter end, with the result that the best team won.'*

The true significance of the 1905 match is that, as a result of this titanic encounter, rugby became the national game of both countries. Distinguished New Zealand rugby writer T.P. McLean wrote that the Deans controversy was to be 'the greatest event in the history of New Zealand rugby because it provided a basis, a starting point, a seed of nationalism upon which all aspects of the game were to depend in succeeding years'. And in Wales, as historian Gareth Williams has observed, the jubilation, 'stitched rugby on the national flag'. Rugby became as much an expression of Welshness as coal and male-voice choirs.

caps, while Harry, Gus and Wyatt all played for Newport. The Goulds could almost field a family team to beat many a town side. At 16 Arthur Gould made his début for the Newport first XV as an emergency full-back against Weston-super-Mare. He had strict orders to kick the ball at all times, but twice routed the opposition by running like quicksilver through their entire ranks. This was a boy born for stardom.

Arthur Gould, the 'Great Crack' of Newport and the first star of Welsh rugby

Gould's subsequent fame owed much to his job as a public works contractor and the fact that he had to travel up and down England and Wales by train. He played for Southampton, the newly formed London Welsh, the acclaimed Richmond team, Hampshire and Middlesex county sides and South Wales. He also won many athletic competitions and by 1890 his winnings exceeded £1000 from running races alone. One of the great rugby writers of the age was W.J. Townsend Collins, who recalled seeing a 'dazzling' Arthur Gould 'swerving left and dodging right' to score a match-winning try for Richmond against Blackheath in 1888. Collins regarded Arthur Gould as the 'greatest rugby player who ever took the field'. He gave that opinion in 1948, some 60 years after his introduction to the sublime skills of A.J. Gould.

In 1890 Gould joined his brother Bob in the West Indies on contract work building bridges. The mayor of Newport presented him with a cheque for 50 guineas and a gold ring. Gould promised to return if he found fortune, and within 18 months he was back playing for the town of his birth and for Wales, for whom he was still to play his greatest game. That came against England in the first match of the 1893 international season. England had beaten Wales seven times, with one draw and just one narrow loss in the past nine games between the two countries. The prospects of improving that record in front of 20,000 people at the national stadium in Cardiff appeared bleak when Wales changed over 7–0 down. The English side had played with the wind, and their forwards, large and robust as ever, were proving far too strong for their opponents. They increased their advantage just after changing ends, with a third try, and a feeling of gloom descended on the Welsh crowd. But cometh the hour, cometh the hero, and Gould suddenly had the ball on the half-way mark. He beat two men before outsprinting the English full-back Edwin Field to score between the posts. But with less than ten minutes to go, England were still ahead by 11–7 when Gould scored his second try, gliding through the English defence. The conversion was missed, but close to full time a penalty on the English 25-yard line, wide on the right, gave the Welsh one last, difficult chance. Swansea full-back W.J. (Billy) Bancroft stepped forward. The ground was by now too frozen to place the ball, so with what Gould described as a 'grand kick', he dropped the ball over the bar. Thus did Wales, in the most exciting manner imaginable, cross the most threatening hurdle on the way to their first Triple Crown.

Gould proclaimed the victory as a triumph for teamwork and hard training in the Newport gym, but the crowd would have no truck with such modesty. They carried him shoulder high through the streets of Cardiff while men and women leaned from windows and balconies cheering and waving at their national hero. Gould planted the seed of national rugby fervour that the great Welsh team of 1905 was able to harvest 12 years later. The 1890s saw a contrast in the styles and ambition of England and Wales, which translates easily to the game of 1999 – Welsh flair and opportunism against old-style English brawn and forward power. In 1893 Wales had triumphed. In 1896 it was the turn of England to administer a 25–0 thrashing, but at Wembley in 1999 it was Wales who overcame the might of the English pack to snatch a 32–31 win in a thrilling final.

Between January 1897 and March 1898 Wales played no international fixtures, effectively ostracized following what became known as the Gould Affair. It began the year before when rugby lovers, in effect the whole of South Wales, and the regional newspapers decided that they wanted to honour their most famous son by a national testimonial to mark his imminent retirement from the game. By January 1896 he had played in more first-class matches, scored more tries and dropped more goals than any other player on record. A national testimonial was endorsed by the Welsh RFU and more than £500 was collected to buy Gould a house in Newport. The Rugby Football Union in London, and subsequently the International Rugby Board, were outraged, especially considering the fragile nature of

There is no more passionate a crowd than the Welsh: here supporting their boys at Wembley (Wales v England, April 1999)

the game after the breakaway by the Northern Union just a year before. Here was the issue of professionalism yet again but the WRFU were not about to buckle to the wishes of London. Instead, in February 1897, they withdrew from the International Board in a defiant gesture that guaranteed nobody would interfere with the national sport in the future. It would be Home Rule for Wales. Dai Smith explains, 'Wales was castigated by the other home unions, Scotland, Ireland and England, as having gone professional. They were told to take Gould's house away but Wales essentially told them to go away, we are going to do what we like. We are standing up for ourselves. England caved in because English clubs wanted to play Welsh clubs. Scotland and Ireland didn't play Wales for a season in a fit of pique.' (In fact Scotland didn't resume fixtures with Wales until 1899.)

A few weeks later, on the night of Easter Monday, 250 of Wales's great and good gathered in Gould's home town to pay tribute to the man lauded as the 'Great Crack of Newport'. The public galleries of the Drill Hall were overflowing and a marching band struck a majestic note or two. Gould was presented with the keys to a magnificent detached villa in his home town. The nearest Victorian sportsman to Gould in terms of achievement and adulation would be the cricket legend W.G. Grace, but even that great man could not unite a nation. On and off the field Gould was to set the agenda for the game in Wales. If the country had followed the industrial North into a professional game, it would have lost the chance for glory in a wide, global arena – the sort of international isolation that so tormented South Africa over the issue of race in the modern era. By using its greatest player as a figurehead, Wales was able to have the best of both worlds: to keep its international status and to reward its players, while retaining their amateur status. It was a uniquely Welsh brand of amateurism. It flirted with professionalism, but those players who needed more than flirtation could go to Rugby League, and many followed that route.

The 'Great Crack' himself continued to serve his sport and his country as a referee and a national selector until his untimely death in 1919 at the age of 54.

THE GREATER WAR

Every year in March the Barbarians play a team from the East Midlands in the annual Edgar Mobbs Memorial Game. Mobbs, a free-running Northampton three-quarter, lost his life at Passchendaele when he led his men 'over the top' by kicking a ball into no man's land and following it up, an act of heroism and bravado that typified the wastefulness of the First World War. Rugby was the game that personified the character of that war: head down, charge at the opposition, get knocked down, get up again to have another go...unless you're already dead. Nine days after the outbreak of war in August 1914 the Rugby Football Union sent out a circular urging all its players to enlist. The players did not need a second invitation. They were the first to sign up and, as a result, rugby was the sport that suffered the greatest casualty rate. Historian Richard Holt observed, 'They came tumbling out of the public-school clubs, straight off to the trenches to be shot down.'

In war rugby's ruling classes had found the ultimate expression for the values they held so dear, an ethos of individual strength and teamwork born on the playing fields of the early Victorian public schools. It was as if rugby had been a way of training men to be officers without joining the army. Whichever way you looked at it, rugby players made good soldiers, and equally soldiers made good rugby players. New Zealand's legendary captain Dave Gallaher had been a veteran of the Boer War. He took his muscular valour with him on to the rugby field, up until the Great War where he fell at Passchendaele.

In the years immediately preceding the war, English rugby had gathered itself after the blood-letting of the northern breakaway. The leanest period in the nation's rugby history came to an end. Twickenham was opened for internationals in 1910 and quickly became the nucleus of everything that the middle class had sought to achieve in the previous 20 years. It became an administrative home, a national stadium synonymous with rugby. And it was in London, nowhere near the North of England. The Harlequins played the first-ever match on the ground against Richmond, and it is interesting to note that many of the club's players followed a path from public school to Oxford University and then to this corner of Middlesex. The first international match was against a Welsh side grown accustomed to routing the English, winning 14 matches out of its previous 20. But this was a new-look England, with a dazzling back line led at fly-half by Adrian Stoop of the Harlequins. Here was a player who took the best elements of the passing games of Wales, New Zealand and South Africa and adopted them for his club and country.

For Stoop, passing was a science. He had three basic principles, which he listed for the first *Rugby Football Annual* in 1913: 1. The passer and receiver must be running on parallel, if not diverging lines. 2. The ball must travel in a horizontal direction. 3. It must fly without spin and with one end pointing towards the receiver.

Harlequins became a successful side practising what Stoop preached, and so did England. From the first international kick-off at Twickenham, Stoop caught the ball, but instead of kicking routinely to touch, he dummied the slumbering Welsh forwards, surged through on a diagonal run and placed an accurate little kick ahead. England retained possession from the ensuing forward mêlée and a deft passing movement to Frederick (F.E.L.) Chapman on the wing put him through for the opening score before the Welsh had drawn breath. England eventually ran out the winners by 11–6, a result that ushered in a new, hugely successful era for England, broken only by the war. Two Triple Crowns and a Grand Slam immediately preceded the conflict. A chief architect of this golden age was the legendary three-quarter Ronald Poulton-Palmer, who rattled up 17 caps before losing his life in the war. He was a player for whom that well-worn sporting phrase 'elusive runner' must have been invented.

In 1913 he was at centre when England achieved their second consecutive Triple Crown against Scotland at the Inverleith ground. It would be the final Calcutta Cup match before the Great War cast its giant shadow, and, fittingly, it was one of the most exciting, a valiant recovery from Scotland in the second half falling just one point short of England's total of 15. Of the 30 players who trudged wearily from the field, 11 would fall in the war. Poulton-Palmer was among them and he, more than any other, became a symbol of rugby's heroism. Thirteen Welsh internationals also lost their lives, including Charlie Pritchard, the star forward in the 1905 winning side against the All Blacks. Ireland lost nine, including arguably their greatest player to date, the flamboyant back Basil Maclear, who lost his life at Ypres. Maclear was an English officer with the Royal Dublin Fusiliers and was stationed at Cork when first picked for Ireland, whose selectors recognized his worth ahead of their English counterparts. He was regarded as something of an eccentric and could often be spied playing in a pair of splendid white calfskin gloves. Scotland lost 30 internationals in the war. On the last day of the season in 1914 London Scottish fielded four teams com-

prising a total of 60 men. The war claimed 45 of them.

The contribution of so many great rugby players in the First World War was a victory, albeit a hollow one, for the public-school image of rugby: they participated for king, country, school and rugger. Historian Stefan Collini explains, 'At first 1914 was seen as one big away game, testing team sprit and bravery under fire. They set off for war with high spirits, only to encounter the appalling destructiveness of trench warfare. Public-school chapels were soon displaying huge lists of casualties – sometimes a quarter or more of any class would be wiped out within a month of leaving for France. A memoir by Paul Jones, *War Letter of a Public Schoolboy*, was published by his father in 1918. Jones, formerly of Dulwich College and Balliol Oxford, was killed in action in France in July 1917. Some of his observations are, in their innocence, a savage reminder of the cavalier wastefulness of that war. He wrote, 'Do you realize what a fine part amateur sportsmen are playing in this war? I doubt if there will be many great athletes left if things go on as they are doing.'

RONALD POULTON-PALMER:
THE STANDARD BEARER

On his seventeenth and last international appearance in 1914 the flaxen-haired figurehead of English rugby, Ronnie Poulton-Palmer, captained the team against France and ran in four breathtaking tries from centre – a record at that time. It was a great pre-war send-off for rugby and a memory to cherish during the five bleak years before international rugby resumed. Soon afterwards, Poulton-Palmer was off across the English Channel to add his panache to the desperate war in the trenches. A year later, in May 1915, his death from a sniper's bullet at Ploeg Steert Wood in Belgium guaranteed that he would remain for ever as the

Left: Ronnie Poulton-Palmer, who lost his life in the First World War, was the ultimate hero of Rugby Union

Previous pages: The elusive Jonathan Davies maintaining the Barbarians' tradition for open rugby during the annual match against East Midlands in 1996

ultimate symbol of English rugby and all it stood for. He was just 25.

Ronnie Poulton, as he was then called, went to Rugby School and still leads the table for caps won by old boys of that establishment. He moved on to become an undergraduate at Balliol College, Oxford, becoming part of a formidable university team and scoring five tries in the Varsity match of 1909. He won his first English cap that year, and later moved on to join Adrian Stoop at the Harlequins Club. Stoop and Poulton's careers followed almost identical lines – Stoop, too, was an Old Rugbeian and Oxford man – with the notable difference that only one of them survived the war.

In 1913 Poulton was at centre when England scored their first-ever success against Wales at the famous Cardiff Arms Park, so called because it was across the road from an old coaching inn called the Cardiff Arms. The win was hardly a huge surprise. Wales was going through one of those difficult periods where industrial stoppages, such as the successful minimum wage strike by miners, had disrupted fixtures and forced some clubs into financial ruin. The English victory by 12 points to nil showed that ascendancy in the British game had been transferred back across the River Severn. Poulton marked the occasion with one of rugby's most celebrated drop-goals, which sealed the win. The left-footed effort that split the posts was particularly memorable because the pitch was a sea of mud and to get the ball airborne at all was generally considered to be a feat in itself.

Poulton assumed his double-barrelled name in March 1914 after he was left a fortune by a wealthy relative on condition that he took the name of Palmer. Poulton did not hesitate and became Poulton-Palmer from that day on. He cut a dashing figure both on and off the field and was the most popular player of his generation. One contemporary writer described him as 'the greatest figure who ever played' and 'a man apart'. Truly, the powerful people in the rugby firmament who wanted to keep control of the game for gentlemen and amateurs could not have created a more perfect image for rugby than Ronnie Poulton-Palmer. He went to the right public school, one of the best universities, played for the top club, captained his country and served with the 4th Royal Berkshire Regiment. His death at such a young age assured him of a similar legendary status – albeit in a different sphere – to that of the war poets Wilfred Owen and Rupert Brooke.

After his death, a fellow officer who had witnessed his funeral wrote in a letter of condolence to Poulton-Palmer's family, 'When I went round his old company, as they stood to at dawn, almost every man was crying.'

AFTERMATH

Somehow rugby was not destroyed by the First World War. Perhaps it should have been, leading, as it did, to the untimely and wasteful deaths of so many of its finest. And those who did return, with broken bodies and broken minds, were in no fit state to take to the rugby fields and do battle once more over an oval ball. Fortunately for rugby, it was not perceived as a link in a chain of middle-class destruction. The true horror of the First World War became apparent only gradually and it was many years before doubt was cast over the ideal that rugby had embodied. Now, in the immediate post-war years, the game became glorified, just as the war itself had been. Once again rugby was able to take its place in the forefront of public-school education at a time when mistrust of the working classes increased in leaps and bounds, culminating in the General Strike of 1926.

Internationally, the England team went from strength to strength, replacing Wales at the helm of British rugby in the 1920s. In Wavell Wakefield of the Harlequins, England possessed one of the finest and most innovative forwards in rugby history. He was the king of the breakaway back row, using his speed and strength to swarm all over the opposing backs and force them statically across the field. As historian O.L. Owen wrote, 'Woe betide the opposing back who underestimated Wakefield's speed in the open and loose.' Wakefield fully understood the impact a powerful and mobile back row could have on a game long before the 'gain line' was part of every coaching manual. His England team won the Grand Slam in consecutive years – 1922/3 and 1923/4. In the latter season they cantered past the opposition, beating Wales 17–9, Ireland 14–3, France 19–7 and Scotland 19–0, despite not having a star in the backs. For the first time forwards were proving more important than backs in a successful team. Wakefield, 6 feet tall and 14 stone in weight, would charge around the field with Tom Voyce rampaging at his elbow. These were gruelling physical matches. Wakefield, according to popular legend, used to say he could not begin to play until someone had punched him on the nose. By his retirement in 1927, he had claimed 31 caps, more than any other Englishman up to that time. He was the archetypal English rugby player – minor public school (Sedbergh), RAF, Oxford, Harlequins, Middlesex and England. In 1950 he became president of the RFU.

Conflict shifted from the trenches to a more familiar English battleground of middle class against working class. Historian Stefan Collini observes, 'Immediately after the war

The 1920s were a golden age for English rugby when the inspirational Wavell Wakefield (third from right) led them to victory in 1924 to the second of two consecutive Grand Slams

there was a great deal of anxiety about organized working-class militants, with a series of strikes leading up to 1926. The middle classes once more saw the need to draw their wagons into a circle to preserve their values and social class. Those schools that had played soccer now saw it as a professional game and one increasingly identified with the working man, so once again rugby took the responsibility of being the sport of the middle class.' As a result, the 1920s saw more rugby clubs founded in England than in any other decade.

The inter-war years witnessed the growth of grammar schools, who identified rugby as an important ingredient in their public-school role models. They became slightly inferior images of minor public schools, with houses and inter-house sporting competitions of which the rugby tournament would always be the most important. There were also other class trappings, such as blazers and ties. The grammar school boy – and, more pertinently, his parents – wanted the symbols of the class to which they aspired. As university education became more widely available, so did careers in the professions. Professional people played rugby. These grammar schools were the basis for a new suburban class, particularly in the south-east, who chose rugby as the sport to give these new urban fringes social cohesion. There was no established social structure, so the rugby club provided a hub for the suburban world to build around. As ever, if you wanted to be middle class and get on in the world, you would have to play rugby.

OBOLENSKY:
PRINCE AMONG MEN

Even though history tends to look on the Second World War as rather less futile than the 1914–18 conflict, it is a sobering fact that 111 rugby internationals from all over the world lost their lives during it. The very first of them was a White Russian prince called Alexander Obolensky, who had joined the RAF when war was declared. His Hawker Hurricane crashed on landing in East Anglia and he was killed. His name lives on in the world of rugby because he scored one of the most famous tries of all time in a memorable match in 1936 when England gave the All Blacks a rare thrashing by 13–0. Not surprisingly, it became known as Obolensky's match, partly as a result of the newsreel coverage, which has led to the try being replayed thousands of times over the years.

Obolensky was born in Leningrad, the son of Prince Alexis of Russia. His classical English education saw him attend Brasenose College, Oxford, the Alma Mater of William Webb Ellis. Unlike Webb Ellis, he distinguished himself in university rugby, playing the first of three Varsity matches in 1935 when just 18. He made his England début the following year, when he won the first of his four international caps against New Zealand. Although he is remembered for one particular try, he actually scored twice during the match. The first was a simple job of rounding the full-back. It was his second, exceptional, solo effort that gained him rugby immortality. England fly-half Peter (P.L.) Candler seized the ball wide on the right and fed the flying prince, who immediately cut inside. He sprinted full speed in the direction of the opposite corner, evading both full-back and wing cover. The famed rugby writer T.P. McLean called it 'a stupendous exhibition of the hypotenuse in rugby'. It was rather like having a number one hit with your first record. Fame for the prince was assured, but how could he follow it? In truth, he was a one-hit wonder, whose international career was over by the time war came. There was something exotic about 'Obo', as he was called. Not only did he represent the traditional rugby standards of Oxford gentleman and amateur, but he was actually a member of a royal family, an ultimate class symbol. He did have one other claim to fame. In that same year of 1936 he toured South America with a Rugby Football Union XV and scored a world record 17 tries against Brazil. Not surprising, therefore, that Brazil prefers kicking the round ball.

THE REVENGE OF CLASS

While, perversely, the middle-class game in England was strengthened by the First World War, the social and industrial depression that followed hit Wales hard. During a period in the 1920s and 1930s when England won the Triple Crown six times and the Grand Slam on four occasions, Wales won nothing. Rugby so much represented the demeanour of the Welsh people that the national game sank into a slump. The country had lost its confidence.

In England the public and grammar schools were buoyant and breeding cavalier rugby players but in Wales the working-class bedrock of Welsh rugby was struggling in a series of strikes, marches and demonstrations against massive unemployment and economic recession. The 1920s were a period of intense class conflict in both England and Wales, but it was in the principality that rugby suffered. The middle classes in England were 'all right chum', and their rugby was flourishing. Wales, however, was in mourning. The year 1924 saw New Zealand administer a 19–0 humiliation to Wales in Swansea. Between 1920 and 1927 Scotland beat them seven times, including 35–10 in 1924, with one match drawn. Wales managed just two wins in the first 12 post-war matches against England.

The best revenge the middle-class protectors of rugby could have against the Welsh 'underminers' was to beat them where it really hurt: in their pockets and on the rugby field. Rugby has always been a barometer of the state of the nation in Wales. Dai Smith explains, 'There is no doubt that the expansive success of Welsh rugby before the 1920s was to do

Following pages: Prince Alexander Obolensky, pictured at Rosslyn Park in 1936, lit up the rugby field with some memorable tries in his all-too-brief career

The imposing figure of Wilf Wooller – here was a new kind of centre who would batter his way through 1930s' defences for Cambridge University and Wales

with the power of the economy. Come the 1920s and the bottom was kicked out of the bucket. Great depression and essentially the beginning of the end for the coal trade set in. Rugby was by now very much a working-class game, played and watched by the working class even if still administered by the middle classes. The best players started to go to Rugby League: the working-class spectators were literally leaving Wales.'

The 1930s began to see a gradual social revival in Wales, but with a supreme sense of irony it was with the help of grammar schools and university players that rugby began to strengthen again. In December 1935 the Welsh XV faced New Zealand in a match few gave them much prospect of winning. In the backs the Cambridge University combination of fly-half Cliff Jones and centre Wilf Wooller gave them some hope of making a game of it. Wooller, who had English parents, had been snapped up by the canny Welsh selectors, who recognized his physical presence – 6 feet 2 inches and close on 14 stone – while still at school in North Wales, and he was the most prolific Welsh scorer since the immortal Arthur Gould. He dwarfed Jones by 6 inches. Together they appeared like whippet and lurcher running rings around defences. At Cambridge they had perfected their art of scything through defences. Jones, with a quicksilver break between opposing fly-half and centre, would launch Wooller on an unstoppable inside run. It remains one of the most popular moves in international rugby today, with Gregor Townsend and John Leslie demonstrating its effectiveness for Scotland in the 1999 Five Nations Championship.

Once more, a game against the All Blacks gave Wales a resurgence of national identity and confidence. The ground was hard and unforgiving after a night of frost, and a watery winter sun illuminated plumes of breath as people blew hard into their hands to warm them. The fearsome All Blacks had played 85 matches since Gallaher first led his men off the boat in 1905, and they had lost just two, both on Welsh soil. For this game the Welsh selectors moved Wooller to the left wing, a strategy that was to prove a master-stroke as the match reached an awe-inspiring climax. Tries by skipper Claude Davey and by Wooller, taking the inside pass from Jones just as he had done so many times at Cambridge, saw Wales 10–3 up ten minutes into the second half. The crowd, sensing a famous victory, cheered and shouted every touch of the ball, but gradually the All Blacks clawed their way back until, with just four minutes left, they were leading 12–10. Gloom settled on the stadium when brave Welsh hooker Don Tarr was stretchered off with a broken neck. Wales were being kicked when they were down.

Cliff Jones broke again deep in his own half and, momentarily diverting the attention of the New Zealand defence, passed to Wooller who, using Davey as a decoy runner, broke through and galloped into the All Black half. He bore down on the opposing full-back, Mike Gilbert, and the crowd held their breath waiting for the clash. Instead, he chipped a perfect kick over the full-back's head and a kindly bounce saw fellow wing Rhys Jones scoot over. The match was won 13–12 amid scenes every bit as jubilant as 30 years earlier. The frustrations of 15 years were released in a momentous sporting occasion. The Monday after the match the *Western Mail* ran an editorial saying that this was a victory achieved by Wales impossible in any other sphere. Historian Gareth Williams explains, 'It was making the point that you had workers and college boys in the same team. The backs were virtually all public school, Oxford and Cambridge, while the forwards were working men. They achieved a victory by one point at a time of class conflict, mass unemployment and intense hardship.' Wales was a country looking for confidence, and rugby gave the people the chance to turn the corner of social recovery, an upturn that would reach fulfilment in a new generation of the 1950s and 1960s, which would herald the second golden age of Welsh rugby.

THE COURT OF KING JOHN

Like his countryman Arthur Gould before him, Barry John was a 24-carat gold superstar of rugby. If Gould was the first man in the game to be granted that overused sobriquet, then John was the leading figure in an age when television was the main instrument in creating heroes. In a way that proved a sadness for the sport, it was that pressure of being a popular, recognizable figure at the helm of a country's national game that took John away from the rugby scene at the height of his powers.

Barry John was a miner's son. His father, William, worked for 28 years in Great Mountain Colliery, Tumble. His uncle Lloyd, whose death when Barry was 12 deeply affected the boy, was also a miner 'and had blue scars on his hands and dust in his lungs to show for it'. This was the Welsh heritage that placed Wales apart from its rugby-playing neighbours. This was a world of grit and sweat and gruelling physical endeavour from which rugby proved a dynamic release. John's great rugby-playing partner for Cardiff and country, scrum-half Gareth Edwards, was also from a mining village, and the two men forged perhaps the greatest half-back partnership of all. Their legendary meeting of minds began at a practice session for a Welsh trial at Trinity College, Carmarthan. Edwards, a trainee teacher, was positively gleaming in new tracksuit and boots. His laid-back partner-to-be was in his customary casual mode, wearing plimsolls and nursing a small hangover. They sized one another up. 'Look Gareth,' began John, 'you throw 'em and I'll catch 'em. Let's leave it at that and piss off home.' Edwards retorted, 'Don't you worry about my passes, boy. I can sling 'em from anywhere. Just make sure you catch 'em, that's all.'

John grew up in the mining village of Cefneithin in the post-war days of carnivals, street parties and coal tips. His dad's favourite occupation was trying to pick a winner for a Saturday afternoon bet. The village already boasted an international rugby player in Carwyn James, then the most famous man in the community and the one always surrounded by a group of reverential small boys, including Barry John, who recalls, 'We used to run with him, pass to him and kick to him. At times we must have been a nuisance but he never asked us to go away.' However, James did provide John with a piece of rugby gospel which proved to be invaluable. He told the youngster not always to watch the ball when he went to see a game but to watch the man. John followed the advice, although James never knew that it was he whom young Barry would watch. From an early age John adapted the quiet, almost tranquil, manner that was to guide him through his rugby life and make it appear that he was tearing defences apart without so much as ruffling his hair.

Besides his great natural talent, the most precious commodity John possessed was time. He always read the game that fraction of a second quicker than the opposition. James, however, must take some credit for nurturing John's talent on the village cabbage patch, the 'rugby pitch' that was literally at the bottom of the John family garden. There the king-in-waiting would spend hours practising the fly-half's art of swerve and dummy and kick. The other thing he practised was signing his autograph. He was born to be a rugby star.

The king: in the early 1970s Barry John had the rugby world at his educated feet

Barry John never seemed to boot the ball. He glided it over, even from enormous distances. It was all about timing. Today it seems that everyone in rugby kicks the Barry John way. He had what Carwyn James once described as an 'inner calm, a coolness, a detachment; a brilliance and insouciance which is devastating'. His great contemporary Gerald Davies, master of the try-scoring side-step, had those same qualities.

The pinnacle of his rugby career came just five years after that muddy encounter with Gareth Edwards when they were both part of the British Lions team that toured New Zealand in 1971 under the captaincy of John Dawes. He began the tour as a brilliant fly-half; he finished it dubbed 'King John' and the most famous rugby player in the world, the George Best of the game. He ended the tour with a total of 188 points scored and the series won. The following season for Wales he set a record of 35 points in the Five Nations Championship in the first Grand Slam and Triple Crown-winning team of the 1970s, setting the standard for a wonderful golden age of Welsh rugby. Bill McLaren describes John as displaying 'acceptable arrogance' on the rugby field. He infused confidence into a team as he ghosted effortlessly through packed defences. Former Welsh coach Clive Rowlands once revealed that he was in the players' dressing-room before an international, trying to stir up feelings of pride and passion, of fighting for one's country. He looked around the room at the faces of a team who would die for their nation when he spotted Barry John sitting at the back, whistling quietly to himself.

Just when Barry John had the world at his feet he chose to retire. His 25 caps could have been many more. In a recent television interview with Dai Smith he said that the defining moment of his decision came when he travelled up to Rhyl to open an extension to a local bank. All the bank officials were there and John remembers a woman employee becoming so flustered and nervous that she actually curtsied to him. He recalls, 'I thought, that's it. I've finished with rugby.' John realized he wanted no more of the lifestyle that went with the sport, and promptly announced his retirement at the age of 27, the first victim of a new age of rugby. The king had abdicated. He left a legacy of wonderful tries, goals and drop-goals but left people wondering how much more there might have been. He maintains

The Varsity match of 1928: the Oxford and Cambridge teams are presented at Twickenham

to this day that he loved the sport, and didn't actually want to retire from rugby itself.

Barry John, Gareth Edwards and others, such as J.P.R. Williams and Gerald Davies, were part of a new, optimistic age of Welsh nationalism. There was more money in the economy and more money in rugby. While these players were 25 years too early to become millionaires from the game, they were part of a new culture that saw rugby and its players as marketable commodities. They enjoyed perks of course – cars, some expenses and help with a job – the sort of thing that would have had the Rev Frank Marshall turning in his grave. But since the Arthur Gould Affair, Wales has been allowed to get away with this covert 'shamateurism'. In many ways Barry John is a throwback to the days of Gould. He always knew he would play for Wales. Just 25 years ago that meant playing *rugby* for Wales. There was no doubt of that. If a young man declared he was going to play for Wales today, the answer would be 'At what sport?'

SHADES OF BLUE

The second Tuesday of December is traditionally a day when thousands of grandmothers are supposedly buried. Their imaginary funerals are the well-worn excuse for taking the afternoon off to go to Twickenham to watch the annual Varsity match between Oxford and Cambridge. To this day the match represents the purest example of the amateur spirit that

FRANCE 5 – WALES 9
STADE COLOMBES, PARIS
27 MARCH 1971

Benoit Dauga was a mountain of a man. At 6 feet 5 inches tall and pushing 16 stone, he had been the rock at the back of the French scrum for 54 internationals.

After half an hour of fiery French pressure, he had given the home team the lead when he crashed over for a try, and looked certain to double his personal

Dai Morris, with John Bevan in support, launches another attack for Wales against a belligerent French defence

fly-half, squashing his nose. John, battered and bruised, staggered off for treatment on a badly broken beak, but returned to play his part again, with splatters of blood the evidence of a job well done.

Barry John has no hesitation in naming this match as the greatest he has ever played in. It may not have been his personal best, but for sheer blood and guts the performance of the 15 Welshmen, who kept out a rampant French team, was proof positive that no sport can equal the heroic qualities of rugby when the match is an epic such as this. Both teams were undefeated that season, although only Wales was chasing a Grand Slam because France had drawn with both Ireland and England. It was a prize that had eluded Wales since 1952, when the Blaenavon speedster Ken Jones streaked past opposition defences time and time again. The 1971 vintage was a team Jones would have been proud to grace with his electrifying presence. J.P.R. Williams and Gareth Edwards were there, along with the captain, John Dawes, who that year would take charge of the British Lions. But it was in the pack where the unsung heroes did so much to hold the French. The back row of Mervyn Davies, John Taylor and Dai Morris was the best in the world. Prop Denzil Williams was, at that stage, the

tally when he set off again like a giant possessed for the Welsh line. He was held up near the corner flag, but his momentum was sure to carry him over until Barry John, 5 feet 9 inches and 11 stone 11 pounds of Welsh mining stock, bravely jumped on the Frenchman. He hung on grimly, like a man dangling from the Eiffel Tower. Dauga toppled over short of the line and landed on the most capped forward for Wales. He was to make a crucial impact in the match.

Wales kicked off into the wind and immediately the roars from a packed Stade Colombes urged, 'Allez enfants, allez!' The French team, with the Spanghero brothers in the scrum and the elegant Pierre Villepreux at full-back, mounted wave after wave of attacks on the Welsh line. The Welsh tackled like demons, none personifying the death or glory spirit so much as the redoubtable J.P.R. Williams at full-back. The flying French wing Roger Bourgarel was hurtling towards the Welsh line, with Villepreux a scoring pass away and with only J.P.R. to beat. Bourgarel delayed a fraction too long and felt the full force of a bone rattler from J.P.R., who wrapped up both man and ball and the chance was gone.

Poor Bourgarel was to have a wretched game. An increasingly frustrated France was still only five points up when the wing was off again towards J.P.R. with Villepreux in support. This time he managed to pass, but Williams had read it and made a full-blooded effort to intercept. He grabbed the ball and was off up the field with the French defence in disarray. Over half-way he thundered, with only Denzil Williams, the lion-hearted prop, gasping to keep up. J.P.R. checked inside, wrong-footing the defence, and feinted to pass to his team-mate and namesake. A gap on the left-hand side appeared as everyone swept to the right, and out of the corner of his eye J.P.R. glimpsed Gareth Edwards, scorer of great tries, straining every muscle to get to the action. In a fraction of a second J.P.R. turned and spun the ball out to Edwards, who sprinted over in the corner. Wales turned round only two points down, with the wind at their backs in the second half.

Still the French pounded the Welsh defences with their massive forwards, Claude Spanghero in particular driving through. Wales managed only two worthwhile attacking positions in the whole of the second half, but each time they made them count. The French went offside at a ruck under their own posts and Barry John kicked a simple penalty to put Wales in front for the first time.

A fumble by Villepreux then set up the second attacking movement. A series of scrums on the French 25 ended with Jeff Young winning a ball against the head. Edwards flung a quick pass to John, who cut through the French line, wrong-footing his opposite number, J.L. Berot, and fooling centre Roland Bertranne, who had moved across, believing he would pass. It was a typical Barry John try, apparently effortless, but all down

to a man who always seemed to be thinking half a second quicker than the opposition. 'Gareth flipped it up and I just danced in,' he said afterwards. Wales then just went on tackling until the job was finished and the Grand Slam was theirs.

Afterwards, John Reason, the respected rugby writer, commented, 'The standard of the game was one of the highest ever seen in Europe.' Barry John thought it 'a complete performance in terms of attacking and covering'.

Welsh centre John Dawes looks to close down another sparkling French attack

One of the earliest games for the sartorially challenged teams from Oxford and Cambridge - the Varsity match of 1880

rugby's controllers fought so hard to preserve in the 19th century. Public schools from all over the country descend on the national ground in coaches. The Stock Exchange and the City are ghost towns. Radio and film crews cover the match extensively. For years the evocative images of Pathé News brought the excitement of the game to cinema audiences.

Yet this annual jamboree is not an international, nor, most unfathomably, is its appeal limited to students and graduates of the two universities themselves. For generations it has been the great middle-class day out, a celebration of rugby's role in producing men of which the country can be proud. It doesn't matter one iota if you have never been within sniffing distance of Oxford or Cambridge. In the car parks and the bars you can meet old friends and make new ones, joined in a sense of unity that for this day at least you are as one man. Historian Stefan Collini describes it as an 'odd' institution where, 'Two entirely amateur teams made up of students can draw a huge crowd. A whole social stratum migrate to Twickenham for the day to affirm the essentially joyful nature of the game.'

The influence Oxford and Cambridge have had on the game is no more than to be expected, as the universities are part of the natural progression of a public-school life. Playing rugby is the link in the chain and the Varsity match itself, attended by so many enthusiastic schoolboys, is a way of rugby regenerating itself for the future by encouraging more boys to take up the sport. Although William Webb Ellis went to Oxford, there is no evidence that he took up the game there. However, his old school, Rugby, led the way in taking the game to both Oxford and Cambridge, and the former in particular could always be relied upon to provide a team to take on the school. Competition between Oxford and Cambridge is fought out in many sports, although it is only in the Varsity match and the deeply unexciting University Boat Race that it has truly captured public attention. It is unimaginable that anyone fed on a soccer diet of Arsenal against

Spurs in league and cup would take a trip across London to see the two universities play out a 0–0 draw.

Oxford won the first encounter played at their ground, The Parks, on 10 February 1872, five days after the second-ever international match between England and Scotland. Oxford wore dark blue jerseys from the outset, while on this occasion Cambridge wore pink. Despite the presence of many international standard players, just a handful of spectators turned up to witness the encounter and no 'gate money' changed hands.

Cambridge suffered a set-back before they even took the field, when captain E. Winnington Ingram had to resign because of his imminent exams. Oxford were at full strength, relying heavily on Old Rugbeians. Before the game they held a trial match, Old Rugbeians *versus* The Rest, and the men from Rugby waltzed it. Of the Oxford 20, they provided 16 players, the other four coming from their old allies of Marlborough College. Each team played with three backs, three half-backs and 14 forwards – a crowded pitch. The Oxford captain of the day, W.O. Moberly, later to become a successful county cricketer with Gloucestershire, wrote a report of the match which is one of the first-ever accounts of a game. After ten minutes he was happy to note that Oxford were in the ascendancy: 'The Oxford forwards soon showed their real superiority and by some excellent play, notably by Isherwood, Cholmondeley and Fletcher, took the ball to their opponents' goal-line and forced them to touch it down. On their dropping it [the ball] out, it was returned to the 25-yard post and Isherwood, getting a ball when thrown in from touch, made a good run-in and turned it into a goal by an excellent kick, for the distance was very long.'

Isherwood's goal – try and conversion – proved to be the only score on an afternoon when he was one of a handful of players his captain singled out for a special mention. He was one of several in that first match to gain international honours, beginning a tradition of the Varsity match acting as an advanced nursery for future stars. It has been a common phenomenon right up to the present day, with some of the greatest names in rugby making a name for themselves while playing for Oxford or Cambridge. More than a dozen players from Oxbridge played for England in the first five years of international competition. The second match in the annual series was played at the Cambridge ground, Parker's Piece. Cambridge won and, as a result, it was decided that all future matches should be played on neutral territory: the Kennington Oval, at Blackheath and the Queen's Club, now more famous for tennis – being favoured until Twickenham took over in 1921.

In 1875 the Varsity match was the very first to be played 15 a side. Perhaps even more significantly, Cambridge decided pink was not an entirely suitable colour for the manly pursuit of rugby and opted for light blue and white hoops.

An incredible number of players in the Varsity match have gone on to play international rugby. In the first 100 years of the encounter more than 500 tasted international honours. From generation to generation almost every match has found a star, and not only from England. Both Adrian Stoop and Ronnie Poulton-Palmer played for Oxford. In 1921 future England captain Wavell Wakefield led a brilliant Cambridge team. The 1928 match saw young Harry Bowcott from Cardiff prove himself a classically gifted kicker, winning his first of eight caps the following year at centre. In 1934 Cliff Jones won the first of three blues for Cambridge when he was selected for Wales at fly-half; over four subsequent seasons he established himself as one of the all-time greats. With the physically formidable Welsh international Wilfred Wooller at centre, he turned the Cambridge University team into one of the finest of all Varsity sides. These were great virtuosos – Jones the Side-step and Wooller the Battering Ram – who formed an intuitive partnership at fly-half and centre. They led Cambridge to a pounding 29–4 thrashing of poor Oxford. Wooller scored with a colossal drop-goal from 5 yards inside his own half. Wales didn't hog all the action, though, with Jones releasing Scottish international wing Kenneth Fyfe for three tries.

Cliff Jones remained a man of rugby all his life, becoming the third president of the Welsh Rugby Football Union in the centenary year of 1981. In 1946 he played at full-back for the British Army of the Rhine XV, which also included Howard Campbell of Cambridge University, whose international career with Scotland lay ahead of him. On one scorching hot day in Trieste they took on a Combined Services XV from the Central Mediterranean Forces. Because of the extremely hard ground, Jones turned out in sand-shoes, something he was to regret when he attempted a clearance kick which was nearly charged down, and when a burly Scotsman landed on his foot, leaving him writhing in agony. The opposing forward was none other than Bill McLaren, who recalls in his autobiography, *Talking of Rugby*, being 'thoroughly ashamed' at hurting a rugby legend in this fashion. Years later, when Jones was president of the WRFU, McLaren reminded him of his clumsy challenge: 'Don't worry, Bill,' soothed Jones, 'I've long since forgiven you.'

Above: The 1984 Varsity match: the young Rob Andrew makes a telling break

Opposite: Hamish Innes (Cambridge) celebrates a try during the 1998 Varsity match

The whole of the Scottish back line of the 1920s was transposed from Oxford: Johnny Wallace, George Aitken, Phil Macpherson and Ian Smith were the best in the land, and in 1924 were largely responsible for dishing out a 35–10 drubbing to Wales. Great names continue to grace the Twickenham turf – men such as maths scholar and Scottish captain Arthur Smith, Mike Gibson, Richard Sharp and Gerald Davies sampled the competitive edge in the annual Oxford and Cambridge clash. Overseas stars, including Chris Laidlaw, Tommy Bedford and New Zealand's World Cup-winning captain David Kirk have also joined them.

One of the great advantages of Varsity rugby is that it brought great players from different countries together in one team, just as the Lions and the Barbarians would do. In the 1950s the Oxford partnership of Welsh wizard Onllwyn Brace and the urbane M.J.K.

Cliff Morgan, one of the most gifted Welsh fly-halves, sends a perfect pass to Ken Jones (France, 1956)

(Mike) Smith, later to be the English cricket captain, was full of flair. Although it was a pity that they never played together outside Oxford, Brace went on to even greater heights with the gifted Cliff Morgan, who many, including Bill McLaren, would put at fly-half in their all-time best team. Although Morgan was not an Oxbridge man, he did make his début for Cardiff against Oxford University in 1950. He too was inspired by the exploits of Cliff Jones a generation before, relating in his autobiography, *Captain's Diary,* how he met the great man, in their native Rhondda Valley, when he was just 14.

In more recent times Rob Andrew and Stuart Barnes enjoyed a rivalry in the Varsity match that was to spill over into the international arena as they competed for the privilege of wearing England's number 10 jersey. Barnes almost did not make the match in 1981.

Rather like E. Winnington Ingram in 1872, the pressing matter of exams at Oxford threatened to rule him out when he discovered that they fell on the same day. Fortunately, he was able to reach a compromise with his college and was allowed to sit his exam at the ungodly hour of 6.00 a.m. He passed, but his performance in the match did not pass quite so successfully: Oxford lost by 9–6.

The advent of professionalism is likely to mean fewer younger players relying on the traditional path to rugby glory that an appearance in the Varsity match often provided. Teenage sensations, such as Jonny Wilkinson of Newcastle and England, are full-time rugby players earning big money at an age when former stars were still attending tutorials in cap and gown. Cambridge won an exciting 1998 renewal by 16–12, their fifth success in a row. It remains to be seen whether any of the two XVs join the past greats as a household name.

THE OLD FARTS

In 1955 Playfair Books published *The History of the Rugby Football Union* by O.L. Owen. Each past president and secretary of the RFU is pictured – a total of 50 in all – and the committees of 1890/1, 1906/7, 1912/13,1937/8 and, of course, the-then current committee of 1954/5 are all pictured with their names, some 48 of them, carefully listed underneath. There's a photo of some goalposts at Rugby School, the famous Webb Ellis plaque, two photos of rugby balls and four pictures of the Twickenham ground. Only two pictures show any players, and these are the first two international teams from England and Scotland in 1871. The book shows more collars and ties than rugby jerseys. Although the text records many great matches and players in the game's history to that date, there is not enough room to include pictures of them among the sea of (self-) important administrators. If any doubt remained as to who claimed ownership of the game of rugby, then this display of aggrandisement dispels it. Here is a bold statement of possession. Only one non-committee person does merit a full-page picture. Alas, the Queen is not renowned for her rugby-playing prowess.

If he had been England captain in 1955, even Will Carling would not have had his photograph in *The History of the Rugby Football Union*. His record-breaking achievements certainly would have deserved some sort of mention. He captained his country 59 times, a

figure unsurpassed in world rugby. For England, the durable Bill Beaumont comes next, with 21 games as captain. Carling was in charge of three Grand Slam-winning teams – in 1991, 1992 and 1995. And in May of 1995 he made an off-the-cuff remark which has become the most famous quote in all of rugby and put the men that ran the game under the brightest spotlight since the battle with the northern clubs a century earlier.

Carling was being interviewed by Greg Dyke for a Yorkshire Television documentary. Afterwards, Carling unpinned his microphone and placed it on the table, not realizing that it was still 'live'. Dyke asked him a question about running sport through committee and Carling replied: 'If the game is run properly as a professional game, you do not need 57 old farts running rugby.' Carling maintains that he had no idea the remark was on tape. Unfortunately, it was recorded for posterity and in this media-run age there was no hope of keeping it a secret, especially when *The Sun* newspaper got wind of it.

Telling the story of 'Me and My Big Mouth' in his autobiography, Carling recalls that he was playing golf with the former England football captain Gary Lineker on the day the programme was to be broadcast. Over a cup of coffee on the ninth, Gary said, 'Will, not even your lot are stupid enough to react to a thing like that, even if you did say it.' As Carling puts it, 'He couldn't have been more wrong.'

The senior figures within rugby were 'hopping mad' and met at the East India Club to decide what to do. Carling had never been particularly popular with top table at the RFU because of his high media profile and his campaign for payments to players. He acknowledges some blazing rows with former RFU president Dudley Wood, and there was clearly no love lost between the pair. Carling tried to call the incumbent president, Dennis Easby, but was told he was in a meeting. He sent a fax explaining the context of his remarks and was told to ring again the following morning. He was on the phone to Easby bright and early, full of apologies. Easby interrupted him: 'I'm sorry to tell you, you've been relieved of the England captaincy. You'll still be able to go to South Africa as a player, but not as a captain. Thanks for all you've done.' The announcement was made official the same morning. With a breathtaking lack of public relations acumen, the committee men of the RFU had, in the eyes of the public, revealed Carling to be exactly right: they were undoubtedly 'old farts'.

By the time the Sunday newspapers hit the streets, it was clear that the RFU had misread the situation. Their attempts to confirm their authority over the game had backfired.

They were generally thought to have over-reacted to what many people considered an amusing remark. Indeed, it was now clearly seen to be an accurate remark. If the committee had consisted of 57 varieties, it might have been different. If the public had noticed some black faces, some working-class people or some women among their number, Carling might have been perceived as being out of order. Instead, the committee was a bunch of middle-class men in blazers and ties collectively behaving like a ballet dancer who had snagged his tights. They were a laughing stock. In his book Carling writes, 'As far as the public reaction went, that was a pretty apposite comment on the egos of a few old men. How anyone could be so upset, react so strongly at being called old farts is beyond me.'

Two leading players and candidates for Carling's job, Rob Andrew and Dean Richards, stated publicly that they would not be interested in taking over the captaincy. The RFU climbed down and attempted to save face. Carling publicly apologized to Dennis Easby, the RFU president, and was reinstated as captain for the next World Cup in South Africa, which was only a few weeks away.

So were there any differences between this row, which split the rugby world, and the most important battle in rugby history which had taken place a century before? In 1895 it appeared that the middle-class men who ran rugby were dinosaurs fending off inevitable change. A century later they were at it again. Both fights revolved around a maniacal desire to preserve amateurism in Rugby Union and a dedication to the idea that professionalism would in some way destroy the game. Both fights were about control of the game and the question of who had authority. There was, however, one huge difference. In 1895 professionalism was viewed with a mistrust based on fear of the working classes. Will Carling, however, was not a cotton-mill worker trying to earn a few bob for using his sporting talent. He was a man who, in a previous age, would have been the darling of the old amateur ranks – a handsome sporting gladiator who represented the best of the public school and military characteristics so vital to the image rugby had of itself over the past 100 years. Carling was *Boy's Own* stuff, a former soldier and public-school boy. He had attended Sedbergh, the same school as the renowned former England captain Wavell

Previous pages: England's Captain Marvel, Will Carling, slips a tackle from Jason Little during the 1991 tour of Australia
Following pages: Lawrence Dallaglio leads England from the front against Wales in the Five Nations (1999) before resigning amid media controversy. His successor Martin Johnson was ready to step up

Will Carling and RFU president Denis Easby look glum during a press conference, after Carling's dismissal as captain

Wakefield. Later, Wakefield became president of the RFU, a course his young counterpart is unlikely to follow. Carling even played for Harlequins, the club of Poulton-Palmer and Stoop, and synonymous with the English revival after the débâcle of the northern break-away. The old farts affair was part of a middle-class civil war, with Carling a traitor who started off Cavalier and turned Roundhead. The prize was not the throne of England but control of the kingdom of rugby. Just as in 1895 when the Northern Union was formed, the game of rugby would never be the same again.

The rough edges that have so clearly defined differences in class in England in the 20th century have been sanded down over the course of generations. Everyone is now vaguely middle class but there are divisions within that caste. A sense of tradition, a mistrust of new money and the desire for exclusivity are new markers of social status. Professionalism in rugby still, to some extent, represents a lower social class than amateur. Anything with mass appeal, such as soccer or *The Sun* newspaper, is perceived as working class. A middle-class mistrust of the press and media as instruments of the masses is a common thread running through life in Britain today. Ironic, therefore, that the hand that fed Will Carling should so vigorously have bitten him just four years later.

Carling's media profile undoubtedly helped him to remain as England captain. Yet any public popularity he had was effectively lost when he dumped his partner and baby. He was roundly reviled in the newspapers. There was talk that he cashed in on the trauma in his private life by timing the publication of his autobiography to coincide. The superstar status that money and professionalism brings also invites intense public scrutiny. The ghoulish interest in Carling's domestic arrangements proved that rugby was no longer a game enjoyed and controlled by a middle-class masonry. The nation owned the sport now, as they were effectively paying for it through television and gate receipts.

The handling of Carling by the press revealed the pitfalls for modern rugby superstars. However, the incident paled into insignificance compared to the news that his successor as England captain, Lawrence Dallaglio, had resigned in May 1999, after allegations of drug taking. In this climate of increased media coverage, Dallaglio had to justify his reputation, not only to the RFU, but also to the increasingly cynical public. The Carling and Dallaglio revelations showed that there were more important things than rugby on the nation's minds.

THE EMPIRE GAME

THE STORY OF NEW ZEALAND
AND SOUTH AFRICA

The All Blacks and the Springboks
have been the two giants of world
rugby for a century. The history
of the two nations has been
interwoven with a mutual passion
for the game introduced to their
shores by British colonials.
Together they formed a bond of
excellence that no other countries
have been able to match. Their
prowess at rugby gave them
international status. Only Wales
could claim to have taken rugby as
much to its heart as these two
outposts of the British Empire. Former
New Zealand prime minister David Lange
described rugby as the one thing that a
country with three million people could do
superbly. 'Rugby is New Zealand,' he said.

Throughout the 20th century New Zealand and
South Africa have slugged it out in a series of
heavyweight contests with neither side being able to
claim long-term advantage. The greatest team to leave
New Zealand shores is often amusingly described as the
1937 Springboks. Revenge for the All Blacks came in 1956 –
and it was sweet. But New Zealand's desire for competition with
their great rugby rivals almost tore both apart as racial division
spilled over into violence during the Springboks' 1981 tour. Ultimately
both nations put the dignity of their people before their desire for sporting
success. It was not always so.

IN SEARCH OF AN IDENTITY:
THE POWER OF RUGBY IN NEW ZEALAND

New Zealand in the 19th century was a pretty strange place, the British Empire's most loyal and distant colony. It was a tough, uncompromising country, and the few hardy souls who migrated across to the other side of the world were a resilient breed. Historian Jock Phillips describes the life as 'stressful with a lot of drinking, swearing and yarning. Rugby built on the culture of that particular male community of pioneers.' They had come to this country to seek their fortune in gold but stayed on as sheep farmers or white-collar workers in the increasing number of small towns that sprang up as railways snaked their way into the more remote parts of the territory. They did not go to New Zealand to play rugby football. But by playing rugby football they became New Zealanders.

The first recorded game of rugby in New Zealand took place in the town of Nelson on 14 May 1870. It was the brainchild of Charles James Monro, whose parents had sent him to England to complete his education at an English public school, Christ's College in Finchley, north London. Rugby was popular at the school and the 18-year-old Monro returned home with the laws of the new game packed in his suitcase. Monro was very much of the higher social class in New Zealand, as his father, Sir David, was a Member of Parliament and Speaker of the House of Representatives. He watched his son play in the first match and, in doing so, bestowed instant social acceptance on the new game. It did not remain the private game of the ruling classes for long.

The majority of settlers in New Zealand were working class and, as in the Welsh mining communities, they placed great emphasis on physical strength and male bonding. They embraced the game that had been fostered by English public-school boys and turned it into something altogether more violent and dangerous. A player was actually killed during a match in 1877 and the coroner subsequently declared that 'the game of rugby football was only worthy of savages'. The *New Zealand Herald* was moved to complain that 'bull-baiting and cock-fighting have more to commend them than rugby football'. Rugby became a physical expression of 'mateship', without any homosexual undertones. A player from those pioneering days recalled, 'St Jacob's Oil, at first bought by the bottle, was afterwards procured by the case, and the pungent smell of this embrocation used to pervade our quarters; the spectacle afforded visitors of half a dozen men vigorously rubbing each other's legs in the sitting room of our hotel must have been rather startling.' Historian Jock Phillips explains, 'Rugby was very rough at first and society as a whole was feeling anxious about it. Male communities where so much drinking is involved become socially dangerous, so it was important to impose a strict code on the game so that the pioneer values could flourish within a controlled setting.' The New Zealand Rugby Union, which was established in 1892, quickly set about doing just that, empowering the referee to stop the violence at the blow of a whistle.

As the rail network in New Zealand developed throughout the 1870s and 1880s, so rugby reached small communities and helped to bind them together. A match between the towns of Christchurch and Timaru drew a crowd of more than 1000 enthusiastic spectators once the rail link between the two towns had been completed in 1875. In that land rugby had a great advantage over cricket and soccer. All the locals needed was a piece of empty ground and sufficient players to make up two teams. It was a bonus if someone knew the rules. The growth of the game depended on its acceptance in the small towns where local businesses, banks and councils had enough employees to easily make up a team. It also allowed the desk-bound a chance for some satisfying physical endeavour at the end of their working week. That provided the nucleus for the 'Saturday' culture in New Zealand, where town and country would meet, with rugby as the centrepiece. Manual workers, miners, farmers and railwaymen would come into town on a Friday night determined to spend their money over the next two days on a boisterous good time. A rugby match gave the weekend a purpose.

By the 1880s, the emerging road and rail network was transforming New Zealand from a frontier society into a colony seeking a national identity. Over the next 30 years a combination of war and rugby would help it achieve that. In 1888 the first representative team from New Zealand arrived in the British Isles. The first official tour would not be until 1905, but the 'Natives', as the 1888 team became known, embarked on an astonishing schedule of 107 matches across Britain and Australia. The party was largely made up of superb Maori and part-Maori players, 21 out of 26, including the famous Warbrick brothers. The nucleus of the team had been to Te Aute College, in some ways the Rugby School of New Zealand. Situated in the Hawke's Bay region, it was originally the Imperial motherland's attempt to impose a European educational system on the natives. It was a school for 'young Maori gentlemen'. In effect, it prided itself on being able to turn the native people of a far-flung corner of the Empire into middle-class Englishmen.

The most influential of Te Aute's old boys, in rugby terms at least, was Thomas Ellison. He was born into a great rugby-playing family. His cousin, Jack Taiaroa, had scored nine tries on the first New Zealand tour of Australia in 1884. Young Tom, whose middle name of Rangiwahia betrayed his origins, was the first of his generation to approach the sport of rugby with a degree of professionalism. A brilliant attacking forward, he captained the Natives and led by example, playing in more than 80 matches. He is also credited as having invented the position of wing forward. Ellison was a man well ahead of his time, not just with his thinking on the pitch. On his return from the tour he wrote *The Art of Rugby Football*, in which he put forward cogent arguments for the players to be paid. He pointed out the unfairness of expecting the players to perform for nothing while spectators were actually paying for the entertainment provided. It was an argument far too advanced for the burghers of Rugby Union, who were to take another 100 years before admitting that amateur sport had no divine right to a higher morality. In his book *The Game of Our Lives*, Finlay Macdonald pays tribute to Ellison as a man of vision. The rugby writer Ron Palenski maintains, 'If Tom Ellison was living in the 1990s instead of the 1890s, he'd be Sir Tom Ellison and he'd be revered as one of the great New Zealanders.' Sadly, Ellison died at the young age of 37, perhaps burnt out by the huge physical demands he placed on himself in playing the game of rugby.

His legacies to the sport are great, not least in the unlikely introduction on the Natives' tour of two institutions that subsequently became part of New Zealand's national identity. First, the Natives wore an all-black strip with a single silver fern on the jersey. Second, they chanted and performed a Maori ceremonial war-dance known as the *haka* before the game. The British crowds had never seen or heard anything like it before. In his book *Maori Games and Haka*, Alan Armstrong defines the haka as 'a composition played by many instruments. Hands, feet, legs, body, voice, tongue and eyes all play their part in blending together to convey in their fullness the challenge, welcome, exultation, defiance or contempt of the words. It is disciplined yet emotional. More than any other aspect of Maori culture, this complex dance is an expression of the passion, vigour and identity of the race. It is, at its best, truly a message of the soul expressed by words and posture.' The best-known *haka* is called *Ka Mate* (I die) and was composed by a Maori chief called Te Rauparaha in the 1820s. Originally included as a publicity stunt to entertain the crowd, the *haka* has been moulded by the All Blacks over the years into a menacing challenge to the opposition, masquerading as an essential piece of New Zealand culture. It remains a vital part of the pageant of an All Blacks' match.

The fearsome warrior spirit demonstrated in the *haka* was soon to be tested on the battle-fields of the South African veld but not yet on the rugby field there. This was the Boer War, the bitter fight for white supremacy between the Afrikaans-speaking Dutch settlers and the British Empire-builders. As a taste of what was to come on the rugby fields, the Maoris were left behind, ironically as a result of a British decision that this was exclusively a white

The haka – *The All Blacks scare the opposition during their 1953 tour against Southern Counties*

man's war. Jock Phillips explains. 'It was a tragedy for Maori culture that they weren't allowed to go and fight. Being a warrior was part of the very core of Maori identity. Thomas Ellison, in particular, talked about rugby as a soldier-making game. He saw rugby as a way of training future soldiers for the Empire.'

As an emerging nation, New Zealand was proud of its contribution to the Imperial victory. It was as if both rugby and war gave the colony the opportunity to show the 'old country' how well it had turned out. Ironically, their opponents in war would become their fiercest rugby rivals, a competitive edge sharpened by this bloody conflict.

At this stage in the development of rugby in New Zealand, politicians became involved. Astute strategists recognized the game as the heartbeat of the nation and extremely influential in tipping the electorate for or against. Politics and rugby have been uneasy bedfellows ever since the great success of the 1905 'Originals' tour. The trite maxim that

New Zealand prime minister, Richard Seddon, leads the Originals on their triumphant return home in 1905

politics and sports should not mix, so often trotted out when racial discrimination was an explosive issue in the 1970s and 1980s, has never been more than a hollow ideal. The prime minister of the time, Richard Seddon, was quick off the blocks in linking arms with the Originals. He became known as the minister for football because of his intense interest in the tour and the way in which he manipulated its success to create a national fervour for rugby. He also used it as an advertisement extolling the qualities of life in New Zealand. His High Commissioner in London, Pember Reeves, cabled match reports home that were given maximum publicity throughout the country. The New Zealand Post Office would telegraph the results to every remote area, uniting the people in a common sense of victory.

Pember Reeves followed the team around, acting almost as an unofficial PR, speaking at post-match dinners praising the New Zealand lifestyle and drawing favourable comparisons with the congested cities of Great Britain. It was an extension of the idea born in the Boer War that these sons of the Empire were fitter, stronger and had a better quality of life than their British male counterparts. On Seddon's instructions, Reeves placed advertisements for immigrants in local papers on the day of each match. The subliminal message was that if you went to New Zealand, you and your sons would turn out like All Blacks. It was a hugely successful ploy.

In the little town of Eltham in Taranaki Province the rugby ground has by tradition been the centre of the community, as it is in many such settlements all over New Zealand. Above the changing-rooms hangs a painting showing a soldier, a sailor and an airman locked together as if they are the front row of a scrum. It stands as a tribute both to the game of rugby and to the men who lost their lives in battle. The First World War took a huge toll on sport, and rugby was no exception. It seemed that whole teams had enlisted as one and subsequently died as one. At least the New Zealand troops could console themselves that they had shown the Empire to be in safe hands. At the end of the war former All Blacks throughout the ranks were assembled in

'Ranji' Wilson, All Black vice captain and the first victim of South Africa's racist policy in Rugby Union

London to represent the New Zealand Expeditionary Force in the British Empire Championships for the King's Cup. Unforgivably, they lost an early round-robin match against Australia, but recovered to face England in the final at Twickenham. Not for the last time, they triumphed on that famous turf, and King George V was there to present the trophy and give the men in all black a congratulatory royal word.

On their way home to New Zealand, the team had been invited to play a series of games by the South African Rugby Board. The vice-captain of the team was a dashing wing forward called Sergeant Nathaniel Arthur Wilson, who had an English father and a West Indian mother and was known by the nickname of 'Ranji'. But before the team left England, the New Zealand high commissioner in London received a confidential communication from the South African Board. It stated that if the visitors included 'coloureds', the tour would be wrecked and immense harm, political and otherwise, would certainly follow. They were urged to 'try to arrange exclusion'. The New Zealanders obliged, and when the boat docked at Cape Town, Sergeant Ranji Wilson stayed on board, good enough to fight with but not worthy to play rugby.

DAVE GALLAHER:
ORIGINAL HERO

Rugby and war have always enjoyed a close relationship. Fearless men on the playing fields have become great warriors in uniform. Dave Gallaher, captain of the famous 1905 All Blacks, was such a man. Already a veteran of the Boer War, he enlisted for more action when the First World War broke out. Sadly, he did not see out the final whistle, falling at Passchendaele in October 1917. He was one of 18,000 New Zealanders who died in the service of the Empire during that war. His death at least helped to define the sense of identity that New Zealand, as a far-off colonial frontier, had been striving to attain. Historian Jock Phillips explains: 'We were a man's country, defined by the achievements of our men, particularly the achievements of our men in war. We boasted a pioneering past, a place embracing the qualities of strength, courage and team spirit. Rugby was a means of keeping alive all those virtues.'

Unlike Gallaher and his fellow soldiers, the majority of New Zealanders were not particularly big, nor strong and warrior-like. But their wonderful rugby players were able to preserve the nation's self-image. Gallaher was, in fact, an Ulsterman by birth, but had been raised in New Zealand. By the time he served as a corporal in the Boer War, he epitomized that idealized image of colonial manhood – 6 feet tall, a dashing yet taciturn figure in uniform, his thickly cut drooping moustache a fashion of the Edwardian age. He was also an outstanding wing forward, a position on the field of the play which at that time excited much controversy. Opposition teams were aghast at this innovative position and for years they complained about wing forwards flouting the offside law. That was especially true of the British teams when the Originals became the first All Blacks to tour in 1905. They swept aside their opponents in contemptuous fashion, starting with a 55–4 victory over a battered Devon. They followed it up by beating Bristol 41–0, Northampton 32–0, Leicester 28–0, Middlesex 34–0, Hartlepool 63–0, Ireland 15–0 and England 15–0. By the time the tour ended, they had lost just one game in 32 played. Gallaher's men had scored 830 points (at three for a try) and conceded a miserly 39 points. The one loss, a 3–0 defeat by Wales, served only to focus public interest on the tour.

Gallaher's vice-captain was Billy Stead, who was part Maori and whose inclusion was apparent proof of New Zealand's enlightened attitudes to racial integration. The *haka* was performed before every match and Stead and other Maori teammates made a significant contribution on the pitch. Just 14 years later that policy of inclusion was tested against the South African principles of racial segregation and white domination and found wanting.

The Originals returned home great heroes, as if triumphant from war. Gallaher's achievement was to captain a team that led directly to rugby becoming his country's national game. By

Dave Gallaher was a superb leader of the All Blacks and the epitome of colonial manhood

the time they docked in Auckland, they had such status that a crowd of 12,000 gathered at the quayside to welcome them. The prime minister, Richard Seddon, eager to cash in on the celebrations, was there as well. It is no surprise to learn in this more politically cynical age that it was Seddon and not the stoical Gallaher who led the team down the gangplank. But as 1980s' premier David Lange concedes, 'Rugby is New Zealand. You cannot explain New Zealand except in a context of being embraced by rugby.'

MYRTLE GREEN:
SOUTH AFRICA UP TO 1937

Rugby in South Africa has never been a traditional Afrikaner game. The misleading notion that it has, became true only after the 1920s, when Afrikaners took a grip on their country's society and its national sport. Rugby in South Africa began as a quintessentially English game played by a relatively élite group, and spread through the English-speaking schools of the western Cape. The man usually credited with introducing rugby to the Cape is Canon George Ogilvy, an old boy of Winchester College and Wadham College, Oxford, who introduced a version of the game to the Diocesan College in Cape Town when he became headmaster there in 1861. It was a sanitized version of the game peculiar to Winchester, and it contained elements of rugby and soccer. It was played with a large round ball with the goalposts a generous 150 yards apart. Ogilvy rejoiced in the nickname of 'Gog' because that was, apparently, the only legible part of his signature. As a result, the version of rugby played at his school was called Gogball. As author Paul Dobson explains, 'When Canon Ogilvy came to Bishops [another name for the Diocesan College], he found a whole lot of boys running wild in the bush and so he decided he would get them to play football to work off some of those wild energies. It spread by imitation – largely where there was a conglomeration of physically active males who were cut off from the debilitating effects of females.'

The first recorded match took place on 23 August 1862 and was announced in the *Cape Argus* newspaper two days before:

'We are happy to find this fine old English school-game has been introduced among us. On Saturday next sides consisting of fifteen officers of the army and a like number of gentlemen in the civil service will open the Ball with a game on the race-course at Green Point. Of course, this example will be speedily followed, and we shall have foot-ball treading closely on the likes of cricket and other imported manly games.'

This is hardly conjuring an image of massive Afrikaner farmers knocking their heads together. As author John Nauright comments, 'Rugby, as with cricket, was initially tied closely to concepts of British civilization, culture and imperial power. Similar to its English origins, white rugby began as a private school and old boy clique.'

Rugby rules – as opposed to the Winchester game of Ogilvy, who considered real rugby too barbaric – were brought to the Cape in 1878 by former England international William Henry Milton, later to become governor of Rhodesia. Just a year later, the first two authenticated clubs, Hamilton and Villagers, were founded in Cape Town. Around this time the game began to take root in Natal where, rather as in New

Canon George Ogilvy, father of South African rugby

Zealand, it helped to bind together pioneering white settlers. It reaffirmed ties with the motherland and enhanced the masculinity of its players. But unlike New Zealand, where the game has always been a great social leveller, South African rugby remained steeped in class prejudices nurtured in the élitist school system.

South Africa became a very popular destination for international (Imperial) rugby in the 1890s, and for a side that was to become the dominant world force, the home team came off decidedly second best. In 1891 a British Isles team consisting of 21 English and Scottish players won all of their 20 matches. The tour was more of a social event than a sporting encounter, with concerts, dinners, picnics and a formal ball at Government House. The team representing South Africa was hardly a national side: a captain was appointed and he would cobble together his rugby-playing mates. The three tests were lost without the home side registering a point. There was a degree of anarchy in these early encounters, with players able to claim a penalty if they thought they deserved one, the Victorian equivalent of 'That was a penalty ref!' Although the final decision was up to the referee, it did put a lot more unwanted pressure on the beleaguered official.

In 1896 the British visitors were almost as good, applying coaching science to scrummages; for the first time everyone straightened their legs in a united heave when the ball was put in and shoved. The captain for the fourth test at the famous Newlands ground was the first great South African forward Barry Heatlie, known affectionately as 'Fairy' Heatlie. He decided that his men would play in the jersey of his club, the Old Diocesan Rugby Club (Bishops Old Boys). It was predominantly a dark myrtle green. Amazingly, they won 5–0, the first time South Africa had triumphed in a test. The home team employed lots of enthusiastic 'dribbling rushes' and, after exerting a great deal of pressure, scrum-half Alf Lerard popped up to score under the posts and the match was won. It was the start of a glorious run of success for South African rugby. The new green jersey was considered something of a lucky omen.

The British colonialists of the period viewed the Dutch settlers as little more than second-class citizens, not far removed from the black natives. Novelist and colonial politician, John Buchan, made the memorably absurd remark in 1903, 'The Afrikaners are not a sporting race – they are not even a race of very skilful hunters.'

It is easy to see why the Boer War became such a bitter landmark in South Africa's history. It was an uncivil war in which the British distinguished themselves by introducing concentration camps where 26,000 women and children died. These camps initiated bitter resentment and hatred of British domination. By the end of the conflict, a ruthless war waged by greedy Imperial forces determined to run the gold and diamond economy of their Cape colony, there were 27,000 Boer prisoners of war. To put things in perspective, more than 450,000 British and Imperial troops, including detachments from New Zealand, took nearly three years to overpower 40,000 Afrikaners – a ratio of more than ten to one. In some ways the war sowed the seed for rugby becoming South Africa's national game. John Nauright explains, 'It was played by prisoners of war in the camps with British troops. This is how it spread into the interior of the country, into Transvaal, Northern Transvaal and Orange Free State, the real core of Afrikaner rugby. After the war they took it back to their homes and the game started to spring up in Afrikaner schools.'

In 1903, just two years after the end of the Boer War, a touring team arrived from Britain, perhaps seen as some sort of wound-healer. Barry Heatlie was again captain for the last test and once more he brought out the green jerseys, which had proved so effective in 1896. They did the trick again and, after two drawn tests, victory 8–0 in the third at a muddy Newlands gave South Africa its first series win. Green became established as the sporting colour of South Africa and they would not be beaten again in a test series until the titanic 1956 battle against New Zealand, who would soon overtake Britain as the rugby-playing enemy.

PAUL ROOS:
FIRST AMONG EQUALS

A deeply religious man, Paul Roos, captain of the first official Springbok team to undertake an overseas tour, refused to travel on a Sunday. He would teach during the week in Rustenburg and play his rugby on a Saturday in Johannesburg. Saturday night was a barren time to get a train between the two towns, so Roos used to take his bike with him so that he could pedal furiously the 70 miles home to Rustenburg before the clock struck midnight. This was a man of fierce principle and discipline, a stickler for sportsmanship, who used his skills as a headmaster to mould his 1906 tourists to Britain into a popular and effective unit. It helped having a jumbo pack and flying backs like Japie Krige and Bob Loubser, who could run 100 yards in ten seconds and scored 24 tries on the tour. The full-back Arthur Marsburg was an

Paul Roos, a stickler for sportsmanship, captained the first Springbok tourists to Britain in 1906

heroic figure who would hurl himself at the ball like a soccer goalkeeper to stop a dribbling rush from his opponents.

The 1906 team arrived in the British Isles anxious to demonstrate how rugby in the colony had improved since the Boer War. They wanted to prove themselves just as superior to the motherland as the All Blacks had a year earlier. Roos and his men had heard how journalists had dubbed the 1905 New Zealanders the All Blacks and were aghast that they might be similarly named after the colour of their jerseys, which were myrtle green. The 'All Myrtles' was not acceptable to the rugby players of the high veld, so they suggested to journalists that they should be called the Springboks after a type of gazelle. Roos, an Afrikaner and a teacher, informed one and all that it was a Dutch word and the plural should technically be Springbokken. Fortunately, he was over-ruled and the Springboks were born. To emphasize the point, badges depicting a springbok were sewn on to their jerseys. They gave the team a precious identity.

The 1906 Springboks, while perhaps not quite the equals of the 1905 All Blacks, nevertheless swept Wales aside 11–0 in front of 50,000 spectators at Swansea. In a way it was revenge for all the colonies. After the 'Boks crushed Midland Counties 29–0, the *Daily Chronicle* memorably dipped into its well of metaphors: 'The colonials have met the cream of the Midlands and made them look like thin skim milk.' There was little doubt that the South Africans enjoyed considerable superiority in terms of organization, tactics and physical strength. Some of their success was due to an innovative 3–4–1 scrummage formation, which was designed to be especially effective on muddy British grounds. And it did no harm that Roos communicated with his men in Afrikaans, which, unsurprisingly, seemed like double-Dutch to the home teams. In all the Springboks won 25 matches, lost two and drew against England. They scored 553 points and conceded a miserly 79. One of the games they lost was 6–0 to Scotland when Roos was absent because of a shoulder injury.

Roos was not the best or the most famous player of his time, but he cast a mould for future South African captains. He was upright, imperturbable and strong. Future leaders were picked to preserve this image of South African rugby abroad. On his jubilant return to Cape Town, Roos asserted that the tour had drawn English and Afrikaner South Africans closer together after the bitter divisions of the Boer War. The drawn match against England had, he said, shown them all as 'equals'.

THE BATTLE FOR SUPREMACY

Although Paul Roos was an Afrikaner, rugby in South Africa remained firmly an Empire game until after the First World War. In fact, in the 19th century it was played more by the black population than by the Dutch settlers. The first coloured club was founded in Cape Town in 1886 at a time when, as in New Zealand, the emphasis was on integration rather than segregation. It overtook cricket as the key black sport of the Cape until the late 1960s when soccer started to find a niche among youngsters. The first black players were attached to the school system in much the same way as the game spread through the white population. But as Andre Odendaal, curator of Robben Island Museum, explains, 'Instead of getting greater opportunities for advancement, these people were excluded from the political, social and economic system in South Africa. Increasingly, they played rugby on their own.'

Ironically, the success of the 1906 and 1912 touring teams to England gave white supremacists a strong hold in a sport that they were unwilling to give up. The Boer War also helped them to consolidate this hold as it forced the Afrikaner population to value their own culture and heritage more than the diamonds that continued to fall into British Imperial hands. However, the Afrikaner settlers should not take all the blame for the ensuing policy of apartheid. Racial prejudice and white supremacy were common tools of British colonials. Even where there was no overt racism, there existed an overwhelmingly patronizing attitude towards the natives. One manifestation of this was in New Zealand, where Maoris were excluded from white society for decades under the lame excuse that in some way they were being protected. No legislation was ever passed in South Africa declaring mixed sport to be banned. But from 1910 an unofficial colour bar ensured that the game the world would see as quintessentially South African would be, until the close of the 20th century, the white man's game. The sportsmen themselves created the segregation.

The 1912 Springbok tour to Britain established South Africa at the top of the world tree and they remained there until 1956. Billy Millar's devastating 1912 team achieved the first Grand Slam over all four home nations, including England's first defeat at Twickenham, which had opened in 1910. In the four internationals they scored 66 points and conceded only three. This supremacy began to run parallel to the growth of cultural ambitions in Afrikaner South Africa. The merging of these two strands, which occurred about a year before Ranji Wilson was left aboard a ship in Cape Town harbour, came about when Stellenbosch University was founded. It was the first Afrikaner university and in its fostering of the language and national identity of the Afrikaner it engaged in great rivalry with the English-speaking University of Cape Town. More importantly, it became the centre of rugby power, largely thanks to the influence of two men, August Markotter and his

Billy Millar led the brilliant 1912 South African tourists, who presented this springbok's head to Newport Rugby Club

protégé Danie Craven, both of whom coached the university team. They were the two most important administrators in the history of South African rugby. Stellenbosch became a breeding ground for Springboks and 'true' South Africans. The students had the time both to play rugby and to embrace Afrikaner culture. That culture included rugby as a white man's sport, a philosophy that almost dragged the game in New Zealand into the mud.

Nothing in the history of rugby can match the power and the passion of the contests between the All Blacks and the Springboks. The rivalry intoxicated both countries into inflicting a series of social indignities on their own people. The Ranji Wilson affair was just the beginning. The first South African team visited New Zealand in 1921, this time unable to dictate the racial fabric of their opposition. They had to face a full Maori side in Napier, a match that New Zealand international George Nepia was later to describe in his auto-biography as 'more than just rugby. It was racial conflict.' It was a bloody encounter, which the tourists clinched by just a single point, but the real damage was done after the game when a report by a South African journalist, C.W.F. Blackett, was leaked to the local *Napier Daily Telegraph*. It said: 'It was bad enough having to play a team officially designated New Zealand Natives, but the spectacle of thousands of Europeans frantically cheering on a band of coloured men to defeat members of their own race was too much for the Springboks, who were frankly disgusted.' There was national outcry in New Zealand at these comments, but just seven years later Maoris were excluded from the first All Blacks tour to South Africa. It had quickly become a recognized fact of life that rugby in South Africa was a white man's game – a tacit acceptance of a misconceived tradition.

The curious aspect of Maori exclusion over the decades is that it undoubtedly weakened the All Blacks when they visited South Africa. They lost in 1928 without George Nepia, and in 1949 they were whipped 4–0 in the test series, a defeat so humiliating that it plunged the country into national mourning.

In the 1930s, the golden age of Springbok rugby, the game provided the Afrikaner with a great sense of achievement. Its influence on national identity mirrored the effect that rugby had in New Zealand. Without their success in rugby, neither country mattered a bean in the world. According to historian Paul Dobson, the Springboks of the 1930s had a great sense of being South Africans. A

August Markotter wielded great influence over South African rugby

major part of that influence came from Stellenbosch, where August Markotter was coach until the time of his death in 1957. He had started coaching when he stopped playing in 1903, and he became the first coach/selector in South Africa. He was renowned as such a hard and cantankerous taskmaster that on occasions he would beat his players with a walking stick. He was descended from German missionaries and his proud boast was that he had kicked lots of players into Springbok teams. His impact was enormous and he was regarded almost with reverence by the players, who called him Oubaas Markotter, which translates roughly as the 'Old Master'. He saw rugby as a religion and regarded the players he coached at Stellenbosch as his rugby missionaries who would go out into the world spreading the happy gospel of Rugby Union. Perhaps Markotter's greatest legacy is through the later work of Dr Danie Craven, a protégé and disciple who would often refer to Markotter as a 'great man'. The climax of the Afrikaner golden age came in 1937, when the greatest-ever Springbok team left South Africa for New Zealand. It is rightly judged as possibly the finest-ever rugby side.

GEORGE NEPIA:
'INVINCIBLE'

Just off the roadside at Rangitukia, amid the harsh landscape of the East Cape region of New Zealand's North Island, is a simple grave of polished white stone with a charcoal grey headstone surrounded by flowers and a simple fence of wooden posts. It is the last resting place of George Nepia and his beloved wife. Tourists and rugby-lovers make the trip off the well-trodden urban path to this remote, Maori-dominated community to pay homage to one of the greatest names in New Zealand rugby. Nepia's was the most glittering career of a golden age, but it was blighted because he was never allowed to play against South Africa. To his own country's shame, he was excluded because of his colour. Although he was the world's first rugby superstar, Nepia's legendary status is assured because of that outrage.

Typical of the man's humility and grace, there is no mention of rugby at his grave. Instead, his children and grandchildren share pride of place on his headstone. The only clue that we are near hallowed rugby ground can be found in a little churchyard just beyond the grave. On the right-hand side of the gateway stands a pillar with a carved figure holding a rugby ball; beneath it is the simple inscription 'George'. Nothing more is required. It is a tribute to Nepia from his son, Oma.

G.M. Nepia hailed from Wairoa in the uncompromisingly named region of Poverty Bay, where he had an extremely hard childhood trying to please a stern father, while being raised, in effect, by his grandmother. Nepia later wrote an early acclaimed sporting autobiography called *I, George Nepia*, in which he recalled how, as a child, he was a terrible disappointment to his father: 'My father was ashamed and disgusted with me. He once came on to the field while I was playing and clouted me on the backside as hard as he could; it did no good as I was aware of.'

Nepia's fame as a rugby player was assured when he revealed a prodigious talent as full-back on the 1924 All Blacks tour of the British Isles. It was Nepia, just 19 years old, who led his team in the fearsome *haka* before each game. They won every match and their unbeaten record earned them the unforgettable nickname of the 'Invincibles'. The young full-back was an immovable last line of defence, who seemed to be prepared to die for his country, much in the manner of J.P.R. Williams, the great Welsh full-back of 50 years later. Nepia played all 30 matches on the 1924 tour, unbeaten and unbowed, and he emerged as a hero, especially when the line stood firm against Wales, handsomely avenging the wounding 1905 defeat with a 19–0 thrashing.

In the heady climate of today's professionalism, Nepia would have been guaranteed overnight millionaire status, but the Jonah Lomu of the 1920s returned to carve out a living as a hard-working dairy farmer in Rangitukia, where he had moved with his new wife, Huinga. New Zealand as a nation seemed proud that

The charismatic George Nepia, the greatest of all Maori rugby players

their country's first bona fide sporting superstar was a Maori, a testament to their society's enlightened racial attitudes. In 1928 the All Blacks set off for their first-ever tour of their great rugby-playing rival, South Africa, without their greatest player, a victim of his country's tacit compliance with their opponents' racial policies. Racial prejudice was a staple diet of South Africa long before apartheid became one of the most hated words in the dictionary. The series ended in a 2–2 draw, but few would argue that Nepia and his fellow Maoris would have tipped the balance in the visitors' favour.

According to historian Jock Phillips, George Nepia was 'an absolutely fearsome tackler, brilliant runner, brilliant kicker and someone who played with total courage and became very rapidly a great hero. Yet despite that, when it came to 1928, it was made very clear that Nepia was unacceptable to South Africa, and so the New Zealand rugby authorities accepted that. They colluded, with very little debate.'

In all, Nepia played just nine tests for his country – a criminally small number. Like many of his countrymen, he eked out a 'dismally low income' on his farm during the Depression years of the 1930s. In 1935, to ease chronic debts, he journeyed to England to earn £500 playing Rugby League for the London club of Streatham and Mitcham. He never lost his dignity. His foster-son, Jim Perry, quoted in *The Game of Our Lives* by Finlay Macdonald, recalled, 'I didn't see him as a famous person. He was just another Maori milking cows and trying to make a living. He was an even-tempered bloke. I only ever saw him get really angry once, right up until the time he died. I guess that was part of the thing about him as a rugby player – that he could keep his cool all the way through a game.'

The 1960s' All Blacks captain Brian Lochore played rugby with Nepia's grandson and is full of praise for Nepia himself, whom he knew well: 'George was an absolutely fabulous man and obviously a wonderful footballer. I am sure he was extremely disappointed in not being able to play on all the great stages of the world.' In 1976 Nepia eventually travelled to South Africa as a guest of the South African Rugby Union. He was, according to his daughter Kiwi, treated like royalty and offered a new Mercedes as a gift. He did not accept.

BENNIE OSLER:
THE 'EVIL GENIUS'

Like a comic strip hero, Bennie Osler, the man who revolutionized the kicking game in rugby, used to practise hour after hour booting a tennis ball around a paddock at his parents' house. At least, that's the story of how the lad from Rondebosch became the master of the drop-goal in the days when that means of scoring counted for four points and was an even more effective method of deciding matches than it is today. Like all good legends, it's only partly true. Early on in his rugby-playing career, while still a schoolboy, Osler realized that not enough attention was being paid to drop-goals. Four points was four points, and a drop-goal might involve considerably less effort than a running movement spread over 70 yards of muddy ground to score a try worth just three.

Osler was a great tactician but always modest about his achievements, particularly his drop-goal expertise: 'I don't think there was anything surprising in my methods. I discovered that the best way to hold the ball was so that its long ends were perpendicular to the ground, with one hand on the top and the other on the bottom. This was to ensure that when the ball was dropped it fell on its point.

'Once I had decided to drop, there was usually no time to look at the goalposts. There was just a sense of where they were. The old golfing tip of keeping your eye on the ball is absolutely essential for drop-kicking. My advice to others is: never take your eye off the ball, kick it with the instep and not the toe. And, incidentally, talking in golfing terms, I found it possible to induce hooks and slices into kicks which were most useful in the face of oncoming defences.'

The idea of swerving the ball round a giant All Black forward intent on doing him some serious damage shows just how far

Bennie Osler's kicking game was very successful for South Africa, if not universally popular

ahead of his time Osler was. Typically, he was vilified in certain quarters for the match-winning characteristics he brought to the game. His critics would argue that his superb line-kicking was just to engineer the ball into a position for him to drop a goal and take the glory. The kicking game versus the running game is an ongoing debate within rugby. If a side is successful using the former, they will undoubtedly ruin things by trying to play the latter. It is the classic dilemma that has faced England in recent years, with arguments about whether Rob Andrew or Stuart Barnes should have been first choice fly-half.

What is in no doubt is that Osler was the dominant force in world rugby from 1924 to 1933, during which time he played 17 consecutive tests for the Springboks. Perhaps his finest hour came in the 1928 series against a New Zealand side missing the talisman presence of George Nepia. Following the success of the Invincibles on their tour of Britain in 1908, these All Blacks were thought to be unbeatable. One of the key players, goal-kicker Mark Nicholls, later conceded, 'We went over to South Africa greatly boomed, grossly overrated; the South Africans, by all accounts, were expecting man-eaters and world beaters.' After a six-week journey and an insignificant warm-up game, they encountered the mighty boot of Osler in the second game and were soundly beaten 7–3 by Western Province. That was small beer compared to the first test, when Osler dropped two superb goals and two penalties in a 17–0 defeat for New Zealand, a record defeat at the time for the All Blacks. Osler's personal tally of 14 points was a South African record, and it should be remembered that these were the days when the referees were far less generous with penalties.

After this humiliation, the All Blacks improved to take two of the remaining three tests, but afterwards they acknowledged the lesson they had learned from Osler. Opinion will always be divided on his merits. On the 1931 tour of Britain his allegedly boring safety-first kicking brought him considerable flak, but the fact remains the Springboks lost only one game on that tour – the one in which Osler didn't play. Some contemporaries might have thought him an 'evil genius' for introducing a winning strategy to the game that many rugby-lovers hated then and still hate now. But for many years, whenever young kids got together for a playground game of rugby, the one taking the kicks would declare himself to be Bennie Osler.

SEPARATE WAYS

After fighting side by side in the desert campaigns of the Second World War, South Africa and New Zealand went their separate ways in peacetime. South Africa fell under the spell of apartheid when the National Party came to power in 1948, while New Zealand entered a phase of conservative complacency. In both post-war societies, rugby reassumed its position of great importance. In the South Africa of the 1950s rugby was crucial to the spread of Afrikaner Nationalist power. Indeed, it held such significance that it became a powerful instrument of apartheid during this period. Behind the government was the Broederbond, the secret society that infiltrated the corridors of power at all levels. Founded in 1918, it was a sort of freemasonry taken to an extreme. Most of the Cabinet and National Party MPs were members of the Broederbond, which targeted rugby, the national game, to spread the attitudes and policies of the government, segregation being top of the agenda. Many of the Springbok players and captains were also in the Broederbond. At the top level of rugby, only Dr Danie Craven kept his distance from it (see page 165).

The power of the Broederbond is never better illustrated than by a story involving Craven and the prime minister, Hendrik Verwoerd, the architect of apartheid, in the early 1960s. Verwoerd was being heavily critical of Craven both in public and private, and the 'Doc', as he was known, was getting thoroughly fed up with it. In desperation, he went to see the rector of Stellenbosch University, H. P. Tom, who more significantly was chairman of the Broederbond, and asked him to get Verwoerd off his back. A couple of weeks later things hadn't improved, so Craven went back and again asked for help. This time Tom picked up the phone, got straight through to the prime minister and told him to leave Craven alone. That, Craven later admitted, was when he 'saw the power of the Broederbond for myself'. From that moment on, Verwoerd left Craven alone.

Away from political interference, rugby took on a similar role in South Africa and New Zealand after the war. A future Springbok captain, Wynand Claassen, once described the special fascination of rugby in South Africa: 'In every little town, in every little school, a rugby field can be found, and the goalposts alongside a corrugated iron pavilion are as familiar as the church towers in these towns. All little boys playing rugby have their heroes – great names running on the field in their green and gold jerseys and Springbok emblem. I am sure most little boys have this ambition, this dream to become one of those special men

NEW ZEALAND 6 – SOUTH AFRICA 17
EDEN PARK, AUCKLAND
25 SEPTEMBER 1937

This was the decider, the rugby heavy-weight championship of the world. A crowd of 55,000 packed into the Eden Park ground to see if the much-vaunted 1937 Springboks could finally gain the upper hand against outclassed but dogged opposition, who had taken advantage of some ramshackle South African tactics to win the first test. That had been avenged in the second clash, thanks largely to a 55-yard penalty kick by full-back Gerry Brand and a try from

Spirited action in the Third Test: Danie Craven foxes the All Blacks with another perfect dive pass to fly-half Tony Harris

the graphically named Ebbo Bastard, which gave them a 13–6 victory.

The tourists were brimming with the greatest rugby players of the age. Besides Brand, who kicked 190 points on the tour (including an Australian leg), there was the charismatic captain Philip Nel, a Natal farmer who used to ride 60 miles on horseback to play rugby for Greytown. A front-row forward, he put the success of his team down to 'honest scrummaging and possession'.

Then there was Boy Louw, pack stalwart and one of the most popular players of his time, who surpassed Bennie Osler's record for caps. When he had toured Britain in 1931, he had visited a West End store to buy some soap. 'Would sir like it scented?' asked the assistant. 'No,' answered Louw, 'don't scented it, I'll take it with me.'

Other members of the pack included Tony Harris, a quicksilver fly-half, who achieved the rare distinction of being capped at cricket as well. The scrum-half was Danie Craven, later to be one of the most influential people in the history of rugby when he became the seventh president of the South African Rugby Board in 1956. As a player, he developed the dive-pass which he used to great effect throughout the tour.

Then there was the dynamic Jewish centre Louis Babrow. He went up to the selection committee on the eve of the match and announced that he could not play. They thought he was injured and asked him what was wrong. He told them he was fighting fit but that he could not play because it was Yom Kippur, the most sacred day in the Jewish calendar. This was a disaster and Brabow was sent away to try and come up with a solution. The next day he came back and declared, 'I'm a South African Jew and Yom Kippur won't have started in South

The strong-running Springbok centre Louis Babrow was at the height of his form during the 1937 tour of New Zealand

Africa until after the match is over. I'm playing.' As it turned out, he was a leading candidate for Man of the Match.

Boy Louw's much quoted philosophy was to 'win by all means but win attractively', and the 1937 Springboks spread this gospel throughout Australia and New Zealand, consigning the safe tactics of Bennie Osler to the memory bin. They averaged 29 points a game and were already being hailed as one of the greatest ever sides when they arrived in Auckland. That reputation would have been destroyed in 80 minutes had they met with defeat and thereby lost the series. On the eve of the third test Nel received a cable from Paul Roos, the legendary captain of the 1906 team. It contained just three words, 'Scrum, scrum, scrum.' The advice proved invaluable against an All Blacks team strong in the line-out.

After just three minutes, the South African backs were in action. Craven took the ball from a rock solid scrum, dive-passed to Harris, who moved it *along the line to Flappie Lochner in space. He slipped the ball to Louis Babrow at just the right moment for the centre to score comfortably. Soon after, Babrow put the All Blacks in further trouble, breaking free of the opposition and sending wing Ferdie Bergh off in pursuit of a well-judged cross-kick. Brand converted and it was 8–0. New Zealand fly-half Dave Trevathan landed a penalty goal to make the scores 8–3 at half-time.*

After the turn-around, Craven executed a beautiful tactical move which effectively finished off the home side. At a scrum close to touch on the half-way line, Craven ostentatiously waved Harris to stand further back, banking on the opposition, particularly Trevathan, thinking that he was going to unleash one of his long-range bullet passes. The All Black fly-half fell for the sucker punch and Craven set winger Freddie Turner off on the blind side. Lochner took the pass before sending over Babrow for his second try. The Springbok forwards were in dominating mood, and the All Blacks for the first time had the air of a demoralized side. Both the wingers put their names on the score sheet. D.O. (Dai Owen) Williams beat three men before crossing the line, and Turner found himself on the end of another move set up by the excellent

Babrow. A late consolation penalty by Trevathan closed the scoring: New Zealand 6, South Africa 17. If Brand had brought his kicking boots with him, it could have been much worse. The score today using the modern points system of five for a try would have resulted in a 27–6 scoreline, which puts the Springbok achievement in perspective. After all, this was the first time the All Blacks had suffered defeat in a home series.

Afterwards the New Zealand critics and press were unanimous in their praise. The New Zealand Truth *wrote, 'The Springboks' magnificent all-round display was one that will live in the memories of all who could appreciate the high-water mark of football. On the day these Springboks would have beaten any other team in the world.'*

One of the most famous rugby jokes of the day was, 'Which is the greatest side ever to leave New Zealand?' Answer: 'The 1937 Springboks.' They clearly deserved to be called champions of the world. Like all great teams who had reached the pinnacle, retirements and careers – not to mention the Second World War – meant they could not scale those heights again. Philip Nel announced his own retirement with great ceremony on the voyage home by throwing his boots into the ocean.

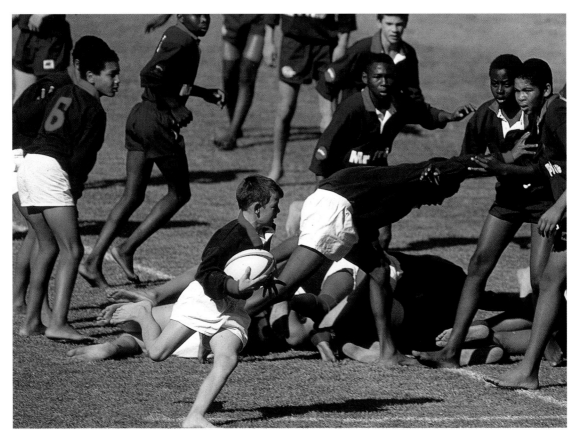

By 1997 rugby among South African youngsters was fully integrated, proving particularly popular among coloured school children

who have worn the green and gold jersey – to become a Springbok.'

Ian Kirkpatrick, Springbok centre in the 1956 series against the All Blacks, remembers getting a pair of rugby boots from an aunt when he was four and running around in them all day. 'I was so proud to have a pair of rugby boots. It's an inborn dream of any person that plays sport ultimately to play for their country.'

WHEN SATURDAY WAS KING

Saturday in New Zealand in winter time was rugby day. Former All Blacks captain Brian Lochore recalls the enormous importance of the game when he was growing up after the

Second World War: 'In country areas it was people's life. It gave a focal point to the whole community in that particular little township. The kids would go along and they would play and be heroes after the game, while the grown-ups were in having a cup of tea or a few beers.' Like many other future All Blacks, Lochore started playing rugby when he was at primary school. 'It was just a little school with 16 kids,' he recalls. 'From the age of five I had to go out and make up the numbers, so I had to face bigger, older fellows.'

Rugby was a family affair, from the very young through to the grandparents recalling great rugby tales of their past, both real and imaginary. Saturday was the holy day. Everyone made a contribution – watching, playing, washing the jerseys or getting the first jug of beer in after the game. In small townships and very remote areas the universal ambition was to have an All Black in the community. Former All Black scrum-half Chris Laidlaw observes, 'If you were the captain of the local rugby team, you were probably more important than the mayor. You would be asked for your opinion on whether the library should be where it is, whether the sail yards should be shifted, or whether there should be a new statue in the centre of town. The local rugby hero would always be asked for his opinion.'

New Zealand was a country very much at ease with itself; it had a post-war feeling of mellowness with rugby as its comfort blanket. The only set-back was the 1949 tour of South Africa when the All Blacks were whitewashed 4–0 in the most disastrous test series in their proud history. They were, says Laidlaw, 'utterly humiliated'. Although there had been some games organized during the Second World War between New Zealand and South African forces, which kept alive the spirit of competition between the two sides, 1949 was the renewal of the real rugby war. But there had been no test matches for 12 years, the pre-war greats had retired and there was no way to judge the relative merits of the two countries.

The year 1949 saw the worst defeat in New Zealand rugby history. A massive Springbok pack and the devastating goal kicking of Okey Geffin overpowered the All Blacks, who were once again touring without their Maori players, including their wonderful centre J.B. Smith. Others 'ineligible' for the tour were J.B.'s brother Peter, Vince Bevan, Ben Couch, Ike Proctor, Alan Blake, Lance Hohaia, Johnny Marriner, Johnny Isaacs, Brownie Cherrington, Ron Bryers, Barry Beasley, Theo Kipa, Angus Douglas, Kingi Matthews, Mick Kenny and Doc Paewai. That made 17 potential star players who didn't make the trip. It is small wonder that the All Blacks were blown away – even if there's truth in the rumour

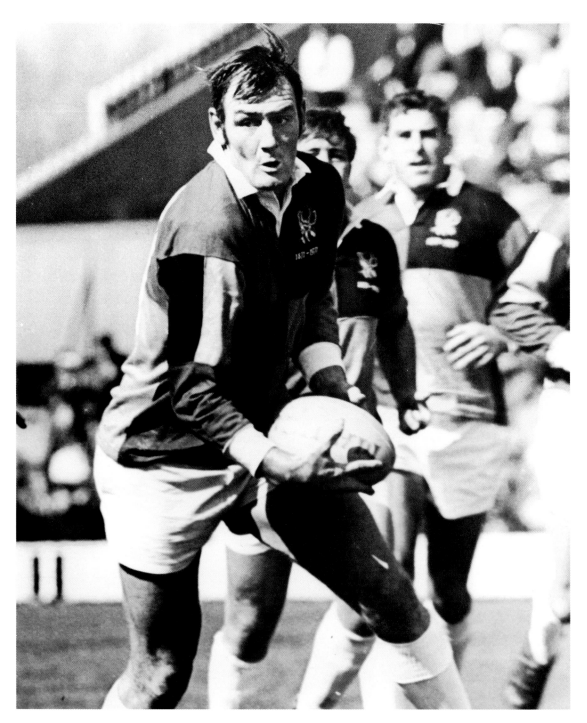

All Black skipper Brian Lochore showing grit and determination for a President's XV against England in 1971

130

that Danie Craven visited the New Zealand hotel in the early stages of the tour to give the All Black pack some lessons in good scrummaging. The humiliation of the tour affected the whole nation. Brian Lochore, like many young boys, had photos of the whole team on his wall. He listened on the radio to commentaries of each defeat. The victors were not a Springbok XV flowing with the imagination of the great 1937 team, but they played to win and succeeded. That success probably set the tone for rugby for the next 20 years. The All Blacks played without a smile for many years to come.

The opportunity for revenge would not arise for a further seven years, when South Africa returned to New Zealand for the first time in 19 years to contest what was universally regarded as a world championship. It was a great occasion and the visitors were treated like royalty. Springbok centre Ian Kirkpatrick described the welcome: 'The first place we arrived was Waikato and they carried each one of us in vintage cars and we were driven along waving to thousands and thousands of people. When we arrived at the hotel, we had to sing for the crowd. If any player said he didn't enjoy it, then he's lying. It went on like that for the three or four months of the tour. You would walk down the street hoping not to be recognized. If you walked into a barber's shop, they'd cut your hair for free. If you walked into a café, they'd give you a cup of coffee on the house. It was unreal to be in a country like this.' After the euphoria of their arrival, however, the visitors were brought down to earth when Waikato beat them 14–10 largely thanks to Don 'The Boot' Clarke.

The two most remembered personalities from the four-match test series were New Zealand prop Kevin Skinner and giant number 8 Peter Jones. Both were heroes to their own country, although Skinner's controversial role made him a villain in many eyes. The first two matches were shared. The All Blacks took the first 10–6 but the Springboks bounced back to grasp the second 8–3. The whole of New Zealand was in a state of nervous anticipation knowing that the unofficial world championship rested on the next two matches. The major problem was in the scrum, where Springbok props Chris Koch and Jaap Becker were dominating their opponents with what many saw as intimidating tactics. Mark Irwen suffered broken ribs during the first encounter when the All Black scrum buckled, and Frank McAtamney endured the same agony in the second. This was war. Enter Kevin Skinner, New Zealand heavyweight boxing champion of 1947. As giant lock Tiny White observed, 'That nonsense disappeared when Kevin Skinner came in for the third test.' The reality of what happened in the match really depends on whether you are an All Black or a Springbok. It is clearly accepted that Skinner smashed both opposing front forwards with his fist. He admitted that himself.

At the first line-out Koch came through on to the New Zealand side and Skinner warned him, 'That'll be the last time you do that, Chris.' At the next line-out the same thing happened, except this time Skinner's fist did all the talking, which stopped the Springboks employing that tactic for the rest of the game.

At half-time the New Zealand props swapped sides. Ian Clarke had been having a torrid time with the powerful Jaap Becker, who would use his massive frame to work his opponent over. In the second half he was opposite Skinner, who described what happened: 'Straight away Becker started to "pop" me, dropping his shoulder and generally making a nuisance of himself, so I hit him.' That settled Becker down and the All Blacks went on to claim victory 17–10, sealed by a superb try by left wing Ron Jarden, who somehow pulled down a cross-kick from centre Ross Brown and acrobatically twisted over the line.

It was an awesome performance by the New Zealand forwards, inspired by the determination of Kevin Skinner. Peter Jones, who had also been brought in to beef up the pack in the third test, said of his team-mate, 'Kevin was not a dirty player. He was a prince of a man in my book.' Springbok James Stark was not so effusive: 'Our front row was the stronger and the All Blacks were looking for an answer, so they put Skinner in the team. He smashed them with a fist in the jaw – both Jaap Becker and Chris Koch – so it was obvious why he was put in the team.' For many years afterwards, the mere mention of Kevin Skinner's name would have South Africans everywhere cursing. In his homeland, however, Skinner was a hero who was elected to the New Zealand Sports Hall of Fame in 1996.

If Skinner was the 'hero' of the third test, then the fourth at Eden Park in Auckland belonged to Jones. New Zealand was full of excitement at the possibility of beating the old enemy in a series for the first time, so it was crucial that they won the final match. Jones was the greatest try-scoring forward of his age, a 17-stone 6-pound battering ram who could steam through 100 yards in ten seconds. He scored 20 times in 37 appearances for New Zealand. His most famous try came when he gathered the ball 40 yards from the South African line and galloped to glory. That put the All Blacks 11–0 up and, hard as the Springboks fought, they could only pull it back to 11–5 at the final whistle. The whole nation rejoiced. Afterwards, Jones and Skinner were interviewed for the radio. With the whole of New Zealand listening, Jones famously declared, 'I'm absolutely buggered.'

Historian Jock Philips, who as a boy had a wall chart keeping a record of all the Springbok matches each year, remembers that victory was announced in the press the next day in type so big that you would have thought war had just been declared. But for New Zealand this was VE day. Victory in Eden Park.

COLIN MEADS:
UNSMILING GIANT

Colin Earl Meads never trained by carrying sheep up and down hills on his King Country farm. It is just one of the many legends surrounding the unsmiling forward who, more than any other, personified the spirit of New Zealand rugby. Here was a man who would die for his country in an All Black jersey, a throwback to an earlier pioneering age when New Zealand was struggling for a national identity. Meads was a farmer, an outdoor man in a remote part of the country, tough as old leather, modest and dignified. His was the masculine image of a New Zealander that the nation wanted to project to the world at large.

The story about Meads' particular use of his flock was all due to one photograph: 'I was carrying two sick sheep, one under each arm, and rushing to get them home, and this photographer who was visiting us that day took a picture as I came through.' You can imagine Richard Seddon, the premier at the turn of the century, using the photograph as a recruitment poster to entice immigrants to the colony. It promoted the right sort of image for both nation and rugby.

Like many of his generation, Meads grew up in an era when Saturday was king. In 1949 his mum and dad would wake him and his brother Stan (another future All Black) so that the family could listen to the test matches against South Africa on the radio. 'It was a national calamity,' he remembers. 'I was terribly disappointed that we would get beaten every time. We didn't have television in those days, so we would listen to the broadcasts of Winston McCarthy. He was the voice of rugby and the voice of New Zealand.'

In the sparsely populated areas of the country, having an All Black — even just a

Following pages: Colin Meads raises his arms as the tourists notch up another try in 1963

potential All Black – living there was a status symbol that every town or village hankered after. Meads and his great contemporary Brian Lochore became the most famous people in their communities. They were local heroes. The person and the place became moulded as one, so it was always Colin Meads from Te Kuite, King Country. That sense of union between man and place became indelible in the case of Meads because of his rare sporting longevity. In 20 years at the pinnacle of rugby he played 361 first-class games, made 133 appearances as an All Black and 55 in tests.

Surprisingly, Meads was a skinny lad, albeit a tall one – 6 feet 3 inches by the time he was 15. Over the next couple of years the rugged physical work on the farm helped to mould the young man's physique into an imposing 6 feet 4 inches and 15 stone. He acquired the nickname 'Pine Tree' on a tour to Japan with the New Zealand junior team and it stuck. Although in the modern game of Goliaths the boy from King Country would be merely average, in provincial games of the 1950s he was the last person the opposition would care to see charging towards their line. He made the King Country senior side at the age of 17 in 1955, and in his first representative game playing at loose forward he made everyone sit up and take notice by scoring a try and dropping a goal from 20 yards.

The national selectors were determined not to rush Meads into an All Blacks jersey, so he missed the 1956 triumphs against South Africa, but he did score a try against the Springboks playing for Wanganui-King Country. It was also his first encounter with the uncompromising South African lock Johann Claassen, whom he

Don Clark was the All Black full-back whose prodigious kicking would launch Colin Meads and the rest of the pack on the opposition defences

marked in the line-out. 'He was the master and I was the young pup,' recalls Meads. 'It was great experience for me and I enjoyed it immensely.' Just four years later they would be opponents again when Meads toured South Africa. 'The test matches were brutal encounters,' says Meads. 'After one game there was some function which was getting pretty stuffy, so I went out to the grandstand to get some air and catch my breath. There was Johann Claassen, sitting out there, the same as me. We were completely exhausted.' Although the All Blacks eventually lost the series, Meads was showing the power and aggression that were the hallmark of his play throughout his golden period of the 1960s. The 14-week tour was the last one to be all white. Maori team-mates, such as Waka Nathan, Pat Walsh and Bill Gray, were not considered. They did not even play in the trials – there was little point. For Meads the most important thing was playing rugby against the best opposition. 'A South African tour was just out of this world. Once you get away, you forget about all those things and you just get on with the rugby and try to play it.'

Away from the rugby field, however, passions were running high. A group called the Citizens' All Black Tour Association obtained 162,000 signatures calling for the tour to be cancelled. That was no mean level of protest considering the total population of New Zealand had still to reach the two million mark. The temperature rose considerably after the infamous massacre at Sharpeville. The New Zealand Cargo Workers Union passed a resolution condemning the killing and declaring that it was now 'imperative that no New Zealand team should go to a country with such a black record of mass murder'. Despite the escalation in domestic and international opposition to playing segregated South African teams, the New Zealand Rugby Union still went ahead with the tour. The brutal nature of the rugby on the pitch, so vividly recalled by Meads, matched the brutality off it.

The All Blacks of the 1960s were a formidable bunch. In 1961 Meads moved to lock for a three-match series against France. They won all three matches, 13–6, 5–3 and 32–3. The 5–3 result was a triumph for grinding forward play, or as Meads himself describes it: 'Heads down, bottoms up and drive, drive, drive for 80 minutes.' These were the days when you could put a blanket over the All Blacks pack. All eight forwards would charge up-field like a massive battering ram pursuing the siege-gun kicks of full-back Don Clarke. Even Meads now concedes that the rugby was 'not the best to look at'. It was effective, however, and Meads was an essential second-row fixture in the teams that beat Wales in 1963 (avenging the 1953 defeat), the Springboks in New Zealand in 1965 and the British Lions a year later. Despite Meads' own modest assessment of the forwards' contribution, the All Blacks were clearly moving ahead of the rest of the world during this period of domination. His captain Brian Lochore said, 'We really caught the rest of the world with their pants down. We actually played a much more expansive game than anybody else, although we never lost the ruggedness, the combativeness and the team spirit – the New Zealand style.'

Part of the mystique of the 1960s' All Blacks, and of Colin Meads in particular, was that they were 'unsmiling giants'. It was, says Meads, just their 'rugby face for the photographers'. He confirms, 'As far as rugby was concerned, we had our joyous moments and we had our times of despair and disappointments like anyone else.' Colin Meads was a true rugby warrior. He faced the Springboks in 1970 while recovering from a broken arm. He played most of a game against the Lions in 1971 with cracked ribs. When he donned the All Black jersey with the silver fern on it, he was playing for keeps.

Like all legends, Meads needed controversy to achieve that status. In 1967 he produced one of the main sporting scandals of the year when he was sent off against Scotland at Murrayfield. He had aimed a large boot at the ball just as the opposing fly-half, David Chisholm, gathered it. His dismissal resulted in a two-match suspension, which meant that he missed playing his one hundredth match as an All Black on that tour. It did not, however, stop him joining Brian Lochore and some Welsh friends for a weekend booze-up in Cardiff. The Saturday game had been cancelled because of snow, so the lads embarked on what Lochore described as an 'enormous' couple of days. 'We sort of lost a day somewhere,' he recalls with obvious relish. 'When Colin and I got back on the Monday morning, we decided we should go for a run and sweat out all the amber liquid. I shall never forget us running through the streets of Cardiff while everyone else was going off to work.' Meads adds simply, 'I was a great believer in not wasting beer.'

THE AMBASSADORS OF APARTHEID

The massacre of 67 peaceful protesters in the South African township of Sharpeville on 21 March 1960 saw Harold Macmillan's 'wind of change' become more than a gentle breeze. Throughout the world it seemed that public opinion was hardening against the grim realities of apartheid. Tommy Bedford, one of the great Springbok flankers, was at university in Durban at the time. 'It was a shock for South Africa and a shock for the whole world. There were riots at the university and I witnessed armoured cars and police and black people marching into town to protest. We were in the "system" but this made everyone uncomfortable.' Far from forcing a policy of appeasement on Verwoerd and his right-wing supporters, world-wide horror at the events in Sharpeville heralded a decade when South Africa dug in and adopted the stubborn 'them and us' attitude to the rest of the world. It resembled a police state, but they still had their rugby. Despite the first signs of real protest at home, the New Zealand All Blacks set off to tour their great rivals again later that year, still with no Maoris. For the first time the idea dawned on the more enlightened members of New Zealand society that excluding the Maoris was tantamount to importing apartheid into New Zealand.

The polarization of opinion was instigated by Verwoerd himself five years later when South Africa were touring New Zealand. With one match to go – the All Blacks had established a 2–1 lead – he made an infamous speech at Loskop Dam in the Transvaal. He made it clear that Maoris would not be welcome when the All Blacks next visited South Africa in 1967. This was a momentous declaration because for the first time it publicly exposed an informal, mutually convenient arrangement. News of the speech actually broke on the day of the fourth test when rugby had centre stage in New Zealand. It was a disaster for the Springboks and it mattered little that the All Blacks won. The series was ruined, which was a pity as it contained one of the most famous comebacks in the history of rugby: the Springboks fought back from 16–5 down at half-time to win the second test in Christchurch 19–16.

Earlier that year the Springboks had their first taste of real protest abroad when they visited Ireland. A group of demonstrators gathered outside the Shelbourne Hotel in Dublin, only to be pelted with eggs from a balcony by the Irish team in an inexcusable display of stupidity. Elsewhere, more enlightened rugby players were beginning to question the morality of playing against South Africa, and were finding it harder to separate politics from sport. The All Black John Graham spoke out against apartheid after he had visited the black townships while on tour. He was a teacher and he revealed racial injustice to a new generation of New Zealand students. Tommy Bedford and Chris Laidlaw, rivals on the pitch and friends off it, were others who found it increasingly difficult to ignore the moral question.

Certainly the weight of world opinion was beginning to tell. The Springboks who came to Britain in 1969/70 were a team under siege. As Bedford recalls, 'Instead of proudly stepping out at Heathrow wearing our Springbok blazers, we were smuggled out in a coach to a golfing hotel. You feel you haven't got a friend in the world.' Demonstrations followed the South Africans everywhere they went and they began to take their toll on the players. They were portrayed as representatives of an iniquitous regime rather than a superlative rugby team. In the fall-out following the tour, the Afrikaner element in the Springboks took over to the extent that Tommy Bedford, the number one candidate, missed out on the captaincy because he was 'English-speaking'. A nadir had been reached in which racial

Sharpeville, the South African township, where a massacre of 67 peaceful protestors on 21 March 1960 sent shock waves around the world

discrimination was directed against anyone who was not Afrikaner. Bedford remembers being told, off the record, that the next Springbok captain after de Villiers would be an Afrikaner and a man sympathetic to the Afrikaner cause. He observed, 'People forget that apartheid was eventually practised against English-speaking South Africans. Sport was totally dominated by the Afrikaners. Everyone was stuck with the Broederbond ethos of Afrikanerdom whether they liked it or not.' The good news for the advocates of change was that the world was finally beginning to shut the door on South Africa. The question on everyone's lips was how much longer would New Zealand tolerate the ambassadors of apartheid?

A TALE OF TWO SCRUM-HALVES

The widening gulf between rugby players off the field is well illustrated by the careers of two famous scrum-halves of the 1960s, Chris Laidlaw and Dawie de Villiers, the New Zealand hero and the Springbok captain respectively. They were fierce rivals on the pitch, although Laidlaw remembers a good on-field relationship, but after their playing careers ended, they stood at opposite ends of the political spectrum. Both were blond, spectacular passers of the ball playing behind a strong pack of forwards. They were adversaries in 1965, when de Villiers was Springbok captain, and again in 1970. In between, Laidlaw led Oxford University when they faced the 1969 tourists on their first match of that hostile tour. Laidlaw recalls trying to talk to de Villiers several times about his concerns over the

Above: Chris Laidlaw is ferociously tackled by two Springboks: lock Frik du Preez (airborne) and centre Albie Bates, in the First Test 1970

Following pages: Bryan Williams burst on to the rugby scene on the historic tour of South Africa in 1969

situation in South Africa: 'Dawie really wasn't prepared to do that. I think he felt uneasy about it all himself. After both our international careers ended in 1970, we parted company. Politically, I found it impossible to countenance more contact with South Africa.

'Dawie became a minister in his government and was a leading member of the National Party, which was allowing atrocities to happen. Subsequently, he was appointed the ambassador to London at the same time that I was working as a diplomat there. We would occasionally see each other from across the room and have nothing to say. Politics had drawn us apart. I was involved in anti-apartheid activities, so I was anathema to his government, as he was to my community. Years later, in the early 1990s, I was visiting Johannesburg for the first time in many years and thought I would give him a call. He had done his bit for the transformation in South Africa and for dismantling apartheid.

'I rang his office and asked if the minister was in and told his private secretary who I was. Moments later Dawie was on the line saying we must have lunch. That lunch proved to be a reconciliation. South Africa was in the process of transforming itself and he had been part of that and I admired the way he admitted, very candidly, that they had been wrong. That was a difficult thing to do. I too had gone full circle because I have a great admiration for much of what the Afrikaner community has achieved. As a result, we now have a lifelong friendship.'

BRYAN WILLIAMS:
BREAKING THROUGH APARTHEID'S DEFENCE

When the plane carrying the All Blacks to South Africa for their 1970 tour touched down at Johannesburg Airport, Bryan Williams was overcome by panic. He was just 19 years old and his hopes and dreams of playing international rugby for his country were about to come true. It was a defining moment in the dubious relationship between the two greatest rugby-playing nations. Williams was no ordinary teenager embarking on a sporting adventure. He was a coloured boy from the Pacific island of Samoa and he was being allowed into South Africa under the grotesque banner of what became commonly known as 'Honorary White'.

The South African premier Johannes Vorster had decided that, for the first time since

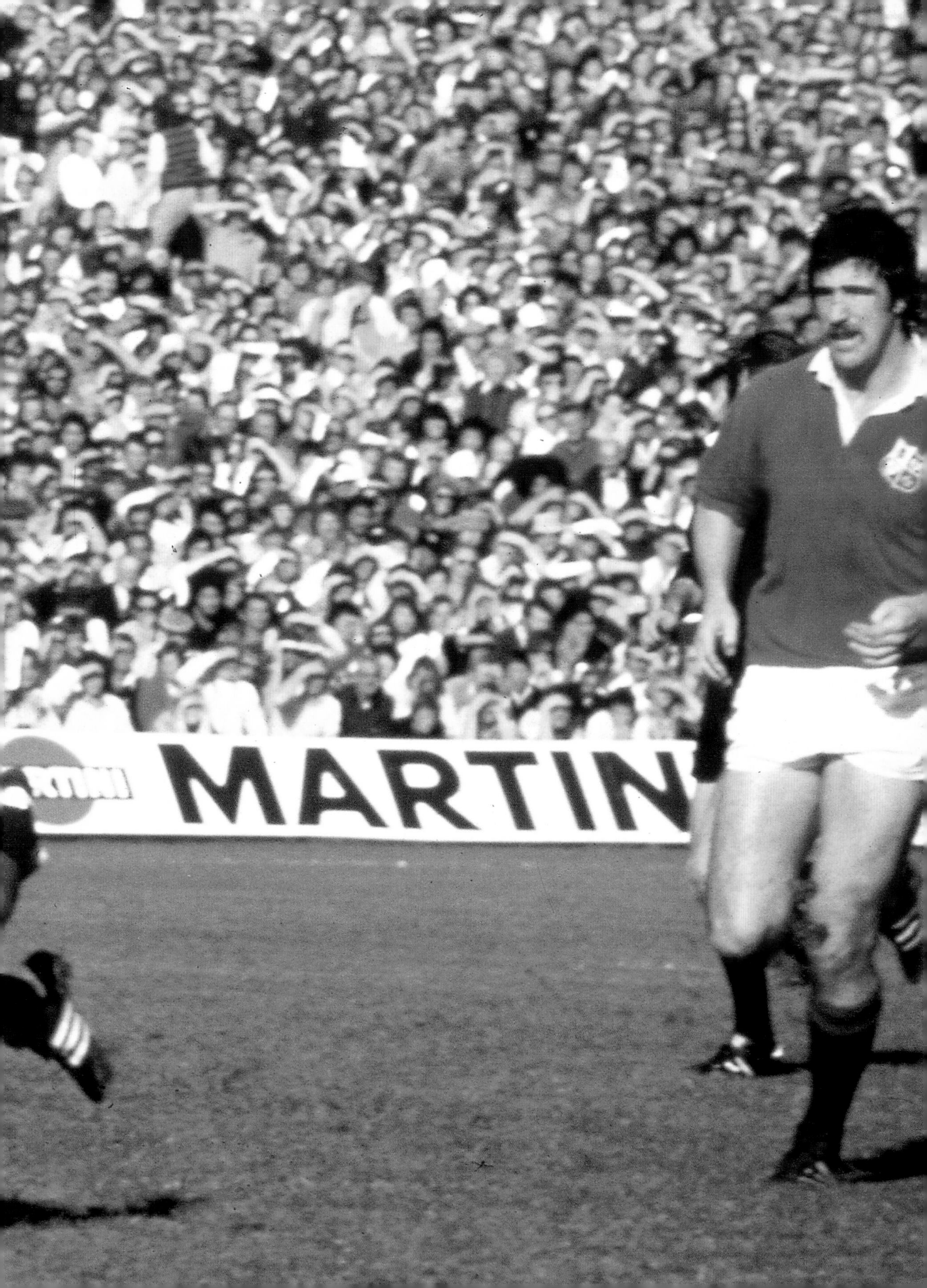
MARTIN

Ranji Wilson was left on board ship in 1919, coloureds would be welcome in the New Zealand team. It was a shallow gesture because it allegedly stipulated that there should not be too many and they should not be too black. In the end, four were selected: Williams was Polynesian, while Sid Going, Blair Furlong and Buff Milner were part Maori. Williams was to be the star of the tour, despite widespread opposition to the trip back home in New Zealand. That opposition included one of the most famous All Black players, prop Ken Gray, who refused to go. When the privileged foursome left Auckland, police and demonstrators clashed over rugby for the first time and 46 arrests were made. Even so, the protests lacked the violent undercurrents that were to explode in 1981.

Williams was born in Ponsonby, Auckland, and grew up in the 1960s when the province carried all before it in domestic competition. Most Saturdays he would watch the game at Eden Park. His mother would give him ten cents to catch the bus home, but the commercially minded youngster would walk the four miles so that he could buy a bag of chips instead. When he was surprisingly picked for the 1970 tour, he was studying law at Auckland University. He says, 'I was well aware of the ramifications of being one of the first people of dark blood to go to South Africa. I just felt that if I could go to South Africa as a "darkie", if you like, and illustrate to people that I could compete on the same level or even better, then I felt I was putting my little chink in the armour of apartheid.' In many ways Williams was right about the chink, although you would hardly have guessed as the visiting All Blacks were greeted as heroes on their arrival, a welcome that eased the dazzling winger's panic attack: 'I was really willing the plane to take off down the runway again and head straight back to New Zealand. But once I dragged myself off the plane and the tour started, I realized how pleased the South African people were to see an All Blacks team. It became very clear right from the start that rugby was number one and any political implications were secondary.'

The rugby Williams played on the tour was sublime and he quickly achieved hero status among the home-grown black population. He thrived in the conditions, his electrifying teenage pace and side-step leaving the Springboks clinging to his shadow as he raced over for try after try. He scored 14 in all, topping it up with six successful goal-kicks for good measure. He made his international début in the first test at Pretoria and scored the All Blacks' only try in a dismal 17–6 defeat, a personal confidence boost even if the team needed a pick-me-up.

It had been a brutal encounter, typical of the savage 'win at all costs' mentality that has been the distinguishing feature of both New Zealand's and South Africa's rugby thinking for a century. Even the hard man Colin Meads, who played on despite breaking an arm early in the tour, admits that the test matches were 'pretty intense'. The South Africans had done their homework, and the All Blacks, having been fed on a diet of easy provincial games where they were able to show dazzling skills, seemed unprepared for the onslaught from the national side. Captain Brian Lochore observed, 'They obviously felt they were up against a very good All Black side and they came on to the field in what was almost a state of dementia. They were very determined and nothing was going to stop them.'

That determination saw All Black scrum-half Chris Laidlaw smashed by an infamously ferocious double tackle from both Frik du Preez and Albie Bates. Despite obvious concussion, he soldiered on until early into the second half, when Sid Going replaced him in time to set up Williams' try. Laidlaw, an Oxford graduate, subsequently wrote a book entitled *Mud in Your Eye*, which was highly critical of South Africa and its sport. Tellingly he said, 'Whether we like it or not, New Zealand is a major factor in the survival of the present structure of South African sport.' Laidlaw's contests with his great South African counterpart Dawie de Villiers, the Springbok captain, were one of the highlights of the tour. But away from rugby they became divided by their political careers. Laidlaw, vociferously anti-apartheid, rejected the idealistic view of Williams and Lochore that sport should be above politics. He explains, 'It took me some years to realize that apartheid was bigger than international sport and in many ways it was more important than rugby. I believe rugby really needed to be an agent of change rather than an agent of resistance.'

Away from the rugby field, the players were soon to realize that one small chink would not breach apartheid's defences – at least not yet. Bryan Williams and other team-mates invited coloured people back to the All Blacks' hotel. 'We deliberately did it,' said Williams. 'I just felt that if I was able to be there, so other people of the same coloured skin should be allowed there. It caused a lot of consternation and there were quite a few incidents with hotel management. A lot of threats were made and it became quite clear that apartheid was an evil thing and we should be rid of it.' Brian Lochore felt that having 'black' friends visit white-only hotels was breaking down barriers in a small way.

Beneath the general celebration of rugby the more sinister aspects of apartheid and white supremacy were constantly lurking. That simmering hatred of white for blacks boiled over after a tour match at Kimberley when coloured supporters ran on to the field to hoist Williams on to their shoulders. They were attacked by a group of resentful whites and all hell let loose. Williams recalls, 'The white people started abusing the coloured and before we knew it there was a huge riot, which was frightening at the time. It brought home to me how volatile apartheid was. It was sobering.' At the matches the coloured spectators were all herded into one area of the ground, into the 'cheap seats' as Chris Laidlaw scathingly puts it. When the New Zealand team scored, they would erupt with delight, while the rest of the crowd remained frozen in silence. It seemed that the majority of South Africa's population was supporting the opposition.

Williams' own playing went from strength to strength. 'I was growing in confidence and I just seemed to get faster,' he said. Perhaps he had an advantage over his team-mates in that he was the least-known All Black when he arrived. He was the new boy at school, slightly in awe of his fellow players and diffident about his own contribution. Colin Meads roomed with him: 'I got a room with this guy to get to know him. He was too shy and didn't want to come near the big boys of the team. He was only 19.'

In the second test New Zealand scraped a 9–8 win when full-back Fergie McCormick booted home a last-minute penalty kick. Williams, however, is convinced that he scored an earlier legitimate try in the corner which the referee disallowed after first blowing for the score. That narrow victory perked up the tourists and Williams celebrated by scoring two tries against Western Province and three more against South African Country at East London. All seemed set fair for the third and fourth tests, but the All Blacks were comprehensively beaten in both. Williams scored their only points in the third – a penalty kick – and managed a bravado try to close his own contribution in the fourth and final encounter. His youthful arrogance included side-stepping three tackles in the in-goal area so that he could touch the ball down between the posts.

More than 1000 fan letters, which he dutifully answered by hand, were testament to the impact the young Samoan made on the tour. Unfortunately, he never recaptured the same form again. Williams himself believes that the principal reason for this was his newly acquired reputation: 'I was far more closely marked from that tour on and I never really trained again like I trained on that tour. The training wasn't very scientific then.'

Colin Meads, All Black colossus, has the final word on the flying wing: 'The rugby Bryan played in 1970 is the best I've seen from a winger in all of my playing career.'

ERROL TOBIAS:
A STEP IN THE RIGHT DIRECTION

President Nelson Mandela once invited Errol Tobias and his family for a private dinner at the presidential house in Pretoria. While they were eating, Mandela turned to the first coloured Springbok and told him that he was still in jail when Tobias was selected for a tour of South America in 1980. 'At the time the whole of our initiative was bleak,' said Mandela. 'Everything was getting darker and darker, Errol, but when you were selected, we saw a light. We started saying to one another that we must keep up the pressure because there is something happening. It didn't matter if it was a political move to quiet us. We knew if you came through with your honour intact, then we would all be the winner.'

That simple exchange reassured Tobias, who has had to endure the handicap of being far more famous for his colour than for his rugby. He has also had to face criticism that he was only being used for political ends when he was first selected at the almost veteran age of 30. 'When the President told me that story over dinner, I just thought to myself, "Errol, I would do the same a hundred times over".'

One of the great myths of Afrikaner culture is that rugby is a white man's game. That is clearly true internationally, but not in South Afica, where fabulous players, such as Eric Majola and Gilman Noqholi, were legends within the black rugby-playing community, where the game was a focal point of people's lives. The black rugby culture was kept a secret, as if to say to the white population and the rest of the world that it was acceptable to keep the sport white because the blacks were not interested anyway. Former Springbok captain and government minister Dawie de Villiers is much remembered for once declaring that there was no such thing as black rugby.

The massive hurdle that needed to be overcome before white and black could play side by side wearing the same jersey is well illustrated by Andre Odendaal. He recalls that, as a boy growing up in the 1960s, one of the biggest issues for white people considering sporting integration was imagining going into a scrum with a black person. He recalls, 'Segregation was so rigid at that period and social interaction so based on apartheid power that it was unthinkable that could happen.'

At least Errol Tobias showed it could happen. Just like the great New Zealanders of the 1950s, he grew up listening to international rugby on the radio: 'We were rugby mad but we never thought any coloured man could become a Springbok.' The progress in the 1970s that made it possible was not universally embraced by all black sportsmen who did not want to concede any black sporting identity until apartheid was dead and buried. They did not want to be integrated into any sport that was still effectively white-controlled. A key slogan of the day was 'You can't play normal sport in an abnormal society'. Tobias was 17 when he first entertained thoughts of one day becoming a Springbok, encouraged by Dr Danie Craven's efforts to promote integration. Some argue that Craven's shortcoming was his desire to be all things to all men, but Tobias is in no doubt that 'he worked incredibly hard with us'. It would be another 13 years before Tobias would achieve his ambition but he still maintains he was at his peak: 'I was 30, but I had never smoked or drank and I was a fitness fanatic, which kept me strong for the big break which eventually came.'

Although Tobias does not believe himself to have been a political pawn, he was disappointed that the whole black community was not behind him when he was first selected. 'There was sadness but there was a change of tune when I actually started playing. Some black players phoned me and wished me good luck. There was a lot of responsibility on my shoulders. At home I'm usually a very talkative guy, but I didn't really talk for the last week before we left on tour. My wife knew me well and she just told the kids to leave me alone. I was just thinking about the game. I knew some people would see me as a token, but I knew I could be a trump card. I knew something good would come out of it and I believe I gained a lot of ground for coloured people.'

A year later Tobias was on the notorious 1981 tour to New Zealand, during which his family back home received death threats and he himself admits to being scared: 'I told Doc Craven that I thought a madman might come out of the crowd and shoot me. It was very rough and I seemed to be the main focus point. I think people thought that if they could get Errol, then the tour would be lost.' To his continued disappointment Tobias was not actually selected for the tests, perhaps a victim of the volatile situation. The tour manager, Johann Claassen, a member of the Broederbond, came out with a memorable quote when asked about Errol's request to be considered for the tests in a different position. It demonstrated, he suggested, 'the inability of people without proper education to stand up to pressure'. Fortunately, Claassen did not speak for everyone on tour. Team-mate Rob Louw, godfather to one of the Tobias children, said, 'All true South African sportsmen have been delighted with the success that Errol has achieved. At the same time some short-sighted people have regarded him as some sort of threat and have tried to play down his achievements. For some time it has been hard to acknowledge that Errol was actually one of the great Springboks.'

Amid all the controversy that dogged his career, Tobias was able to play some classy rugby, perhaps most memorably against the England tourists of 1984 when he scored a try against the visitors in three games, including a test match. Rumour has it that one commentator watching Errol said, 'That's a great black rugby player,' whereupon his companion retorted, 'That's not a black rugby player, that player's all gold.' His legacy, however is far greater off the field. As a famous Springbok, he was eating with his family

Opposite: Errol Tobias made history as the first coloured Springbok in the early 1980s, a signpost of greater changes to come

Following pages: Errol Tobias, wearing the Springbok jersey he was so proud of, runs with the ball against England in 1984

in a restaurant when another coloured man came in with his wife and was refused service. The manager informed a concerned Tobias that it was the law, so the Springbok and his family promptly walked out. A month later the restaurant changed hands and the new owner rang Tobias and said, 'My restaurant is open for each and every one.'

MUCH MORE THAN A GAME:
THE STORY OF THE 1981 SPRINGBOK TOUR

New Zealand was split down the middle. On one side were the conservative old guard cherishing images of a national culture where rugby was king. On the other were the modernists, a younger generation who believed that it was time to call a halt to what they saw as their country's unforgivable moral slide. The chosen battlefield was the 1981 Springbok tour, which political activist Trevor Richards memorably described as the closest New Zealand came this century to civil war. The whole social fabric of the country was torn apart. Just how such an explosive 56 days in New Zealand's history was permitted to happen is largely down to the-then prime minister, Robert Muldoon, who believed that his chances of re-election would be increased if he let the tour go ahead. His declared policy was that you should be able to play sport with whomever you like. That dangerous strategy had led to the 1976 tour of South Africa by New Zealand, which prompted a boycott of the Montreal Olympics by the other African nations.

Muldoon believed in a world of politics where small percentages meant the difference between success and failure. It was his cynical view that the 1981 Springbok tour would give him that vital edge. Chris Laidlaw is one who is convinced that Muldoon knew precisely what he was doing: 'He knew in advance the kind of mayhem the tour would produce. He believed the majority of the population wanted rugby and, just as importantly, did not want the breakdown of law and order.' David Lange, who became the next prime minister in 1984, explains Muldoon's tactics: 'He had to win provincial New Zealand and he had to win red-neck urban New Zealand. 1981 was the last time anyone could have got away with it because there was a great improvement in the ability of the general population to understand the world. We knew what happened in Soweto — we were getting footage of the terrible indignities inflicted upon human beings in the name of apartheid. In 1981 Muldoon

Above: New Zealand premier Robert Muldoon used Rugby for electoral advantage in the 1970s
Following pages: Graham Mourie, the superb All Black captain, in action against France (1981)

got away with it because it was about the last time the majority of the people were in favour of playing rugby with an apartheid nation.'

That dwindling majority was adamant that they did not wish their government to interfere with their entitlement to enjoy sport with the devil himself if they saw fit. Away from the rugby field there would be bedlam, but the tour brought about bitter divisions within the rugby-playing community itself. The captain of the All Blacks, Graham Mourie, declared himself unavailable for selection, opting instead to watch the test series on television. It was a momentous decision because Mourie was one of the greatest wing forwards and one of the most repsected skippers in the history of world rugby. He gives three reasons for his decision: 'The first consideration was apartheid and whether it was right or wrong. The second issue was the tour itself and whether it would be good for New Zealand

rugby, and thirdly whether it was going to be good for New Zealand as a country. I knew it was going to be bad on all three counts.' Mourie was destined never to play international rugby against the Springboks, the only major country he never competed against.

The dashing centre Bruce Robertson also bowed out of the 1981 series on moral grounds, and Mourie maintains that there were others who would have preferred not to play, but they were frightened they would never be an All Black again if they took a stand. 'It did create some friction within the team. Some people thought I should never be selected again, and I had considered that possibility when I made my decision. As it was, I was fortunate to get back in the following year.'

Mourie looked on sadly while his countrymen were at each other's throats. Families, schools and workplaces were dragged into the seething cauldron the country had become. Mourie himself acknowledges that his own views were at odds with those of his parents, who thought the tour should go ahead. But, in a throwback to the old New Zealand way, they never argued about it simply because it was never mentioned. The anti-anpartheid activist, Trevor Richards tells a story that reveals a wonderful vignette of New Zealand life. A friend living in the suburbs told him how glad she was when the Springboks finally left. Although she wasn't the slightest bit interested in rugby herself, they had, she confided, completely ruined her dinner parties for the 56 days they were in the country. All her guests apparently could talk of nothing else and would be furious with each other by the time the main course arrived. In the end, she had to cancel the dinners for the duration of the tour.

Out on the streets protests were leading to violent and bloody clashes. Some remained peaceful, as when 15,000 banner-waving protesters marched through Wellington. That was not the case at Hamilton, where the Springboks were due to play Waikato in the first live televised match to be transmitted back to South Africa. Just 25 years earlier the Springboks had been treated like royalty as they travelled through the town's streets. This time protesters broke on to the pitch and occupied the playing area, forcing officials to call off the game. In South Africa itself, the nation that had set its alarms in anticipation of another exciting Springbok rugby match was faced with proof before its bleary eyes of the enormous feeling of animosity towards its country's rugby team in a land for so long its friend. The jubilation the protesters felt – perhaps even believing the tour would now have to be cancelled – was quickly dampened by the realization that the massive crowd

Strong-running All Black centre Bruce Robertson makes another electrifying break (France 1977)

of rugby spectators was after their blood. They had somehow to get past a jeering, drunken mob.

'The way the crowd saw it,' explains Trevor Richards, 'the protesters had won. Protesters are fine as long as they're never successful. When they actually stop a game, it's a serious business. In order to get off the field, the protesters had to run the gauntlet of thousands of extremely angry rugby supporters. There were bottles and bricks being hurled at them and as they left their faces were covered in blood. It's probably the worst example of New Zealander bashing New Zealander. It was vicious and it's a miracle no one was killed.' Politician David Lange's brother was a protester in Hamilton and was arrested by police. According to the-then future prime minister, 'He told them his brother was deputy leader of the Labour Party, so they broke his finger.'

The mayhem continued throughout the tour. The country began to resemble a police state. It was a commonplace to see riot police complete with crash helmets, shields and long batons patrolling the streets. Lange remembers them having 'all the regalia of certain fascist countries'. Barbed wire was put round the perimeter of grounds to keep protesters off the pitch. Rugby's fall from grace continued its march around the country until, after 13 matches and two tests, it arrived at Eden Park in Auckland on 12 September 1981 for the 'decider'.

THE BOMBING OF EDEN PARK

The pilot was a man called Marx. He and an unidentified friend hired a light Cessna plane from a local Auckland air club and proceeded, in the words of eye-witnesses, to 'terrorize' the 49,000 crowd watching the concluding match of this tour of rage. Already police had been fearing the worst after 60,000 demonstrators had marched through the centre of Auckland on the morning of the game. But they failed to foresee the astonishing finale as the plane made 62 runs above the ground with the very real risk that it might crash into the packed stands. Marx and his co-pilot hurled flour bombs, nets and other objects, some alight, down on to the pitch below. Mighty All Black prop Gary Knight was knocked over by a direct hit from a flour bomb. Police in another aircraft desperately tried to persuade the pilot to stop, fearing the worst. Ignoring their pleas, the plane headed straight for a goalpost, only for Marx to pull back hard on the controls at the last minute so that the Cessna climbed steeply to safety. Deciding that would be his final pass, he flew off to land near the welcoming arms of the police.

Incredibly, the only injuries inside the ground were caused by spectators hurling beer cans at the plane which actually fell within the crowd. Outside the stadium the situation escalated into more violence as riot police clashed with protesters who, according to reports, were armed with large wooden shields, smoke bombs, flares, stones, acid-filled eggs and even Molotov cocktails. It was the armoury of a war zone. Some 45 people, including 32 policemen, needed hospital treatment mainly after being hit by stones. The worst injured was a policeman who had both collar-bones broken by raining stones. The officer in charge,

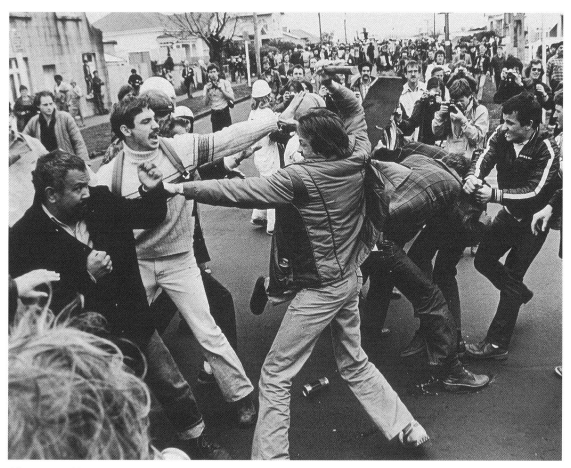

The nearest thing to civil war in New Zealand: anti-apartheid protestors and rugby supporters clash violently at Eden Park, Auckland in 1981

Superintendent Maurice Cummings, told the press, 'They threw everything at us.' A total of 148 people were arrested, including Marx, who subsequently spent six months in jail.

Amazingly, the match went on and proved to be one of the most exciting in the history of games between the two great rugby-playing nations. Despite all the problems that dogged their progress on this unhappy tour, South Africa rallied to produce a match and series-winning performance on the day. Yet somehow they lost (22 points to New Zealand's winning 25). It was a match of fist-clenching tension. Thanks to an inspired pack, the All Blacks had their noses in front 19–9, but then the deadly accuracy of the great blond Springbok fly-half Naas Botha and three tries by superb wing Ray Mordt edged the

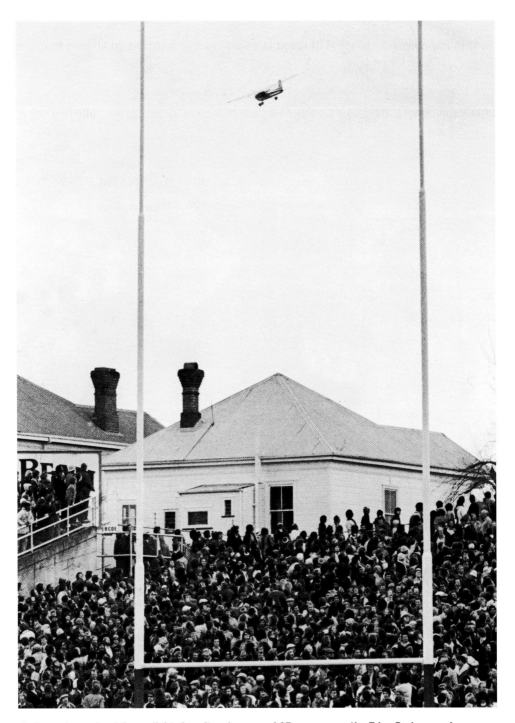

A stunned crowd watch as a light aircraft makes one of 67 passes over the Eden Park ground

visitors closer until, with time almost up, the scores were dead level on 22 all. The crowd went totally quiet with a feeling of dread as Botha lined up a conversion attempt from the right-hand touch-line. It was a case of shut your eyes and pray for New Zealand because Botha never seemed to miss. He struck the ball beautifully and it glided just wide of the right-hand upright. The collective relief was audible as the home support waited for referee Clive Norling to blow his whistle. A draw would have been a welcome result because the backs had made a succession of handling errors, and the kicking of counter-attacking full-back Allan Hewson looked amateurish against the efficient Botha. But Norling didn't sound the final whistle, instead playing more than five minutes of injury time because of all the interruptions on that eventful afternoon.

Seconds remained when the Springboks were penalized some 50 yards out, and replacement scrum-half Mark Donaldson took a quick tap penalty which caught the tiring 'Bok forwards still making their way back 10 yards. That made it 40 yards out. All Black captain Andy Dalton called up Hewson to have a go. It was the last kick of the game and the only option, even though the full-back had lead in his boots all afternoon. Rugby writer John Reason said of Hewson's play: 'Strong men could not bear to look, even when he kicked at goal from 12 yards in front of the posts.' At least this penalty attempt was on the better side for Hewson, who was a left-footed kicker and could, with a bit of luck, draw the ball in from the far post. Dalton could scarcely bear to watch. 'Allan took the kick and it seemed to be fading past the post. I thought, "Oh, jeez, everybody will be saying rugby is the winner again," but somehow it crawled over.' The match and the series were won.

Afterwards the post-mortems were all about the protests and little about the rugby. Who had won the moral match – those for or those against the tour? The events at Hamilton and Auckland, and all 56 grim days of the 1981 tour, dragged New Zealand kicking and screaming into the 20th century. Up until 1981 rugby had been a comfort blanket for the country – now it was a hair shirt. Where once it had brought people together in the days of Richard Seddon and the 1905 Originals, it had now become an agent of social destruction. The question of racial prejudice in New Zealand was one the average (white) man in the street had never had to address before. The British Empire had historically been a breeding ground for racism, but New Zealand was able to ignore the issue for generations because the Maoris were not a majority. The hypocrisy of claiming to be a multi-racial society and then failing to condemn the evil apartheid regime in South Africa shamed the country. Its citizens were no longer prepared to tolerate that. The events of 1981 proved that the game of rugby was no longer a hiding place from basic human morality. Chris Laidlaw believes it was the time when the country realized it had to grow up. 'There were issues that loomed larger than the God-given right to go and play rugby on Saturday and to play rugby with whoever you choose. New Zealand went through the wringer on this, came out of it a great deal more sophisticated and a good deal wiser, and took a step up on the ladder of maturity.'

THE PROFESSOR OF RUGBY

If the Springboks lost, Danie Craven got the blame. He had nothing to do with selecting the team but he was blamed anyway. He was 'Mr Rugby' in South Africa for more than half a century, so who better to take the flak? In 1964 the Springboks lost a poor match to France at Springs. Everyone was depressed, and when Craven returned to his hotel after the post-match dinner, he was confronted by a group of supporters who had been conducting their own post-mortem in the pub. Craven had been planning to go straight up to his room, but joined the lads to talk about the game. After a while, he jumped up and declared that they should choose the next Springbok team. The barman was enlisted to provide everyone with pencils and paper and each fan picked his team. Afterwards Craven, or 'the Doc', as he was also known, checked through the selections and said, 'Not one of you has got the same team. Now which of your teams is going to play the next test?' With that, everyone laughed, and to murmurs of 'Fair play, Doc,' went happily off to bed. As Paul Dobson, a friend and admirer of Craven, puts it, 'He was a man of the people; he could mix with guys like that.'

Dr Danie Craven was born in 1910 in the unassuming small town of Lindley in the Eastern Free State. At the age of 19, although no great academic, he made it to Stellenbosch University, where, under the influence of coach August Markotter, he took up rugby which was to be his passion from 1930 till the time of his death in 1993. His longevity and his determination not to desert the game he loved meant that he became one of the most influential men in the history of rugby. He was a leading figure in all the action and reaction involving South Africa and the rest of the rugby-playing world, particularly New

Zealand. He was scrum-half in the great 1937 team, where he used his famous dive-pass to devastating effect. He was subsequently manager and coach, before becoming president of the South African Rugby Board in 1956, the year the All Blacks won a series against the old enemy. He was forever thinking up brilliant new strategies; some worked and some didn't. To prepare for 1956, he added lead weights to his players' rugby boots so that when they trained it would be just like playing on the muddy pitches of New Zealand. That was an idea that didn't work.

Springbok scrum-half Danie Craven demonstrates his devastating dive pass in the mud of Newlands (1932)

He presided over the years that saw his great team increasingly marginalized. Rugby isolation was a fatal disease to Craven. The man himself remains an enigma, with one major unanswered question. Were his efforts at making rugby a multi-racial sport in South Africa genuine or were they the desperate measures of someone who wanted rugby for his country at all costs? He was a lifelong Stellenbosch man, the institution at the heart of Afrikanerdom. And yet of all the top people in South African rugby, he was the one who remained aloof from the Broederbond. In the late 1960s and early 1970s it was strikingly obvious to Craven that South African sport was in big trouble. The country was no longer welcome in the Olympics, and great cricket players, such as Graeme Pollock and Barry Richards, saw their international careers wrecked by apartheid. Somehow rugby kept going, despite the cancellation of the proposed 1973 New Zealand tour because of premier Norman Kirk's fears that it would lead to the cancellation of the Commonwealth Games.

Danie Craven, legendary president of the South African Rugby Board

In order to remain a world power at rugby, South Africa had to be seen to be implementing change. The problem for Craven was that rugby was so clearly central to white control of sport and the whole apartheid ethos that it became a target for those seeking to undermine the regime in South Africa. Nelson Mandela's minister for sport, Steve Tshwete, explained that the African National Congress (ANC) saw the isolation of South African sport as one of their 'strongest weapons in the fight against apartheid tyranny'. That included cheering for the British Lions when they toured in 1974 so that the white regime could not revel in the success of the Springboks. Tshwete listened to the matches on the radio inside Robben Island prison. He recalls, 'We derided the Springboks. We laughed at them and even at the prison warders, and we said it was good the team was getting a hiding. That was an indication of the power of sport in pushing forward the process of change.'

Meanwhile, an embattled Craven found himself more and more having to defend his country's politics instead of their rugby. Author and historian John Nauright explained, 'The first reforms to racist policies in South Africa came in rugby because the government believed it was too important to sacrifice as they had done with the Olympic Games. It was too central to the Afrikaner. The issue was so contentious that members of the government actually left the party because they were afraid it would be the beginning of the end for apartheid. In some senses it was.' The honorary whites of the 1970 All Black tour were the first small chink in the armour of apartheid.

Throughout the 1970s the South African government tried to persuade the rest of the world that they were instituting reforms by holding black and coloured trials or by allowing international teams to play against black sides. 'Nobody bought it,' observed Nauright. 'They saw it as a sham and a cover-up. It wasn't changing anything.' The South African Council of Sport, founded in 1973, adopted the slogan 'No normal sport in an abnormal society', and it was one that even Craven found impossible to combat. It did not help that he is alleged to have remarked that 'there would be a black Springbok over my dead body'. He may or may not have said it, but it was a stick that would be used to beat him until his death. Certainly, black sportsmen never forgave him for it.

Errol Tobias became the first coloured Springbok in 1980. He was a product of the South African Rugby Federation, an organization that kept coloured players separate but affiliated to white unions. He also had enormous respect for Doc Craven, whom he saw as a 'good, well-balanced thinker'. Perhaps it is not Craven's fault that he was not a politician or a member of the Broederbond and did not wield the influence in the centre of power that many thought he did. He could stand up to the political bosses, but he could not decide for them. After the débâcle of the 1981 New Zealand tour, it was become increasingly clear that rugby in South Africa was going to suffer the same fate as the Walls of Jericho. There would be no official test matches between Springboks and All Blacks for 11 years.

By the time the proposed 1985 tour was due, David Lange was in power in New Zealand and he was in no doubt that 'rugby was a bane of the government'. He tried unsuccessfully to persuade his home union not to undertake the tour on moral grounds, before the New Zealand High Court came to his rescue and granted an injunction effectively stopping the

Pierre Berbizier, the French scrum-half, tries to rally his team in the first World Cup final. Meanwhile, the forwards get stuck in

THE FIRST WORLD CUP FINAL
NEW ZEALAND 29 – FRANCE 9
EDEN PARK, AUCKLAND
20 JUNE 1987

Fifty years on from when the South African tourists of 1937 triumphed at the heart of All Black rugby, New Zealand tried again to be hailed as the world champions – only this time South Africa, beaten by politics and isolation before the competition began, were not the opponents. Instead, a French team full of flair and invention with, ironically, a coloured full-back, Serge Blanco, as its star stood between New Zealand and the world recognition for which the nation had always craved. This was an All Black team that had cantered through the earlier games. They had the leading try-scorers in the competition in wings John Kirwan and Craig Green, not forgetting the scorching pace of full-back John Gallagher or the enterprise of scrum-half David Kirk, who marshalled his forces so intelligently behind a pack that dominated throughout. And then there was fly-half Grant Fox, who scored 126 points, which was nearly double the tally of the second highest scorer, Michael Lynagh of Australia. Fox was at the top of his game, missing nothing

with the boot, yet ensuring that his wings were given every opportunity to run.

The New Zealand points total was frightening. Italy were blitzed 70–6, Fiji 74–13, Argentina 46–15, Scotland 30–3 and Wales, in the semi-final, 49–9. There seemed no stopping the Kiwi juggernaut, but France had proved themselves at the highest level, showing greater discipline than ever before and triumphing in the most exciting game of the tournament when an heroic Blanco sealed a 30–24 victory in the semi-finals against the more fancied Australians. In reality, the All Blacks pack, with flanker Michael Jones widely acclaimed as the player of the tournament, established an early grip on the game that the French could not shake. Just a year before, Jones had been only a reserve for the Auckland team in provincial games and was almost a novice in terms of senior rugby. Yet here he was in the final of the inaugural World Cup, producing a masterly display of pace and power.

Not surprisingly, it was that man Fox, ignoring a gusting wind, who *established an early lead for the All Blacks with a confident drop-goal following a line-out. Another attempt was fumbled disastrously by French wing Patrice Lagisquet. Jones, with the speed of a three-quarter, was first to the loose ball and he contemptuously dismissed Blanco's tackle to cross for the first try. Fox converted and half-time saw New Zealand comfortably placed on 9–0. Didier Camberabero opened the scoring after the break with a penalty from far out on the left after the All Black forwards had piled over the top. Any fears the home crowd might have had that France would now get into the game were swiftly allayed by the boot of Fox, who kicked two more penalties to re-establish a points cushion. New Zealand began to enjoy themselves. Some neat handling by Fox and Jones let in Kirk, who eluded three tackles to cross for a captain's try. A blind-side break from the scrum-half shortly after the restart saw powerful number 8 Wayne Shelford set off at a gallop for the French line. A pass to flying wing John Kirwan and the match was all but over. Some further kicks from Fox, who took his tally to 17 points, were the icing on the cake. All the French could manage was a late consolation try by their artful scrum-half Pierre Berbizier. It made the 29–9 scoreline look a little better.*

David Kirk gleefully received the Webb Ellis trophy. Afterwards he said, 'It's not just unrestrained joy. There was a feeling of deep satisfaction, a sense of a burden being lifted because we had done what we were capable of doing and we hadn't let people down. There had been a great national expectation on us.' No one could argue that the All Blacks did not deserve it. They scored 298 points in the tournament and conceded a miserly 53. They crossed for 43 tries. In Kirk they had found a polished, charismatic and media-friendly leader. Here was a doctor and a Rhodes scholar who represented a modern New Zealand image, far removed from the frontiersmen of the past. The country had found itself again after the disaster of 1981. Experts were divided on whether this great side would have been the champions if South Africa had taken part. But Nelson Mandela still languished in jail, and while sporting enthusiasts could feel only sadness that many great Springbok players would never play a World Cup match, New Zealand had fulfilled its rugby destiny with the ultimate recognition on the world stage. After the match David Kirk said, 'Any opportunity to demonstrate the qualities that make our country great is gratefully accepted. It has been wonderful to take part in such a tournament.'

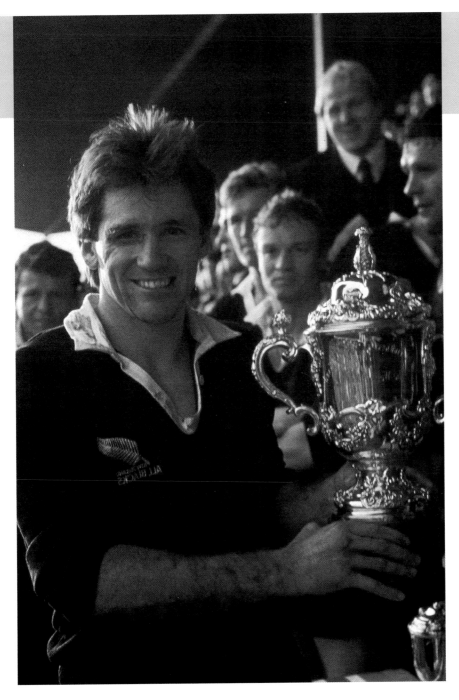

The New Zealand scrum-half David Kirk was the lucky man who collected the trophy at the end of the match

tour, which Lange believes 'rescued us from international ignominy'. The situation was desperate and, behind the scenes, Craven and key players in New Zealand conspired to set up a rebel tour which was called the Cavaliers Tour – a sparkling name for so tawdry an event. Just how much they were paid remains a secret, but acclaimed rugby writer T.P. Maclean reported that the tour fund was estimated to be 2 million rand. Although scrum-half David Kirk and winger John Kirwan turned it down, many leading rugby figures were involved. Colin Meads was coach and Andy Dalton, captain of the 1981 side, was made skipper.

The announcement of a rebel tour was an enormous embarrassment to Lange, who had just completed a three-week trip of southern Africa, which included meetings with ANC leaders. He recalls, 'I told the African leaders that I would not stop New Zealand people travelling but that they would not, I hoped, be in the receipt of news of a New Zealand tour of South Africa.' He still regards the timing of that announcement as a 'singularly cowardly thing'. In effect, the Cavaliers Tour had two major consequences. First, it ushered in the era of open professionalism in rugby. Second, and more importantly for Craven and South African rugby, desperate for international contact, it made them even more isolated. At the time, Colin Meads said the tour 'would open a door that should never have been shut'. In reality, it not only kept the door shut, but locked it as well. The New Zealand Rugby Union, outraged by the underhand way the tour had been organized, suddenly found itself on the same side as the anti-apartheid forces – the worst possible scenario for South African rugby.

Just a year later New Zealand was at the forefront of plans to launch the Rugby World Cup, but South Africa was not included in those plans. Back home Craven was still trying to promote integration, believing it to be the only way back into the world arena for the Springboks. Ian Kirkpatrick, a 1950s' Springbok, worked with the Doc throughout the 1980s and recalls that Craven would travel to five or six towns a day and in every town he would have to convince the local white population to play against the coloured or black community. He instituted coaching clinics for all and was considered by the government to be moving things along too fast. 'If it was a publicity stunt,' says Kirkpatrick, 'it was a very expensive one.' Craven might have been moving too fast for the government in Pretoria, but it was not fast enough to see his beloved Springboks take part in the first World Cup. He could only watch as his greatest rivals took the glory.

A year after New Zealand won the 1987 World Cup, Craven agreed to talks with the

ANC in the Zimbabwean capital, Harare. It was a massive step. Looking back, minister for sport, Steve Tshwete, is convinced that Craven was absolutely serious about the deracialization of rugby: 'It was always quite clear in his mind that the only people who could open the doors into international participation were the African National Congress.' For the first meeting Craven had to send a deputy because he was in a Cape Town hospital after a heart attack. He made the second meeting, along with Tommy Bedford, Chris Laidlaw and Steve Tshwete. There was outrage when news reached Pretoria. Craven was summoned to President F.W. de Klerk to account for why he was conducting discussions about rugby with terrorists in exile. To his credit, Craven refused to go. He was realistic enough to know that the ANC in exile could bring the All Blacks back to South Africa; De Klerk could not.

Craven's biting of the bullet was a vital part of a gathering momentum. Crucially for him and his beloved game, the ANC endorsed sporting contacts in 1990 when the political momentum was clearly going their way. It was not soon enough to allow South Africa's participation in the 1991 World Cup, but by the following year, negotiations were well advanced to bring the All Blacks back in 1992. Despite continued violence and atrocities in South Africa, the ANC decided to draw a line of distinction between the perpetrators of violence and the ordinary rugby player. They agreed to support an All Blacks match in 1992 provided that there was no singing of 'Di Stem', the Afrikaner national anthem. It was an agreement that had Craven's blessing, and he took his seat in the stand at Ellis Park next to Steve Tshwete. Just as the teams were about to take the field, the crowd struck up 'Di Stem' in direct breach of the agreement. Tshwete remembers that he saw Craven crying at this apparent betrayal. At least the South Africans lost the match.

Craven may have been downcast, but the ANC adopted a realistic approach. Tshwete observed, 'It was clear statement by Afrikaners that rugby was still their property and they were not going to part with it. They still had a strong notion that they were going to remain superior even at a political level. There was a resistance to change, a resistance to the transformation of South African sport, particularly rugby. We had no qualms about that. We knew they would be defeated and that's why we were happy to support the Rugby World Cup because it would have a role to play in nation-building and conciliation after the elections of 1994.' Those elections and the conciliation that led to South Africa staging the 1995 World Cup were denied to Craven, who died in 1993.

THE RAINBOW

There was no rugby on Robben Island in 1964 when Steve Tshwete was sent there to serve his 15-year jail sentence for being a member of the ANC, a banned organization. Rugby had been an important part of his life growing up in the Eastern Cape, where he admits he became 'a rugby person altogether'. He was part of the strong tradition that white South Africa tried to pretend did not exist. It began in primary school and went right through his education to college. Tshwete was a promising player with ambitions of playing for his province and perhaps even the African Springboks. But life on Robben Island was very different: 'There was no sport. We were locked up in our cells at weekends, and during the week we would be hewing stones in the lime quarry, pulling bamboo from the sea and mending old dilapidated roads on the island. So we mounted a huge struggle to get the sport and recreation we were entitled to. We went on hunger strikes and even engaged the international committee of the Red Cross to try and help.'

Eventually, the authorities conceded, but would allow the inmates to play only soccer, arguing that rugby was too dangerous and would result in too much medical attention. Tshwete was still determined to campaign for rugby, stressing that they would not be playing as robust a game as those outside prison because their level of fitness, health and diet were so poor. Ultimately, the Afrikaner prison authorities agreed, perhaps because of a love for the game, and Tshwete was elected as president of the Island Rugby Board. They formed a championship league, held knockout competitions and tried to include as many prisoners as possible, even those who saw rugby as an Afrikaner sport. Rugby became a way of binding this incarcerated community together, just as generations before it had united rural communities in New Zealand and the Afrikaner farmers of the high veld. The power and passion generated by rugby was clear to the ANC, who used it as a weapon in their armoury against apartheid. When Nelson Mandela joined Tshwete and other freed political prisoners in 1990, negotiations were advanced to bring the rugby World Cup to South Africa, by which time political power in the country would have shifted for the first time since the White Supremacist National Party swept into power in 1948. Tshwete explains, 'We were clear in our minds that the World Cup would act as a catalyst in the promotion of nation-building and conciliation after the 1994 elections. The people of South Africa would come together.'

The source of these expectations lay in the personal power and charisma of Nelson Mandela himself. In his autobiography, Will Carling remembers being introduced to Mandela before England's first test against South Africa in Pretoria in 1994: 'It remains one of my most cherished memories. Most dignitaries move quickly down the line with a routine comment for every fourth person. Not Mandela. He moved along the team and spoke to each player as he shook their hand. That was rare enough, but he also listened to what they said in return. The dignity and grace of the man were remarkable.' He certainly inspired England to one of their best-ever performances abroad – they won 32–15, with Rob Andrew scoring 27 points.

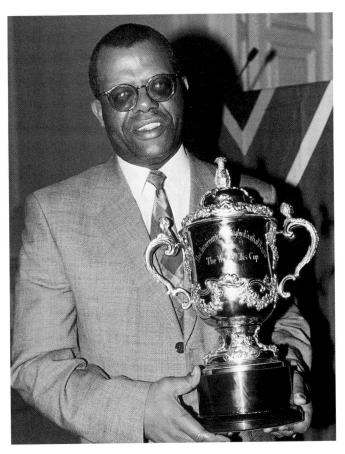

Steve Tshwete, South African minister of sport, holds the World Cup, a trophy he always dreamed his country would win

Mandela's inspirational qualities were never better illustrated than during the 1995 World Cup, when he personified a new spirit in his country. He rallied his people around a fresh look at rugby. Here was a sport that would bring the people together and not, as of old, be a despised icon of white supremacy. He told anyone who would listen that the Springboks were 'Your boys – your pride'. The people took the hint. And on that uplifting afternoon no one could forget the sight of the ageing leader, who had spent so much of his life in jail, proudly wearing his Springbok shirt and cap and joyfully throwing his arms in the air when victory was there for him, his team and his people. As Hugh McIlvanney observed, 'His presence was no mere decorative addition to the wild swirl of jubilation that swept across the ground in response to South Africa's late, tense and unforgettable triumph.' It was a day on which the Rainbow nation danced with happiness. Jonah Lomu, the player of

THE THIRD WORLD CUP FINAL
SOUTH AFRICA 15 – NEW ZEALAND 12
ELLIS PARK, JOHANNESBURG
24 JUNE 1995

This was the day Hollywood came to rugby. For drama, excruciating tension and joyous conclusion this was a scriptwriter's dream. The Springboks *had battled dourly to reach the final in their first World Cup – a disallowed try robbing France of victory in the semi-final. But few could have wished for*

*Springbok captain François Pienaar
refuses to give up the ball during this
epic encounter between South Africa and
New Zealand*

during the All Blacks 45–29 win), they
had the superstar of the tournament. Who
could have believed that in the same
century Lomu would have lined up on
South African soil against a Springbok
side that contained Chester Williams, a
coloured wing?

Both teams had played their best rugby
before the final. They started uncertainly,
neither wishing to be the first to concede
a precious advantage with a silly error or
over-elaboration. Opposing fly-halves Joel
Stransky and Andrew Mehrtens were
content to hammer the ball 60 or 70
yards into the thin air of the high veld in
the certain knowledge that it was safer to
play the game in the opposition's own
25-yard line. In the end, Stransky and
Mehrtens were the only two men to put
their names on the scoresheet all afternoon. They traded two penalties and
two drop-goals to bring the scores to
9–9 after 55 minutes.

The All Blacks, who had scored tries
at will in the competition with a philosophy
of playing a 'wide game', started to make
handling errors as they desperately tried
to rifle passes across the midfield in the
direction of Lomu. Just once he seemed
to have the line at his mercy, only to be
called back for a forward pass. In fact, it
was South Africa who came closest to
scoring when a blind-side break down the
left saw tenacious winger James Small

anything less than a battle against their
century-long rivals for the title of the
Kings of Rugby, the All Blacks. The New
Zealanders were firm favourites, having
cast aside the opposition throughout in
the manner of men taking on boys. In
Jonah Lomu, the 20-year-old Polynesian
winger whose massive physique had
scattered the defences of every team he
had come across (most notably England,
when he ran in four bulldozing tries

head for the New Zealand line, with Joel Stransky poised outside him to receive a try-scoring pass. Incredibly, Stransky, like a striker caught offside in his anticipation of a goal, strayed a yard ahead of Small and the pass was forward.

As the 80 minutes drew ever closer, bringing the prospect of extra time, so Lomu and centres Frank Bunce and Walter Little ploughed into the South African defence. However, Small stood up bravely against Lomu, and the back row of Ruben Kruger, captain François Pienaar and Mark Andrews were magnificent as they covered every inch of turf. It remained a stalemate and, incredibly, the drama was to be prolonged by extra

time for the first time in a World Cup Final. Rugby is not yet decided on penalties, and South Africa knew that if the scores remained level with no tries scored, it would be their arch enemies who took the trophy. The rules were that the deciding factor would be the number of men from each side who had been sent off throughout the tournament. No New Zealander had been dismissed, but Springbok hooker James Dalton had been shown the red card in Port Elizabeth during his country's match against Canada.

Andrew Mehrtens, blond-haired and ice-cool, gave the All Blacks a precious lead with a 50-yard penalty in the opening minutes of extra time after

South Africa had chased a Stransky kick from an offside position. Stransky's nerve held, with an accurate penalty after the New Zealand pack went offside at a ruck – 12 points all. Players' nerves were clearly beginning to fray on the pitch with handling errors increasingly creeping into the play. A knock-on gave the Springboks a sniff of a chance eight minutes from the end of time. The strong men in the Springbok pack produced a rock solid scrum, and Joost van der Westhuizen hurled the ball to Stransky giving his half-back partner just enough time to measure a drop-goal that soared between the posts. The crowd went wild with delight, but then had to endure the closing minutes as the All Blacks strove in vain for the try that would have given them the trophy. When the final whistle sounded, the Springbok captain François Pienaar closed his eyes and raised his arms to the heavens in jubilation. The whole nation joined him. It would have been Doc Craven's proudest moment – world champions at last.

It had not been a classic match, but it was an epic battle, an Oscar-winner for sure. As he made his way across to receive the trophy from his president, Pienaar was asked what it had felt like to have 65,000 supporters behind him. 'No,' said Pienaar, 'we had 43 million people behind us.' For one glorious afternoon the country was united at last.

Springbok full-back Andrê Joubert comes off second best, as All Black battering ram Jonah Lomu launches another attack on the South African line

179

the tournament, remembers the honour of meeting Mandela at the final. He recalls, 'We saw a nation come together that had been shut out from the rest of the world for so many years.'

Winning the World Cup, combined with the new commercialism in rugby, has injected massive amounts of money into the game in South Africa, just as it has done in New Zealand. There is still a battle for ownership of the game, with the Afrikaner die-hards clinging to what they regard as their property. Too much money is available to too few and not enough is spent at the bottom of the pyramid to promote rugby in the poorer areas and among young people. Politically, white power in South Africa has gone for ever. After the

Above: England captain Will Carling meets Nelson Mandela in Pretoria in 1994. He describes it as one of his most cherished rugby memories
Previous pages: Nelson Mandela, proudly wearing the Springbok jersey, inspired his country during the 1995 World Cup

glorious combined triumph of state and sport at the 1995 World Cup, perhaps rugby can never again be used as a political tool in South Africa. It remains to be seen, however, how many non-white players make the Springbok side for the 1999 World Cup and beyond.

Shortly after the 1995 victory, Nelson Mandela visited New Zealand for the first time. It was a momentous occasion, during which he was greeted with enthusiasm and emotion wherever he went. He attended a church service for veterans of the local anti-apartheid movement in Auckland, which had witnessed such violent scenes in 1981. During his time in prison, New Zealand played four official and one unofficial test series against his jailers. They played without Maoris, with honorary whites and finally with a fully racially integrated team. At last rugby was not the most important thing in the world.

PART THREE

THE ADOPTED GAME

RUGBY TRAVELS TO FRANCE

Rugby has been traditionally a game played by countries belonging to a kind of British Empire club. Only France has had the nerve and talent to challenge the principal rugby-playing nations. It was the first country outside the Imperial Anglo-Saxon world to adopt rugby and, over the past century, it has stamped its own identity on the game. (The French have always been determined not to be seen as copycats.) Rugby has been closely entwined with the history and development of France in the 20th century. However, as in the other countries, French rugby has had more than its fair share of controversy and strife.

Being no more than a Serge Blanco siege gun punt away from Twickenham encouraged the French upper and middle classes to adopt the most popular game in the public schools of Victorian England. But as its popularity spread away from the cosy environs of Paris, it became a game of such violence and professionalism that France was thrown out of the international playground for a decade in the 1930s. In modern times the term 'champagne rugby' has come to describe the gallic flavour France brings to the Union game. There was, however, nothing to celebrate about its association with the collaborationist regime of Vichy during the Second World War.

TOUCHÉ – EARLY DAYS IN FRANCE

Baron Pierre de Coubertin, the founder of the modern Olympic Games, paid a visit to Rugby School in 1883. It was just one stop on his journey around Europe and the United States studying educational methods. He had, by all accounts, been moved by the description of the school – and the game – in the French edition of *Tom Brown's Schooldays.* He obviously valued the same principles as the school's headmaster, Dr Thomas Arnold, who had done much to refresh the vigour and moral fibre of the young men of England. The baron, a forward-thinking member of an aristocratic Norman family, famously had a vision in the school chapel. He was, so he later said, moved to imagine the Olympic Games. He saw in the team sports of Britain the chance to strengthen the French élite classes which had been so humiliated by defeat in the Franco-Prussian War of 1870–71 and the loss of Alsace and Lorraine. He could foresee Frenchmen playing these traditional English sports and playing them well. He and his fellow countrymen who visited the public schools, as well as Oxford, Cambridge and other colleges in England, were not especially fascinated by the game of rugby, but they were enthusiastic about what the sport represented.

De Coubertin was a great supporter of physical education and saw sport very much as the making of the man, an ethos well ingrained in the playing of Rugby football. It is a little surprising that the game that fought so hard to retain amateur status could not find a place in the first Olympics. Perhaps de Coubertin found the French slow to adapt to the masculine game preferred across the Channel. When rugby was first introduced into the middle and aristocratic classes of Paris in the early 1880s, it was a game where physical contact was not encouraged. They prized style and elegance, combined with speed of thought and foot. Physical strength was not admired in French society at this time, so the game more closely resembled a traditional French pursuit called *la barrette*, where a player had only to brush lightly against the man with the ball and yell 'Touché!' to stop play. Imagine the fearsome Benoit Dauga, Jean-Pierre Bastiat or Daniel Dubroca responding to a cry of *touché* as they flattened some poor opposing wing.

The ingredient that allowed rugby to establish a broader appeal across all social classes in France was the country's need to re-establish a national identity after a crisis. This was clearly the case after the defeat of 1870/1, but also in the 1950s when President Charles de Gaulle recognized that sporting excellence could give France status. Rugby had been proven in countries such as New Zealand and Wales to be a sport that could enhance a nation's self-esteem and sense of achievement. Rugby prowess could also provide greater status to a country in the eyes of the world. These virtues mirrored the thinking of de Coubertin, who believed that sport could improve a sense of nationality. 'Je veux rebronzer La France,' he declared, which roughly translates as, 'I want to bring glory back to France.' Author and historian Jean Pierre Bodis observes, 'He no longer wanted an anaemic France with an anaemic youth. Sport in general, and rugby in particular, was a good means of making the real men, the soldiers who might win back Alsace and Lorraine.' The Olympic movement, supposedly founded on a philosophy that taking part was

Baron Pierre de Coubertin advocated rugby as a sport the French should adopt

more important than winning, was swiftly usurped by a feeling of nationalistic fervour, where a country's medal count became far more significant that the honour of competing. Sports historian Richard Holt observes that, 'Olympic medals soon came to be seen as a barometer of national virility.'

Strangely enough, the early competition to the popularity of rugby in France came from those who believed gymnastics to be the sport that would make the nation great again. Gymnastics, a staple element of German education, was perceived as a route France should

The Racing Club de France, pictured here in 1912, was one of the most famous sporting clubs in the world

take to be more like the victors of 1870/1, a case of if you can't beat them, join them. Gymnastics in schools were similar to paramilitary training for the nation's youth, who would climb ropes, vault and swing on bars as if attempting a difficult army assault course.

Others, like de Coubertin, believed that the British Empire was the role model French society should be following. They saw the sports played every afternoon on the playing fields of English public schools and decided they would import them wholesale to France. Rugby became the most important of these imports, although athletics, rowing and soccer were also endorsed by the Union des Sociétés Françaises de Sports Athlétiques, which was formed in 1889 and administered French sports for the next 30 years. The idea that sport could make schooling fun was a totally new concept in upper- and middle-class France. When Napoleon set up the *lycée*, for instance, students were not allowed to speak to each other and had to march around between classes to the beat of a drum.

A group of Oxbridge expatriates formed the first sports club at Le Havre in 1872, playing their own particular combination of football and soccer, which seemed specifically designed to multiply the number of bashes and bruises participants would suffer. Although English expats did play rugby in Paris, the impetus for the game taking off in the capital came from the élite classes and Anglophiles who saw it being played on visits to England and decided to copy it on their return. In 1882 the most privileged young men of Paris formed their own association, the Racing Club de France, which would soon become one of the most famous sporting clubs in the world. When the clubhouse was built in 1886, it was, fittingly, opened by the minister of war. In the French capital towards the end of the 19th century upper and middle classes were merging into one professional and business class. Playing rugby was an indication of that class, a sport played by like-minded young people, the *grands bourgeois*. Its amateur status kept it exclusive. The extremely exclusive Le Stade Français was founded in Paris by students of the Lyceé Saint-Louis, the year after the Racing Club was formed. From an early stage soccer was seen as unsuitable for polite French society because it was played by tradesmen and people in the street.

LE RUGBY EST ARRIVÉ

If rugby in France gained its footing in Paris, then it gained its soul in the rural areas of the south-west. Beyond Bordeaux, rugby became part of small communities just as it had done in the farming areas of New Zealand and the mining districts of South Wales. For a time the same was true of the industrial towns of Yorkshire, until the breakaway of 1895. Although Paris was very much the centre of the country, the distance to Toulouse, Perpignan, Bordeaux and all the little villages who adopted rugby as their game meant that it was impossible to exercise the iron rod of amateurism with which London had managed to beat Yorkshire.

The spread of rugby to the south-west owed much to the influence of British businessmen, particularly the wine merchants who used the great provincial capital of Bordeaux as a base. From there Bordeaux men founded famous clubs in the region, such as those at Pau, Bayonne, Agen and Bergerac. There was also a close affinity between the students of the *lycées* in Paris and the University of Bordeaux. One of the leading figures of the time was a doctor called Philippe Tissié, who sought to adapt the British game of rugby (as played in Paris) to make it more French. He was a Protestant and a republican and, although of humbler origins than Baron de Coubertin, he had many of the same ideas of reinventing a powerful country by concentrating on the nation's youth. He devoted most of his life to promoting a generation of healthy young men who could 'win back' Alsace and Lorraine. Historian Richard Holt explains, 'It was part of trying to Frenchify British games. No one wanted to be seen borrowing from the British.' Tissié introduced rugby at school festivals throughout the south-west so that, by the turn of the century, it had secured a popular base.

In the extreme south-west members of the local rowing club in Bayonne were persuaded to try the game when the son of a local official brought an oval ball back from a school holiday trip to England. The club, called L'Aviron Bayonnais, which means the Bayonne Oar, was to become one of the most famous rugby clubs in all France thanks to a young Welshman called Owen Rowe, who arrived from Penarth in 1911 to work as a ship-broker. Rowe taught the locals the Welsh style of rugby as played by Gwyn Nicholls and his famous 1905 team which defeated the All Blacks. Bayonne were so proud of their distinctive free-flowing, quick passing style and their achievement in winning the national club championship (Championnat de France) after Bordeaux, that the road leading to the rugby ground is called after Owen Rowe.

The rivalry between the south-west and the Paris élite quickly became established, and in 1899 a national championship pitted the Paris champions against the best club from the provinces. At the time, this was uniquely French, using a British sporting blueprint and making it work in a completely different country. Even today, teams from Scotland and Wales do not compete in either the English league or cup competitions. (There is no United Kingdom cup.) In the first encounter the top Bordeaux club, Stade Bordelais, beat the Stade Français team from Paris. The next year it was the turn of Racing Club to regain the honour for Paris.

Gradually the south-west began to dominate, until a new system arrived at the first all-provincial final in 1909, when Bordeaux took on its great rival Toulouse. When the Bordeaux team disembarked from their train at Toulouse railway station, they were greeted by enthusiastic home supporters shouting 'Vive Bordeaux!', to which they responded 'Vive Toulouse!' Even though there was fierce local rivalry, they were united in beating the swanky Parisian enemy. Rugby was harnessing local identity. The regional papers looked to the teams to avenge the 'injustices and humiliations' inflicted on all provinces by Paris.

Nowhere is rugby more keenly fought than in the final of the French club championship. In 1995 Toulouse beat Castres 31–16

When the final whistle sounded and Bordeaux had won by 17–0, the spectators, victors and vanquished, shouted as one, 'Vive les provinces!' (Long live the provinces). Author Thierry Terret calls it, 'the conflict between the southern ideal of the strong man and the northern ideal of the urban intellectual'. By 1915 some of that bonhomie had vanished and Toulouse supporters stoned a train carrying their great rivals home. These games were attracting vast crowds of more than 30,000 and, as always in rugby, the larger the crowd, the greater the passion.

Rugby was taking its place alongside other essential ingredients of south-western culture: bullfighting, festivals, eating good food and drinking much wine. The peasants of the rural areas were like the Welsh miners, who endured a hard physical working life and to whom the family unit was particularly important. Rugby became part of a rural tradition that provincial men did not want to give up. It is the difference, as in New Zealand, between playing rugby and living rugby. Rural France lived its rugby. The village or town that you came from was more important than your status within the community. Just as in South Wales and Yorkshire, people went along to matches to support their local team, even if they knew nothing of rugby. They certainly had no pre-set ideas of how to behave at a rugby match. This was a culture of machismo glorifying the *castagne*, a Gascon word for 'fight', which accounts for the amount of violence that has always accompanied domestic rugby in France. There was and is nothing *touché* about the barbaric encounters between the villages and towns of a region where accepted brutality set France aside from the other rugby-playing nations – and not just on the pitch.

Rugby matches began to resemble bullfights, where an atmosphere of drama and death was ever present. The same crowds that went to rugby in winter would go to the summer bullfights and shout, scream or fight at both. Spectators would regularly become involved in pitch battles, especially if the rugby match involved one of their own teams against Paris.

THE RUGBY OF DEATH

To the English middle-class amateur, there was something very strange about French rugby players. As academic Jean-Pierre Bodis explains, 'They ate garlic, they attended matches without their shirts and they drank aniseed. These are not things you find in the clubhouses

The French team that played Ireland in 1923, at a time when France had an unwelcome reputation for violent play

of Blackheath or Edinburgh.' International matches between the two began in Paris in 1906, and France were minnows at that stage. Nine games were played before the First World War and England won all nine, including 41–13 in 1907, 37–0 in 1911 and 39–13 in 1914. The French team was very much Paris-based, and during this period rugby was still trying to establish itself as a national sport. They managed their first International win against Scotland in 1911. After the First World War, rugby was able to get a much stronger grip, partly as an antidote to Association Football, which was gaining in popularity.

The administration of the game was taken over by the Fédération Français de Rugby (FFR), which was formed in October 1920 – the same year the French beat Ireland in Dublin to secure the first-ever victory away from home soil. Rugby spread rapidly through the country, a symbol of post-war national pride, and by the end of the 1920s there were 783 teams. After the humiliation of 1870, France was now a nation of victors, and the concept of defeat on a rugby field at any level would not be entertained. When the French team lost the 1924 Olympic championship in Paris to, of all things, an American team, pandemonium broke out. The American flag was torn up and the Welsh referee roundly abused. Unsurprisingly, that was the last time rugby featured in the Olympics. France, like so many international teams, has often considered itself the victim of appalling refereeing. That was certainly the opinion a few years earlier, in 1913, when Scotland beat France in Paris. The crowd were so incensed by the English referee, a Mr Baxter, that he had to be escorted from the pitch by soldiers brandishing fixed bayonets. The outraged crowd then took it upon itself to enjoy an evening of rioting and fighting in the French capital.

The men who played rugby in France played a violent game. The attitude was such that if they wanted to try something more skilful, then soccer was the game for them. It seemed that the more rural the player, the more violent his behaviour on the pitch. The ultimate example of this was probably in the most infamous game of all time, between Quillan and Perpignan, where intense local rivalry boiled over into a terrifying encounter. It also highlighted the threat that professionalism brought to the sport in France. Quillan is a little Southern town in the Aude *département* at the foot of the Pyrenees, notable in those days as a centre for the manufacture of hats. An industrialist called Jean Bourrel was passionate about rugby and determined to make his local team the best in the region, so he lured players from Catalan rivals Perpignan and Toulouse with the offer of money and jobs at his factory. Historian Richard Holt explains, 'He was a determined man, who was happy to put

Below: The peaceful French town of Quillan, whose rugby team took part in the most terrifying encounter of all time
Rugby league in France was fast, fluid and popular game throughout the 1930s
Following pages: Rugby League in France was a fast, fluid and popular game throughout the 1930s

his hand in his pocket to get the best player. It worked because he did win the French national championship three times in succession from 1927, but he won it at a price.' That price was hatred towards Quillan, who were perceived as a team of mercenaries. In the 1927 match against Perpignan the Quillan hooker, Gaston Riviére, received such a kicking that he died from his injuries.

The home unions (England, Ireland, Scotland and Wales) were clearly disturbed by the behaviour within French rugby. It was bloodthirsty, it flouted the amateur rules and it wasn't British. Jean-Pierre Bodis says that the morality of French rugby at the time was 'quite detestable'. A player from Pau was also killed on the pitch, and then, in 1930, an 18-year-old wing called Michel Pradie playing for Agen was killed in a cup match. In the final against Quillan the Agen full-back, Marius Guiral, sent a drop-kick soaring over from all of 50 yards to secure a 4–0 victory. It was said that the kick had the 'breath of poor Michel Pradie carrying it towards victory', a sentiment which would be almost poetic if he had died a hero fighting for his country instead of on a muddy rugby field in Bordeaux.

By now the home unions had seen enough. The middle-class, amateur forces that controlled rugby on the English side of the Channel decided that the French were not for them. Rugby in France was being controlled by unscrupulous forces who had lost sight of its amateur foundations. The French were expelled from the Five Nations Championship and would not return until the end of the Second World War. After all, this was a British Imperial game: we owned it – not the French. The International Board (IB) announced that they were breaking off relations with France owing to 'the unsatisfactory conditions of the game of Rugby football in France'. That ban would remain until the 'control and conduct of the game has been placed on a satisfactory basis in all essentials'.

The shame for France was that throughout the previous ten years their national team had been steadily improving, achieving a victories against all four home countries in the 1920s. Wales had been beaten 8–3 in 1927 in a match that many rated as one of the roughest ever. Wales, which had fought and won its own battles against the middle-class owners of rugby, was broadly sympathetic to the French plight, but was powerless to thwart the IB's wishes – especially as France was not yet a member of the board and, incredibly, was not actually admitted until 1978. If there's one thing the British middle class likes even less than the working class, it's foreigners, especially the French.

THE REVENGE OF VICHY

International isolation was quick to drive disenchanted Rugby Union supporters in France into the arms of Rugby League, which they called *le rugby à treize* (13-a-side rugby). The driving force was an ex-Union player called Jean Gallo, who had been banned in 1932 for violent play amid rumours of under-the-counter payments. He moved to Rugby League so that he could have a contract and be paid in a proper professional manner that everyone could see.

Unofficial contact with British Rugby League officials led to the first showcase match in Paris in 1933, when Britain faced Australia in what would today be called a friendly. The French liked what they saw. The prospect of international competition combined with the financial rewards of this professional sport was too great a temptation for many Union players and within a few months Gallo had raised a team which left French shores for matches in the North of England. This was quickly followed by a series of demonstration matches in Paris between the French and Yorkshire. The game he and his fellow players brought to the fields of Paris and Bordeaux was spectacular and fluid, and, more importantly, an immediate success.

The response of die-hard French Union administrators, particularly those in Paris, fearing that it would ruin their game and their chances of ever being readmitted to the Five Nations Championship, was to try to squash the threat. That merely drew attention to it. Players, administrators and even pitches were ostracized and/or banned if they had anything to do with the new game. As historian Philip Dine of Loughborough University explains, 'Their heavy-handedness appears to have been seriously miscalculated.' The FFR was forcing rugby to choose, and a depressing number opted for League, with 4000 players signed up by the outbreak of war. The south-west stronghold of Union was particularly thirsty for the competition the new game was bringing.

Desperately, the powers that be in French Rugby Union sought fresh international opponents to try to give their game some impetus. As a result, rugby in France started to take on a sinister political significance. An organization dedicated to amateur rugby – the Fédération Internationale de Rugby Amateur (FIAR) – was formed to arrange international matches with Italy, Romania and, most significantly, Germany. The driving force behind the FIAR was Hitler's Germany, anxious to cultivate closer relations with France and drive a wedge between France and Britain. The countries in the federation – Portugal, Spain, Holland and Belgium – had strong fascist elements which the Germans were exploiting. They also played terrible rugby. Although France had far more rugby-playing experience, the official language of the new federation was German.

The political strife in which rugby found itself was brought sharply into focus when the Popular Front was elected to govern France in 1936, the same year that Hitler invaded the Rhineland. The Popular Front was a communist and socialist coalition which swept into power on a ticket supporting the working man. And just as in England, where Rugby League was perceived as professional and working class, so it was in France where the new game was quickly given the official recognition that so horrified traditionalists. Up until then the Rugby Union bosses had managed to persuade the government not to recognize Rugby League. However, in the radically different political climate the Union game was seen as a game of the right, the military and the pro-Europeans, while the League game represented the left, the 'idle' working class and the British. Amid a flurry of strikes, the new government introduced measures to improve job security, allow paid holidays and bring in higher wages. The working classes in France therefore had more money and leisure than their counterparts in England, thus avoiding some of the issues that had divided the sport in Yorkshire and South Wales 40 years earlier. The division that occurred in France came with the outbreak of the Second World War, when the Union game became associated with Vichy and its collaborationist government.

In 1939, when Neville Chamberlain's peace initiative to Germany of 1938 crumbled, France was still isolated in terms of international Rugby Union. The British were not convinced that the game across the Channel had changed; they believed it to be as violent and corrupt as ever. But more important issues were now at stake. With the prospect of war just around the corner, Britain was desperate to cement a bond with France. Historian Robert Fassolette explains, 'The one little black spot in relations between the two countries was the problem between the British and French Rugby Union. Everything was done by British diplomacy to effect a reconciliation.' The diplomacy even included the offer from the Queen – now the Queen Mother – to try to appease the Scottish Rugby Federation, who, as usual, were being the most dogged about preserving old values. Eventually, the home unions were persuaded to re-admit France to the Five Nations Championship, a well-timed gesture, even if there would be no international matches for six years.

Colonel Joseph Pascot was the minister for sport in the Vichy government, which established close ties with the Union game to help unify the country

The French people suffered the trauma of defeat at the hands of Germany, and subsequent occupation of their land from June 1940. The Popular Front had lost power and with that came the abandonment of one of its initiatives – a programme aimed at creating sports facilities for all throughout France. Instead, German troops took over the northern part of the country, and in the south the notorious collaborationist government of Marshal Henri Pétain was formed at Vichy, with the result that many of the old guard, who opposed the Popular Front in 1936, were back at the helm in France. In many ways the Vichy attitude towards sport reflected the same ethos of de Coubertin and his friends after the 1871 defeat by the Prussians. They saw team games as a way of re-focusing the national identity after humiliating defeat.

Rugby found a champion in the famous 'Bounding Basque', Jean Borotra, who had won the men's singles at Wimbledon in 1931 and was one of France's most famous sportsmen, renowned the world over. He became minister of sport and a keen advocate of rugby as a game that could infuse a mixture of discipline and dynamism to the youth of the country. His right-hand man was a former rugby international called Joseph Pascot, who would himself become minister of sport in 1942. Both men reflected the desire of the Vichy government to use sport as an instrument of unification. Vichy was in no shape or form a democracy, so whatever the regime decided quickly became law. There was no opposition. Rugby League had little chance of a fair crack of the whip in the prevailing climate. Quite apart from its allegiance with the left, it was thought to promote individualism to an unhealthy degree.

Vichy and the old guard of Rugby Union wanted revenge. Historian Robert Fassolette explains, 'They wanted to eradicate the playing of Rugby League because it was a dangerous rival. They wanted to take their revenge on the success of Rugby League, so they began to suppress it as a sport.' Incredibly, Pétain himself signed a decree in 1941 banning Rugby League as a sport and dissolving its ruling body, the Ligue Française de Rugby à X111 (LFR). The government was, in effect, insisting on the reunification of the game as Rugby Union. Fassolette graphically describes it as the 'Aryanization' of Rugby League. The result was that all the assets of Rugby League, which had been flourishing in France, were handed over to the National Sports Committee, which promptly gave them to Rugby Union.

The new status of Rugby Union allowed an amnesty for players previously associated with the dreaded League game. It also saw the reintroduction of the national club competition, which had been halted in 1939. Gradually, the Union game found renewed popularity and the slump of the 1930s was reversed. Close to 2000 new players were introduced to the game in 1942/3. Just as de Coubertin and Tissié were proved right in the 19th century, so it seemed that Vichy was right in wartime: Rugby Union was the great patriotic, masculine, rallying sport. When the Vichy regime fell into disgrace at the end of the war, there was no backlash against Rugby Union. It was too deeply entrenched and was able to withstand the renewal of Rugby League and the post-war success of the 13-man code. The Union game had two great advantages over its younger relative. First, it arrived in France before Rugby League, and tradition, once established, is very hard to dislodge. Second, the leading rugby players found that they were far better off financially as 'amateur' Union players than as professionals in League. The objections the home unions had to France in 1931 continued to exist, broadly speaking, but the Second World War meant that everyone now turned a blind eye.

Some post-war reprisals did take place. National club champions Perpignan had their clubhouse and facilities damaged by angry *treizistes* (League supporters), but the sport of Vichy by and large was let off lightly. Both codes enjoyed considerable post-war success. The League team defeated Great Britain at Wembley in 1949 and, under their leading player, Puig Albert, toured and beat Australia for the first time. The watershed year was 1954. The Union team shared the International Championship for the first time, and the Rugby League World Cup was held in France. In the final at Parc des Princes, Britain narrowly defeated the French team. The Union team went from strength to strength in the 1950s, whereas their League counterparts gradually went into decline. If France had won the League World Cup, it would probably have had a seriously damaging effect on the Union game.

THE SECOND MIRACLE OF LOURDES

Lourdes, a fairly undistinguished small town in the Pyrenees, has been a place of pilgrimage ever since the Virgin Mary appeared before a young peasant girl called Marie Bernarde Soubirous, later St Bernadette, in 1858. Devout Christians, those seeking a cure for illness and handicap, and curious tourists have flocked there in their millions ever since. Rugby

As captain of Lourdes and France, Jean Prat ushered in an era of spectacular French rugby – 'le rugby champagne'

was never the attraction, yet out of nowhere Lourdes emerged as the dominant force in French rugby after the Second World War. At a time when Rugby Union in France needed to cast aside its ugly image from the violent 1920s and its association with the disgraced Vichy regime, Lourdes provided France with a fresh, inspiring, entertaining modern game.

The team that dominated French rugby in the late 1940s and 1950s owed a great deal to the vision and expertise of its charismatic captain, Jean Prat. He was able to introduce techniques that enabled the French game to flourish as never before. Paradoxically, his secret weapon was discipline. He realized that what French rugby needed in order to flower was one leader and 14 players pulling together as a team – it did not need 15 captains running around in an atmosphere of total anarchy. Intriguingly, the worst French performances since then have often been when indiscipline has once more taken over. Prat explains, 'The French game at the time was fairly disorganized. Each player did just about whatever they wanted to, and in rugby that's not really acceptable. It should be a collective game. It was precisely because I wanted to institute this kind of game that I first took on the captaincy of Lourdes, and the success we had there led to me being entrusted with the French team.'

Many of the new players Prat introduced into his method of playing the game had, like him, been juniors during the wartime occupation. The Hautes-Pyrénées region had suffered a considerable German presence because of its strategic significance for anyone trying to reach Spain. The men who had been playing rugby before war broke out went away to fight or were taken prisoner, so there were no players from the old regime to encourage bad habits in the young boys taking up the game. In effect, there was a blank canvas to work on. According to Prat, the youngsters were well trained in the 'spirit of the game'. He believed that rugby was a release from the gloom of war and had become much more spectacular as a result.

In Lourdes the effect of the new rugby philosophy was apparent. Prat's team won the National Championship six times between 1948 and 1960. The man himself was a devastating back-row forward with a penchant for kicking drop-goals. The philosophy was simple: harness the power of the 'locomotive' (the scrum) to release a fast and powerful set of backs. With suitable modesty, Prat maintains that he did not invent a new kind of rugby at Lourdes. He says, 'The rugby we talk about now as champagne rugby was being played by all good French teams at the time. Teams like Bayonne were the first to play it and they inspired us.' The other important influences on Prat were the 1945 'Victory' matches against the British Empire teams when rugby relations were resumed following the disarray of 1931. He saw the kind of rugby, particularly in the backs, that he wanted France to emulate.

The effect on the national team was immediately apparent. France beat all the home countries at least once in the first three post-war seasons, and also won against Australia in 1948. Prat led the team that scored a memorable first win on Welsh soil at Swansea on a freezing cold day when snow had to be cleared and the whole ground covered in a protective layer of straw. An hour or two before the game began, the straw was dragged to the edge of the pitch, where it was piled so high that spectators immediately behind it could not see the game. They had to lie on the straw to watch. On a treacherous surface, a massive French pack, including second-row giants Robert Soro and Alban Moga (combined weight 32 stone) were outstanding and the visitors won 11–3.

Just as memorable was the first French victory against the English at Twickenham in 1951. It was France's eleventh attempt and a personal triumph for Prat. The French 'locomotive' became stronger as the match went on, driving through the wet and heavy conditions. Prat rounded off a fine forward drive by going over for a try, and then in the second half sealed victory with a drop-goal. He converted a try by Guy Basquet for good measure, bringing his personal tally to eight points. Throughout his international career Prat was an amazing points scorer, considering that he was a forward. In 51 internationals he clocked up 145 points – at a time when a try was worth only three.

Prat's team went on to share the Five Nations Championship for the first time in 1953/4 and again the following season. Perhaps the clearest indication that France was now a formidable player on the world stage came in 1954 when they defeated the All Blacks for the first time by a battling 3–0 scoreline. One try was scored – by Jean Prat. Over a period of 11 seasons from 1945 to 1955, Prat missed only one international, when he fell victim to flu. Often he played alongside his younger brother, Maurice, who was capped 31 times at centre between 1951 and 1958. Jean received the ultimate accolade for a national sporting hero when he became known throughout France by the nickname 'Monsieur Rugby'.

Funnily enough, the term 'champagne rugby' is not entirely appropriate as the Champagne area of France is one of the least noteworthy rugby regions in the whole country. It has much more affinity with football. Champagne rugby was, however, a handy epithet to describe the French style that evolved in the 1950s with Lourdes and Bayonne at the helm. That style incorporated the best attacking qualities, a fighting spirit and a strong sense of community. In some ways the great Welsh team of the 1970s, including Gareth Edwards, Barry John, J.P.R. Williams and Gerald Davies, came closest to emulating the philosophy of Jean Prat. The important thing for France was that champagne rugby came near to justifying the vision of de Coubertin and others who saw the game as a way of rediscovering a French identity, a new France full of verve, invention and passion. Casting aside the shackles of the Second World War created a social and economic climate where France could impose its own national spirit on the game. The country was no longer playing catch-up rugby with an Imperial game but pushing back the boundaries of rugby itself.

VINTAGE CHAMPAGNE

The year is 1958, a momentous one in French history. It was the year Charles de Gaulle, the unmistakable face of modern France, returned to power as president. It was also the year when the French rugby team, under the dynamic and dextrous Lucien Mias, won the Five Nations Championship outright and could justly claim to be the best team in the northern hemisphere. Trying to contain the flamboyant French sides of the late 1950s was once memorably described as like 'trying to box an octopus'. Mias took the blueprint of Jean Prat and turned it into something more sophisticated and entertaining. If Prat's team introduced champagne rugby, then Mias turned it into vintage bubbly. He built on the hard forward edge, and he engendered an almost arrogant belief in the backs regarding their own superior ability.

As a nation, France itself was on the road to prosperity and the French backs, including Pierre Albaladejo, Jean Dupuy and the incomparable Boniface brothers, André and Guy, played like millionaires. Albaladejo became known as 'Monsieur Drop' because of his amazing drop-goal feats. Mias, a doctor by profession, was one of the game's great thinkers and he was determined that his team would achieve the highest technical standard. Basketball, which was growing in popularity, seemed to be the inspiration for the flips and lobs and acrobatic takes that brought a new dimension to three-quarter play and, more crucially, to forward movement. Men such as Michel Celaya, Amadée Domenach, Bernard Mommejat and Mias himself had the handling skills and all-round mobility of a centre.

Pierre Albaladejo in familiar pose, about to unleash another of his formidable drop-goals

They had given notice in the preceding seasons that they were the future of European rugby.

Mias is credited with devising what were popularly called 'percussion' moves to break down stifling mid-field defences. His loose forwards would peel round the back of the line-out and engage the mid-field, with their backs in support behind them ready to pounce when the defence was sucked in. Although a common tactic in the modern game, it was revolutionary then and gave the French an extra weapon. The French forwards responded magnificently to being the first line of attack, and with their well-honed ball-handling skills, they would rumble on towards their opponents' lines in great tidal waves until they could spread the ball quickly out to the flanks which, by this time, were often sparsely defended.

France, the country, had been slower than its rugby team to recover after the traumas of war, of collaboration with the enemy and of military conflict. Whereas rugby emerged unscathed and untainted by its association with the disgraced Vichy government, the country took more than 30 years to recover. The old colonial constraints had to be consigned to the dustbin of history and France needed to look forward as an influential European nation. The de Gaulle government gave the nation the direction to do that. Historian Phil Dine explains, 'France needed to appear forward-thinking, dynamic and strong. Against this backdrop, a wonderful rugby team emerged. The year 1958 was especially symbolic because of the strong victory against the Welsh in Cardiff.'

Even the most die-hard Welshman would have to concede that his men were comprehensively outplayed in the 16–6 victory at Cardiff Arms Park, the first and most significant victory at the famous heart of Welsh rugby. The match was broadcast live on television, and even though Wales lost the rugby, they won the singing, with a rousing rendition of the 'Marseillaise' in Welsh. Lourdes supplied no fewer than seven of the 15 French heroes, six of them in the backs. The contribution rugby made to France at this time was one of linking the country together. Better roads and railways, personal wealth and the new television age meant that the game found favour all over the country, not just in the south-west, although that region remains the nerve centre of French rugby. A massive new audience was being introduced to rugby at a time when the French had a fabulous team. It was a team worth supporting if you liked the taste of victory. Crowds in Paris for home internationals regularly exceeded 60,000. De Gaulle and his government recognized the importance of sport for securing national pride and international prestige, and began an intensive programme of financing sporting initiatives. Rugby was a virile figurehead for that investment.

For the heroes of 1958 there was even better to come when they toured apartheid-riddled South Africa later in the year. No overseas team had ever triumphed against the Springboks in a series – at that stage not even the British Lions had taken the spoils. Despite their home success, no one gave the French much chance. The tour didn't start brightly, with the players being read the Riot Act about how to behave. Michel Celaya remembers them being told that players who had relations with black women could expect 15 days in prison and that the management could do nothing to help them. They were told that the powers at home would be happy if they managed to win just one match. But this French team had a great spirit, epitomized by the electric atmosphere in the dressing-rooms before matches. Mias would lead his men in a chorus of the Revolutionary song 'La Victoire en Chantant'. The anthem charged the men with a warlike emotion and from that moment on, to the astonishment of the rugby world, they didn't lose a match. After defeat in a bruising first test, the team recovered to win the next two and claim an historic victory. Not even the All Blacks had achieved that.

As was often the case in other countries, rugby and politics in France were closely linked. Jacques Chaban-Delmas, who would become prime minister of his country in 1969, attributed much of his power base to his rugby heritage. He was actually mayor of Bordeaux while still play-ing for a local club, and rose to national prominence on the back of his sporting fame. Chaban-Delmas admitted that part of his appeal was that in south-west France 100,000 people called him Jacques and 100,000 people called him *tu* rather than the more formal *vous*. He was seen as a friend because of his rugby. Another French prime minister and future president, Jacques Chirac, would, in his days as minister of agriculture, go out of his way to be seen supporting rugby in the south-west. Politicians recognized that rugby, the family sport,

Right: Jacques Chaban-Delmas, future French prime minister, cut a dashing figure in his rugby-playing days
Previous pages: Lucien Mias charging with the ball – he was a dynamic captain who led France to international success in the late 1950s

was a political winner and a vote catcher. De Gaulle, more than any other, manipulated this. He was from the north, but you would never have thought so as he sent telegrams of congratulation whenever a match was won, held receptions at the Elysée Palace for the teams and declared Saturday afternoons a no-work zone for goverment officials if there was an international match to be seen on television. Roger Corderc, like Bill McLaren in Britain and Winston McCarthy in New Zealand, was the commentator of this age and very much the voice of French rugby. Oddly, he appeared to know little of the rules, relying instead on conveying the excitement and emotion of the game – a triumph of style over content which greatly enhanced the popularity of the sport throughout France.

BLOOD BROTHERS

In the villages of south-west France, particularly since the Second World War, the game of rugby is still a festivity and cause of celebration in the community. Grandparents, mothers, fathers, wives and children all go along to local matches to be part of the occasion. More often than not, there is an enormous meal with many courses and much wine. 'It is a game of three halves,' admits the Grand Slam-winning captain Jacques Fouroux. 'There are two halves in the match and then the third half is the party. It's about drinking well, eating well and waging war.' The French game is such a family affair that it seems only natural that brothers would come together to play for their country. Jean Prat and his brother Maurice were two of the mainstays of the post-war era. The massive Spanghero brothers, Claude and Walter, were part of a strong pack in the late 1960s and early 1970s. The two most talked about fraternal pairings are the Boniface brothers, who personified the era of champagne rugby, and the Camberaberos, who, in the mid-1960s, were both heroes and villains of French rugby.

André Boniface, first capped in 1954, was always aware of the importance of the family in French rugby. He remarks that, 'Rugby and the family were a tradition of the south-west. As soon as you were able to run and gallop about in a field, you played rugby. My luck was to have had a brother who played rugby with me.' André and his brother Guy used their fraternal understanding to strike up an international partnership at centre which dazzled the rugby world. André played 48 times for his country, and Guy 36 times. They shared an

Above: The brothers André and Guy Boniface brought flair and inventiveness to the international arena, which personified the spirit of champagne rugby
Previous pages: Michel Celaya continued the tradition of mobile French forwards with fast hands
Following pages: Jacques Fouroux (right) was the masterful scrum-half behind the giant French pack who won a second Grand Slam in 1978

The Camberabero brothers continued a famous parade of brothers playing international rugby for France

intuition that gave them a precious edge. Their empathy began as little children, kicking and throwing a ball around, and was honed to a fine art when they both joined the Mont-de-Marsan Club, the same club as Lucien Mias. The brothers Boniface played a passing game. They were forever seeking one another out. André explains, 'A passing game was an attacking game. A good pass meant giving the ball to your team-mate in the best possible position. Guy and I developed our play, relying on the brotherly blood to anticipate crossing passes, and scissor movements to break down defences. We complemented each other, although it was a strategy with quite a few risks.'

Encouraged by Jean Prat, both as player and later as coach, the brothers would attack from deep inside their own half using their deft, fluid skills and unsettling rapport to spin

The battle-scarred faces of the Spanghero brothers, pictured in 1971, would strike fear into any opponents

the ball into a counter-attack, forcing the aggressors to scurry back in desperate defence. They retired from international rugby together in 1966 and a year later Guy was killed in a car crash on his way home after a match. André's favourite rugby memory is chipping the ball over the Welsh defence in Paris for his brother to win the chase to the line and touch down: 'It is difficult to explain what we felt between us, but I really felt it in my heart, and even more so now because of the accident.'

Ironically, the year of Guy's death also marked the emergence of the next set of brothers to dominate French rugby – the diminutive Lillian and Guy Camberabero, who kicked France to its first-ever Grand Slam, the equivalent then of finding the Holy Grail. Despite the achievement of that team, fierce controversy raged within France over the boring tactics

of the 'performing fleas'. Many yearned for the champagne days of the brothers Boniface, and revenge was sweet when Guy Camberabero was dropped to make way for a return to what was now considered to be the French style. Historian Phil Dine explains, 'They did not win the Grand Slam in the way French people would have properly appreciated. It was a team dominated by two famous brothers but it wasn't the champagne rugby of the Boniface brothers, [it was] the pragmatic, forward-orientated rugby dominated by the Camberabero brothers.'

Unfortunately, success proved too great a temptation and the massive French packs of the 1970s and 1980s, captained and later coached by scrum-half Jacques Fouroux, were mightily successful, winning a second Grand Slam in 1978 but moving around the field with all the grace of a herd of elephants after a rather good meal.

SERGE BLANCO:
EURO STAR

If the dice had fallen differently, the world's most capped full-back might have played football for Nantes instead of gracing the world's rugby pitches for more than a decade. Nantes, one of the major football clubs in France, recognized in the young boy from Caracas, the Venezuelan capital, a natural sporting talent and tried to sign him up when he was just 15. He explains, 'I was a good football player but I had to make a choice. The number one sport in the area where I lived at that time was rugby. I had the opportunity to go and play professional football, but it would have meant having to leave this magnificent area, so I opted for rugby. I didn't want to leave my friends.'

But although he was born outside his beloved France, Blanco always felt a strong affinity to his adopted home, and particularly the town of Biarritz, which had a powerful Basque identity and a strong rugby presence. Blanco was an archetypal product of a community that lived rugby; in the same way that isolated New Zealand communities used their All Blacks as local figureheads, so Blanco came to represent the image of Biarritz to the outside world. Blanco admits that the region he was brought up in has played a key role in his rugby life: 'The culture is important, the passion and the challenge. It is always there in this region. The people of the Basque region are a hardy, courageous people. They need to find challenges and that's one of the reasons why they have always been strong at rugby. There have always been Basque players in the French team. Rugby is very much part of our culture and you cannot avoid that.'

Blanco is probably the most famous coloured rugby player of all time, but that has never been an important issue in his career. He had the fleeting extra second of time that Barry John referred to as the most important commodity in rugby and, as a result, always made the game appear easy. His loping stride and uncanny ability to miss the simplest of penalties while kicking outrageously long and difficult ones gave a false impression of casualness. In reality, Blanco was always fiercely competitive. In his early career he played on the wing before finding a permanent place at full-back in a French team brimming with flair – Philippe Sella, Pierre Berbizier, Pierre Lagisquet, Jean-Patrick Lescarboura were among his partners in a back division, which was the envy of the rest of the world. One aspect of his former footballing days that he never lost was the ability to turn the slightest injury into a five-act Shakespearean tragedy.

In 1983 Blanco scored a then-record 37 points for France in the Five Nations Championship, eclipsing the figure set by Guy Camberabero in the 1960s. He was now a fixture in the French side and would remain so until 1991, after 11 seasons at the top and 93 caps to show for it. Will Carling, the England captain from 1988 to 1996, recalls his team talk before the Grand Slam decider in 1991 against France at Twickenham: 'No penalties, do not kick ball away, especially to Serge Blanco…' You cannot get greater respect than that.

The intriguing thing about Blanco's career was that for much of it, his style of Gallic flair was thought to be at odds with the muscular strategy of coach Jacques Fouroux, who advocated a game based around a pack of strong forwards. Their finest moment together undoubtedly came in the semi-final against Australia in the 1987 World Cup, when Blanco's try, two minutes from the end, sealed a famous victory. Yet it wasn't his best effort. That was three years later in Brisbane, also against Australia, when he picked the ball up on his own line and literally raced 100 yards to score one of the most memorable tries in rugby history. 'I sincerely believed someone would catch me,' he recalls. But no one

Previous pages: Philippe Sella (with the ball), the world's most capped player, in action against the All Blacks at Eden Park in 1984
Following pages: Serge Blanco famously loses his temper in the 1991 World Cup quarter-final

did. Not even the great David Campese, who was left stranded by the pace of the veteran full-back. It was especially sweet for Blanco because he was now captain of his national side and his try set up victory in the second test and ultimately in the third, leading to a 2–1 series win.

His last international appearance in Paris was in a thrilling match against Wales, when his French team brought back the champagne days and ran in six tries. In the last minute Blanco made the scoring pass to Jean-Baptiste Lafond to score in the corner. Then, with the last kick of the game, he lined up a conversion from the left-hand touch-line and, with the cavalier exuberance and skill that marked him out as one of the greats, he thumped the ball between the posts. An adoring crowd went bananas. After the final whistle, Blanco ran over to a little boy watching the game from a wheelchair and presented him with a gold statuette, a memento to treasure.

Blanco's final game in a French jersey was much less satisfying. He led the French team against England in the quarter-final of the second World Cup at Twickenham. The French were as wound up as guitar strings in their desire to do well for their country, but this time their temperament got the better of them. Blanco also failed to distinguish himself when, following one or two annoying challenges from Nigel Heslop, he floored his opponent with a haymaker punch. The resulting penalty goal stopped France dead in their tracks and they never really recovered their composure. Carling described it as the most physically demanding game he ever played. Afterwards, Blanco said his goodbyes in the English dressing room and quietly left the international arena.

Blanco embodied the two best qualities of French rugby throughout its history: a sense of regional pride and champagne flair. His own philosophy is disarmingly simple: 'When you play rugby, the best way to win is to take possession of the ball, to run faster than your opponent and to place the ball behind the line.'

AFTER THE WORLD CUP

Despite all the legend and lore of champagne rugby, France in the past 25 years has had a very pragmatic approach to the game. Their great scrum-half and coach Jacques Fouroux produced teams to win as many games as possible. It's a lovely luxury to have Blanco and Sella in the backs, but the game is won with possession snaffled by a hungry, heavy pack of forwards. Fouroux was not always popular, especially when the backs were so criminally underused, but his team was at the top of the Five Nations Championship four years in a row in the 1980s. Fouroux's style did little more than reinforce early French thinking that rugby was a combat sport more closely linked to boxing than to soccer. It is a philosophy successfully followed by many of the great teams from South Africa to New Zealand and, more recently, England.

After a distinguished playing career, Jacques
Fouroux coached the French team in the 1980s

Everything was set fair for French rugby when the side reached the first World Cup Final in 1987, and just 11 years later France lifted the World Cup. However, it wasn't the rugby team that did the lifting. It was the previously underachieving soccer team that finished the job rugby had started. The national Association Football team had followed a similar pragmatic policy of sacrificing individual skill for greater team effectiveness by jettisoning David Ginola and Eric Cantona from the international set-up. They also filled the team with brilliant players from ethnic minorities, just as rugby had. Where Serge Blanco and Abdel Benazzi had once claimed the rugby headlines, now Zinédine Zidane and Youri Djorkaev were taking the soccer laurels. Benazzi, the Algerian strong man who became captain of his adopted country's rugby team, acknowledges that sport is a very important factor in integration. He observes, 'When I came to this country I could speak very little French and it wasn't easy for me to settle, but I was lucky enough to have

FRANCE 30 – AUSTRALIA 24
CONCORD OVAL, SYDNEY
13 JUNE 1987

The script had already been written. Mighty New Zealand would contest the first World Cup final against their southern hemisphere rivals Australia. It was the dream ticket, the match everyone *wanted to watch. In the absence of South Africa, these two nations stood head and shoulders above the European challenge. In their semi-final New Zealand dispatched Wales 49–6, scoring nine*

Serge Blanco scored one of the best and most decisive tries in history when France edged out Australia in the 1987 World Cup semi-final

stylish boot of Michael Lynagh, who dropped a goal and kicked a penalty. But then bad luck stalled the Aussie Rolls-Royce when centre Brett Papworth and Bill Campbell, Australia's highly effective second row, were struck down with ligament problems. Australia were unable to pull away, and France kept on pulling them back with dazzling running rugby and the inspired boot of Didier Camberabero, who, on the day, managed 14 points to Lynagh's 16. Tries came from the great Philippe Sella, then unquestionably the finest centre in world rugby, from the tireless lock Alain Lorieux, who wrestled the ball clear from a line-out near the Australian line, and from flying wing Patrice Lagisquet, who was so quick that he left the partisan Sydney crowd gasping in admiration. Here, for a new generation of rugby-lovers, was 'le rugby champagne'. In reply, David Campese at full-back set a world record for tries, and Campbell's replacement, David Codey, scored for the home team.

With two minutes to go, Australia seemed prepared for extra time. Not so French captain Daniel Dubroca, who continued to urge his men to keep the ball in play and in hand as much as possible, realizing that France's best chance of winning was within the regulation 80 minutes. Lagisquet booted the ball on towards the Australian 25-yard line,

tries in a devastatingly one-sided affair which highlighted the gulf between the two continents. Only an unconvincing French side stood between Australia and their place in the final at Eden Park, Auckland. Even France's coach, the hugely combative Jacques Fouroux, gave his men 'not much chance'.

After seven minutes, Australia had moved easily into the lead, thanks to the where Campese calmly waited to control the awkwardly bouncing ball. But the lion-hearted Lorieux was charging up and caught him in possession. Somehow, prop Pascal Ondarts was there to act as scrum-half from the mêlée; he passed to Laurent Lagisquet and then a long pass spun out to number 8, Lucien Rodriguez. He seemed certain to miss it, but it sprung up off his boot and on to his hand. And there by his side was the incomparable Serge Blanco, bearing down on the Australian defence like an express train roaring across a desert plain. His diagonal run gave him a glimmer of a gap wide on the left and, in a moment of unconfined rugby joy, he plunged over, sending the corner flag into orbit for good measure. Camberabero hoisted an unlikely conversion from the touch-line and France were through.

Afterwards, Blanco thought the try was a justification of coach Fouroux's desire that his French team show the world that 'we were there; that we existed; that we were capable of playing a good game. The try was a reward for all the boys in the team. They experienced as much pleasure as I did knowing it was for the whole team. We were convinced we couldn't lose and we didn't.'

Although in the short term the French ball jugglers had spoilt the party, they had in fact done the greatest service imaginable for the World Cup of rugby. This magnificent match swept aside any lingering doubts about the competition. Here was one of the greatest matches played under conditions of the greatest pressure. This was no 0–0 FA Cup semi-final with both sides so frightened of missing a trip to Wembley by conceding a goal that they never emerged from their shells. The invention and skill that both France and Australia displayed totally vindicated the competition. Australians might not have agreed, but in the long run, it was a lucky break for the World Cup that the final was fought out between the northern and southern hemispheres. It showed that Europe could compete and gave an enormous boost to the next tournament. France, which had played catch-up with its European rivals for most of the century, now emerged as the leaders of the pack. It mattered little that New Zealand comfortably won the final. They deserved the trophy, and Australia would have to wait only four years for ample compensation.

rugby to help me express myself. Sport can break down language and cultural barriers.'

Soccer has always shared the centre stage of sport in France with rugby. As in England, whichever sport first laid claim to a town always had a stronger footing there. Marseilles, for example, has never been fond of the oval ball. Although neither rugby nor soccer could claim to be France's national sport, rugby has had by far the more colourful history. Of course, that might change with the enormous enthusiasm and public interest generated by victory in the World Cup. Unfortunately, the jealousies and rivalries that characterized the early days of rugby in the 20th century have also cast a shadow over soccer in France, with several terrifying outbreaks of violence reported since the World Cup victory. The amateur game in and around Paris has become so bad that riot police outnumber fans during some matches. In one month alone, 800 incidents of violence were reported to the Seine-Saint-Denis amateur league. In a bid to halt the spiral of brawls and beatings, the whole league was abandoned during the season immediately after the World Cup. Despite Benazzi's fine sentiments on sport and integration, much of the conflict appears to be racially motivated.

Perhaps Rugby Union, despite some traditional associations with right-wing values, will emerge once again as a better representative of France's future multi-ethnic society.

Former captain Daniel Dubroca:
the passion of French rugby

PART FOUR

THE NEW GAME

AUSTRALIA AND THE
DEATH OF THE AMATEUR GAME

Despite a tradition dating back nearly 150 years, Australia is the major rugby-playing nation where the game has had the least importance. No national or local identities have been carved out by the sport. Instead, despite early popularity, rugby was in the second division for generations, a poor relation of its Rugby League cousin. That began to change in the 1970s where, following a disastrous Olympics in 1976, sport became part of a political initiative to raise the profile of Australia. Out of the blue the Wallabies were the most entertaining and free-spirited team in the world. Crowds and television audiences loved to see the Australian team of Campese, Ella and Lynagh play.

The media tycoons who control modern-day sport moved in on a game which was coming fresh to the majority of the Australian public. The World Cup success of 1991 had alerted the money men that rugby was a valuable and desirable commodity. The rest of the rugby-playing world would hastily follow Australia's commercial lead. The amateur game's long-standing hypocrisy towards professionalism would soon be blown away. The latest battle for the Union Game would not be about class, race or politics. It would concern money, greed and exploitation.

A HEAVY DEFEAT

Rupert Murdoch and Kerry Packer are not the first Australian entrepreneurs to try to make a few dollars out of rugby. Throughout the history of the game down under, the issue of money has always been close to the surface. It's part of the Australian way, embracing an attitude to sport that has never found money to be a dirty word. A Mr Fix-It called James Joynton Smith changed the history of the Union game in Australia when he sponsored a series of Rugby League matches in 1909, which effectively demoted Union to a second-class game in the country for 70 years and more. Smith, a Sydney hotelier, had one glass eye and the other trained on the main chance. The impact that League made was so swift and dramatic that the amateur code had no chance to fight back before the First World War arrived.

The introduction of rugby into Australia had been very colonial, traditional and middle class. The University of Sydney is usually credited with forming the first club in 1863, followed closely by the Sydney Football Club, which sprang up from an existing cricket club. Old public-school boys from both England and Australia formed the Walleroos in 1870, confirming that this was a game developing very much along the Imperial lines of exclusivity. Two leading members of the Walleroos were the Arnold brothers, one of whom – Richard – was a

former pupil of Rugby School. There is barely a nook or cranny of the rugby world into which this corner of Northamptonshire has not reached. Interest in the game spread quickly, thanks to the huge influx of British immigrants towards the end of the last century. But already Australia was moving away from the amateur class-ridden ethos, which cast an ugly shadow over the game in England in the 1890s. This was a new society which would have no truck with snobs. Author Murray Phillips explains,

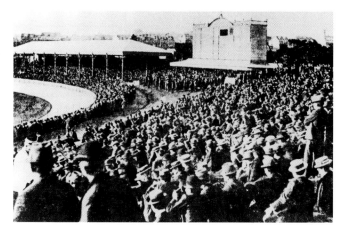

Above: Rugby became increasingly popular at the end of the century – New South Wales play England at the Sydney Cricket Ground, 1899
Below: The Australian crowds loved an open, running game of rugby

'Australia rejected the notion that you should deny working-class people participation in amateur sports on the basis of their occupation.'

In 1874 there were a mere five clubs in Sydney. By the end of the century, that figure had multiplied to 79, and the growth encouraged competitions and rivalries. Sydney itself was entering a boom period and rugby became a key spectator sport in a new confident, extrovert, male-dominated society in which sport was a vital component of culture. The Australians have always loved their sport, had a fierce will to win and liked to make money out of it, either by owning a piece of it or by betting on it. The way in which the whole country closes down to watch the Melbourne Cup horse race every November is testament

to the power of sport in Australia. The Epsom Derby or even the Grand National does not come close to matching the appeal of Melbourne Cup day.

As the popularity of rugby grew, so did the cross-section of classes who became interested in it. The growth of suburban life in Sydney and Melbourne accelerated the game's development and brought a desire for local pride and success. A need to win has always been a close ally of professionalism. As was the case back in Yorkshire and in south-west France, cup matches increased crowds and gate receipts, improved levels of skill and training and attracted the men who made money. There was certainly big money to be made in Australian rugby.

When New South Wales played the All Blacks at the Sydney Cricket Ground (SCG) in 1907, a whopping crowd of 52,000 paid to watch. It is an astonishing figure because the total represented about one-tenth of the entire population of the city. The Union game was becoming so popular that even cricket was relegated to second place in the affections of the Australian sporting public. Cash was pouring in, gate receipts had increased fourfold in five years and the New South Wales Rugby Union (NSWRU) had so much of it that they were able to buy Epping racecourse for £15,000 to develop their own grounds. The players, as usual, saw none of the loot from this amateur game, and the first rumblings of discontent were heard. The NSWRU fanned the flames by withdrawing medical-aid assistance to players and putting that responsibility on individual clubs. In a famous case a barber called Alec Burden was off work for ten weeks as a result of a rugby injury sustained in a representative match. His efforts to gain some form of compensation met with an immovable force, just as similar efforts had done in England, where rugby was perceived as the property of the middle classes, who were intent on making it impossible for working-class men to play through the loathsome weapon of financial hardship.

The catalyst for change was the news that the All Golds Rugby League team from New Zealand would be travelling to Britain to take on the men from the breakaway Northern Union. Those disenchanted with rugby in Australia seized their opportunity. One of the key figures in the move towards a professional game was Victor Trumper, probably the most famous Australian cricketer before Donald Bradman. The charismatic Trumper was a supremely gifted batsman, who scored eight centuries in 49 tests for Australia, including the third fastest double hundred of all time. He owned a sports shop in Sydney, where the conspirators met to discuss the case of Burdon and to plan their campaign. A decision was made to ask the All Golds to play some matches in Australia.

Before any fixtures could take place, there was the small matter of forming an organization and finding a team. The role model for such an organization was the Northern Union, which had been formed in the George Hotel in Huddersfield in 1895. By coincidence, the historic meeting in Australian rugby took place in George Street, Sydney, at the Bateman's Crystal Hotel. The principle of providing financial security for players was established. They were, after all, responsible for the bumper crowds. The New South Wales Rugby Football League (NSWRL) had arrived. The most significant difference between the setting up of the league in Australia and of the Northern Union in England is that Sydney is the most important city in the country, whereas even the proudest of Yorkshiremen would be hard-pressed to nominate Huddersfield as a centre of power. Rugby League in England was always destined to be a regional game and was marginalized because of it. In Australia, on the other hand, the complacent controllers of rugby had a serious threat on their doorstep.

The men at the helm of the new league astutely decided to target the best and most popular rugby player in Australia, H.H. 'Dally' Messenger, for their new scheme. Four of Dave Gallaher's 1905 All

HERBERT HENRY ("DALLY") MESSENGER

AGE, 28.   WEIGHT, 12¼.   THE CELEBRATED NEW SOUTH WALES RUGBY FOOTBALLER   HEIGHT, 5ft. 7½.

Above: At the end of his career, H.H. 'Dally' Messenger's supporters presented him with this portrait
Opposite: Master cricketer Victor Trumper was a key figure in the introduction of Rugby League to Australia

Blacks had already joined the All Golds, so the precedent of persuading top players to join the new code had been set. Messenger, a scintillating three-quarter and deadly goal-kicker, demonstrated typical Australian machismo and left the decision up to his mother. She listened to the arguments of Trumper and the NSWRL secretary, a former commercial traveller called J.J. Giltinan, and gave her approval. The All Golds played three games in Sydney on their way to London against a New South Wales team including Messenger, who were known as the All Blues. Although these matches were not a runaway financial success, they did capture some public attention and Messenger himself was the acknowledged star of the proceedings. In fact, so successful was he that when the All Golds boarded the boat for England, Messenger was with them. It was as if Will Carling had celebrated the Grand Slam of 1991 by joining St Helens.

While the All Golds team did not set the world on fire in the manner of Gallaher's Invincibles, they proved a big hit with spectators. They won 19, lost 12 and drew three matches out of 34. At the end of the tour the players shared a pool of £5461, which was a tidy sum for their efforts. Despite that, the amateur game was flourishing to such an extent that it had nothing to fear from the new professional code. To enforce the point, the Wallabies, the international Union team, toured Britain in the winter of 1908/9 at the same time as a hastily assembled League side from New South Wales called the Kangaroos. The Wallabies, under their rugged front-row forward Dr Herbert Moran, were more than a match for the home sides, winning 25 out of 31 matches and clocking up an impressive scoring total of 438 points against 146 conceded. They lost narrowly (9–6) to Wales in Cardiff before comfortably beating England 9–3 at Blackheath. Rugby featured in the 1908 London Olympics and the Wallabies took the gold medal. Meanwhile, the Kangaroos lurched from one defeat to another before dwindling crowds. While the Wallabies returned home much fêted, the poor Kangaroos limped back, bankrupt and beaten – their fares being paid for by the Northern Union.

The new League game was struggling. The original board, including Trumper, were dislodged. Covertly, in a manner that would be repeated in the 1990s, members of the Wallabies team were approached with promises of much loot to take part in a series of games against the Kangaroos. Businessman James Joynton (J.J.) Smith became involved and promised to bankroll the venture, guaranteeing the defecting Wallabies £100 a man. By the time the controllers of the Union game knew about it, the deals were done and three matches had been arranged for September 1909. They played 15 a side and the Kangaroos won the series 2–1. A fourth match, played to bolster receipts, was also won by the Kangaroos. Although the cost of luring the Wallabies across the great professional divide meant that the venture was not a huge financial success, in terms of publicity, the future of Rugby League in Australia was assured. Crowds as big as 18,000 flocked to see the new rugby and declared the fast, open, flamboyant game a hit. After all, the men playing were the best rugby players in the country. The Union authorities promptly banned the Wallabies who had taken part.

J.J. Smith's career went from strength to strength. He would later be mayor of Sydney and, in a neat foretaste of what was to come during the Murdoch *v* Packer financial battle for rugby in the 1990s, he became a media tycoon when, in 1919, he founded a newspaper called *Smith's Weekly*, which was published for the next 20 years.

In just a year, League outstripped Union in terms of popularity. The Australian public, not weighed down by the inhibitions of tradition, loved the game, as it satisfied a thirst for greater entertainment on the sports field. There was no need to have played the game or to know much about it to enjoy the spectacle. New fans were not burdened by interminable line-outs or scrummaging. It quickly became a working-man's day out. In 1910 a Union international between the All Blacks and the Wallabies was watched by 10,000, while a League game between the Kangaroos and the visiting English Northern Union was seen by 39,000.

The First World War polarized the two camps even more. The amateur game followed the British lead, where achievement on the field of battle was a natural extension of success on the rugby field. Ronald Poulton-Palmer was a good example of this, a hero at Twickenham and in the trenches. While Rugby Union effectively closed down because so many players and administrators signed up to fight, Rugby League stayed open for business and stole an important march on its rivals. Author Murray Phillips observes, 'Rugby Union decided that all their efforts should be geared towards winning the war. League took a far more pragmatic view and decided, while being patriotic and supporting the war, they would play on and donate large sums of money to the war effort.'

Within Australian society there was bitter division between the patriot and the shirker, the Protestant middle class and the Catholic working class. A referendum to introduce conscription was a bitter and close-run thing, with the no vote just prevailing. Despite the criticism levelled at League for not encouraging enlistment, it was the working-class supporters of the game who suffered most from the economic hardships brought by war. The year 1917 witnessed the Great Strike, when 173,000 workers from the roads, railways and mines stayed out for three months. Religious division also entered the equation after the 1916 Easter uprising in Dublin. Australian Protestants were openly questioning the commitment of the Catholics to war. Gate receipts during this period increased sixfold. When the war ended, the Union game was in disarray, while League went from strength to strength. Incredibly, it took until 1929 for a proper Union administration in Queensland to become effective. As if things were not gloomy enough for Union, the state school system in New South Wales introduced Rugby League in 1920. It was no coincidence that the Labour Party was in power at the time.

The conflict between Union and League showed an Australian society dangerously close to unmendable strife: the conservative middle-class Protestant old guard against the Labour working-class Catholic new man. Rugby League also represented a break from the umbilical cord of Imperial England, something Australia has long sought to attain. For most of the 20th century the new Australian has had the upper hand.

BOOT MONEY

Shamateurism is an ugly, modern word for a problem almost as old as Rugby Union itself. In Wales and France in particular, under-the-table perks and gifts have been normal practice for a century. Occasionally, a fuss about a particular flouting of the amateur rules has escalated into a crisis. The Gould Affair in Wales and the infamous Quillan *v* Perpignan game in south-west France are just two examples of how the structure of the game had to endure some mighty blows before carrying on as usual. The concept of amateurism in the Union game involves much more than adhering to a strict policy of no payments for playing. Murray Phillips explains, 'The amateur ideology concerns gentlemanly behaviour, sportsmanship and character-building.' The fear of the middle-class old guard is that professionalism will act like a cancer on those amateur values until they no longer exist.

Throughout its history Rugby Union has sought to protect itself from that cancer. While its rulers kept rugby as an insular, exclusive club, they could keep a lid on the increasing clamour from players for pay and deny them their right to be paid. After the Second World War, renewed interest in sports fuelled rivalry. Australia continued to lose its best players to League, and from the 1950s onwards, clubs striving for success in the various cup competitions realized that they had to keep the stars happy if they wanted success. It was, observes Phillips, 'a period where the players were paid under the table, given accommodation and meaningless jobs'. Social events, bar takings and gaming machines were all encouraged as they brought revenue into the clubs. It was clear from 1970 onwards that the more prosperous the club, the more successful it would be. Players would roll up in their big free cars to so-called jobs in the social clubs. The more staunchly amateur a club remained, the less likely it was to taste success. The University Oval Club in Sydney, for instance, last won the premiership in 1972 and has patently failed to move with the times.

Not everyone, however, was taking the palmed fiver. Andrew Slack, captain of the great 1984 Wallabies, says he never received a cent. He adds, 'I never got any boot money and I don't know of anyone who did. If you wanted to make a few bob out of rugby, you went to Rugby League. I was quite clear that rugby was an amateur game and I had the empty wallet to prove it.' But boot money, a discreet form of bribery, clearly had existed for years in the game in the northern hemisphere, even if the authorities liked to pretend it hadn't. It was common knowledge in Wales that you would be better off playing for a big club, such as Llanelli or Cardiff, than for a small team in the valleys. In France there was talk of mortgages being paid.

Mike Burton, the former England prop of the 1970s who has done more than most to expose the hypocrisy of the Union game, remembers being offered the princely sum of £50 to wear a particular brand of boot before a match against France. Burton had been brought up in the era when the same pair of boots would last you for years. You just soaked them in water overnight and they would do you proud. The new age of sports footwear was

England prop Mike Burton trudges from the field after being sent off during the second test against Australia in 1975

totally different, a multi-million pound business. The boots Burton was offered were made of the softest calf leather and fitted like a pair of comfy slippers. Burton explains, 'They were almost disposable. The rep gave me a pair to try and I went into his hotel room bathroom and sat on the toilet with the seat down to try them out. I undid the laces and discovered five tenners in the boot. I went out and the rep asked, "How did they feel?" and I said, "Super" and I wore the boots.' For the match all 15 England players wore the same boots. Burton and others of like mind were aggrieved that the whole England team had been bought for a measly £750. Clearly, in terms of a game watched by millions of people, that was a laughable amount. But for another 20 years it would also be an illegal practice.

Trying to deny the professional virus was becoming increasingly ludicrous. There was the classic occasion when the popular England number 8, Andy Ripley, wore a different manufacturer's boot on each foot because he did not want to upset either one. Other incidents were not so funny. J.P.R. Williams, the great Welsh full-back, was involved in a legal wrangle after allegations that he had taken boot money from Adidas and accepted 'beer money' of £20 after games. J.P.R. was vilified for returning to Rugby Union after publishing a book on his career. He had to give all the proceeds to charity and remembers the whole thing leaving a very sour taste in the mouth, especially as his family also had to put up with criticism. It appeared to be perfectly acceptable to take a few pounds in official expenses so that the girlfriend or wife could be treated to a nice meal, but

Above: The great J.P.R. Williams was embroiled in a row over payments that soured his last years of playing rugby
Following pages: The dazzling skills of Mark Ella gave Australian rugby an enormous boost in the 1980s

woe betide anyone who legitimately joined Rugby League to play professional sport. When the talented and much-vaunted Welsh captain David Watkins joined Salford for a king's ransom of £13,000 in 1967, it was as if he had suddenly contracted leprosy. He was friendless in the valleys. Scott Gibbs was one of the least popular men in the principality when he cashed in his Union status for a handsome cheque from St Helens in 1994. He was, of course, welcomed back with open arms when the game went professional and players could swap codes like well-worn overcoats. In 1985 Andy Haden led the unofficial New Zealand Cavaliers on a generally unpopular tour of South Africa after the official trip had been cancelled. The exact sums the players were paid has never been revealed, although Haden once said that leading South African businesses had put substantial sums into the kitty. The Cavaliers' booty has been estimated at as much as $40,000. On their return, each member of the party was called before the New Zealand Rugby Council and swore an oath that they had not been financially reimbursed for taking part in the tour. They admitted receiving a daily allowance of $50 a day as laid down by the International Board – although they were not officially representing their country. There is little point now in raking over the question of payments. In 1986 Andy Haden was asked his profession and he replied, 'Rugby player'. That was the simple truth for him and many others well before the death of the amateur game.

Sports journalist and former Wallaby Peter Fitzsimons remembers that on the tour of New Zealand in 1990 the players sold T-shirts that plugged the tour like a rock concert. They cost $3.50 wholesale but were sold for $15. The players also had tickets to sell. At the end of the tour they split $19,000, collecting about $650 each. They thought it was a fortune.

MARK ELLA:
THE DAWNING OF A NEW AGE

He was black, he was working class and he captained his country at the age of 23. Mark Ella was one of three Aboriginal brothers who, for the first time in decades, brought the game of Rugby Union on to the front pages instead of its customary subservient role to Rugby League. The Ella brothers were spontaneous, born entertainers, who exploded upon a dormant game like a starburst. Their arrival trumpeted a golden era for Australian rugby which, to be frank, it had never enjoyed before. They were part of a schoolboy squad that came to Britain in 1977/8, remained undefeated and was one of the most successful of all touring teams. It included two men who would captain their country: Mark Ella at Rugby Union and the superb Wally Lewis at Rugby League.

Mark, his twin brother Glen and younger brother Gary were born in the poor area of La Perouse, Sydney, and were three of 12 children. Unkindly, La Perouse, or Larpa as it

Above: *Just like his brother, full-back Glen Ella shone on the 1978 Australian schoolboy tour of England*
Following pages: *Australian captain Andrew Slack leads by example as he strains to reach the ball at a ruck*

is known locally, is often described as Sydney's Soweto. Gary was just a year younger than the twins and the brothers could have been mistaken for triplets. They grew up in close company and developed an affinity that was to make them both intuitive and unpredictable on the rugby field. Mark Ella remembers that as children their mum would kick them out of the door early in the morning and they would spend the day together caddying on the local golf course, diving for coins in the bay, eating hamburgers and playing pinball. In the evening they would go home and their mother would have dinner on the table. Mark remembers, 'We were never separated, so we each knew what the others were thinking. When it came to playing rugby, we were of one mind. We were going to enjoy it, we were going to attack and we were going to score tries.'

This rapport made the Ella brothers stand out. They went to Mattraville High School, opposite the notorious Long Bay Jail. Unusually, the school favoured Rugby Union because the headmaster had once played for the Randwick Club in Sydney and believed that the old amateur values turned out the best type of young man. The boys had no choice in the matter, so they took up the game with what Mark describes as 'a little trepidation and found that it wasn't that bad'. One of the teachers, Geoff Mould, took the brothers under his wing and guided them up through the junior ranks. Mark was a fly-half, Glen a full-back and Gary a wing. They would try anything to bamboozle the opposition – miss moves, short passes, double dummy scissors.

Rugby Union remained very much the preserve of private schools in Australia, with the majority of international players having been drawn from their ranks. The Ella brothers from a state school were immediately different. And they were Aboriginal: 'We were the odd ones out,' says Mark, 'but we were so dominant as a trio that we forced our way in. We had a carefree spirit and didn't think about being different. It didn't worry us.'

Aborigines have always been the poor relations in Australian society. Racial prejudice is something they have had to bear for centuries, and the success of a few sporting heroes, such as tennis star Evonne Goolagong and the magnificent Rugby League star Mal Meninga, has not opened the door of opportunity to the majority. They have remained disadvantaged in terms of employment, health and income. That the Ella brothers should have broken out of these social handcuffs is remarkable. They needed the financial help of a mystery donor to pay their £750 a week expenses on the schoolboy tour of 1977/8, but grasped their chance with adhesive hands.

Timing is of the essence in the creation of sporting heroes: success is all about being in the right place at the right time. Despite some progress over the previous decades, particularly when the 1966 tourists beat Wales in Cardiff 14–6, nothing Rugby Union did could grab the sporting headlines. That changed when the British media in particular realized that the exploits of the young Aboriginal boys made great copy. There was nothing patronizing about the interest of the press: these Ella boys were great players. The schoolboy team was an exciting side and the first to remain undefeated on a British tour since the 1925 All Black Invincibles. They scored 110 tries, with an average of nearly eight every game. The brothers were responsible for a third of all the points, with Mark at fly-half

proving the star, displaying a mesmerizing change of pace and deft handling ability. He scored a try in each of the three international matches, missing out on a full set only because Scotland was not included in the itinerary.

Geoff Mould coached the team. He insisted on a running game and made it clear to his boys that he was not interested in anyone kicking the ball. Mark Ella was happy to oblige. The tour began in Japan, and over 14 weeks the schoolboys played in France and Holland as well as Britain. Wally Lewis played scrum-half with Mark as his partner. He recalls, 'The first time I played alongside him I remember shaking my head and thinking this bloke is a freak. He could do anything with a football. All three brothers together were amazing.'

The most famous match of the tour was against England at Twickenham, not because of the amazing skills on display but because the whole 80 minutes was played in fog. You literally could not see from one side of the ground to the other. When the Australians walked on to the famous pitch, they could not make out the upper tier of the grandstand. However, they were on a tight schedule, so the match could not be postponed. Wally Lewis was on the bench that day and remembers one of his team running to the side and saying, '"Ladies and gentlemen, Australia have just scored." And we all said, "Yeah, you beaut – Australia have scored." It was a lot of fun on the day.' For the kicks at goal a linesman had to position himself half-way between the kicker and the goalposts to try to show him the line. For the record, although none of the crowd had a clue, Australia won by 13 points to 9.

Australian sport needed a boost after the débâcle of the 1976 Olympics, when the country failed to win a gold medal. The Australian Institute of Sport was established to promote a more 'professional' approach to sport. Rugby Union was able to cash in on the success of its youthful new stars. When the boys returned home to La Perouse, they were exhausted after the journey and went to sleep, only to be awoken by their excited mother. 'You made the papers,' she declared proudly. Mark remembers grabbing the paper, the Sydney *Daily Telegraph*, and turning to the sports pages. He couldn't see the Ella name anywhere. His mother said, 'Turn the paper round.' Sure enough, there on the front page was a picture of the three boys on the front page caked in mud and wearing their souvenir England shirts. They knew they had arrived.

By 1984 the promise shown in the late 1970s had blossomed into a senior side that boasted a back line even the respected New Zealand journalist T.P. McLean ranked among the finest in history. Sports pundit Bill McLaren is on record as saying that they were the team on which he most enjoyed commenting throughout his whole career. An innovative and enthusiastic new coach, Alan Jones, moulded a unit that took the running game to new heights. Nick Farr-Jones joined Mark Ella at half-back. Michael Lynagh and captain Andrew Slack were at centre, the incomparable David Campese and Brendan Moon were on the wing, and Roger Gould was poised at full-back to join in one of the devastating attacks for which the team became famous. This was a back division to merit comparison with the great Welsh names of 1971. Mark Ella had made his début in 1980, and by 1982 was captain of the touring team to New Zealand. He lost the captaincy to Slack when Jones was appointed coach in 1984, but, perhaps enjoying freedom from that responsibility, he played his best rugby on that year's tour of Britain, when the Wallabies won the Grand Slam, beating all four home nations. Ella scored a try in every game and kicked two drop-goals against Ireland for good measure.

As is always the case in rugby, the backs could not play without the ball. For the first time on a tour to Britain, the Wallabies boasted a pack that could match the home countries. Number 8 Steve Tuynman and flanker Simon Poidevin were outstanding. Tuynman scored one of the most memorable tries on the tour when, to the astonishment of everyone watching, the Australians scored a pushover try against Wales. David Campese saw it all from the wing and recalls, 'Everyone who was there will always remember it. Everything was very quiet. I think the crowd were in shock.' This was a pack that offered more than brute strength, however, and they linked up with the backs in broken play that established Australia as the most sophisticated rugby team of the 1980s.

Just when it seemed that nothing could spoil Australia's march to world supremacy, Mark Ella retired from international rugby. Here was a man whose very difference from the norm would have made him the most marketable player in the world in a professional age. Yet a mere ten years before the whole game went professional, he was gone. He confirms, 'I can honestly say that I didn't earn one razoo out of the game. I might have got a free meal every now and then, but no monetary rewards.'

Financial consideration is the first of three reasons Ella gives for leaving the stage. The second is that he married and wanted to settle down when he returned home from five months working in Britain in 1985, and the third is that he wanted to start a career in business. At the time there were rumours that he and coach Alan Jones were not on each other's Christmas card list, but neither party has ever admitted that. Ella explains, 'If I had retired at 30, I would have had lots of accolades and prestige, but it would have been hard to start a life outside rugby. I played the game because I enjoyed it. I didn't want to be an athlete who retired past his best, so I retired when I wanted to and not when the sport told me I had to go.'

When news of Ella's retirement broke, many observers assumed that he would be off to earn a fortune in Rugby League. Within three weeks he was offered a wheelbarrow of money to swap codes and, he discovered, earn more than Wally Lewis, who was then captain of the Australian team. In the end he could not desert the Union game. 'It made me think about going to Rugby League, which is something I had never contemplated before. But in the end I would never leave Union. I retired probably no better off than the day I started, but I was a lot happier and more content with what I chose in life.'

Mark Ella's career might well have been the last great fanfare of the amateur game. He succeeded in reaching the top, despite having apparently every disadvantage for playing Rugby Union. He was black, from a minority ethnic group. He was from a modest, working-class background in an area where most of the youngsters played League. He went to a state school. These are not the usual ingredients of a boy born to play the Union game. He opened the door to a professional age by showing that

Roger Gould was a cool figure at full-back during the golden age of Australian rugby

the game need not be so exclusive as it had always appeared. He chose not to walk through the door himself, but soon players would be falling over themselves in the rush to get through. Perhaps Mark Ella could only have precipitated such change in a forward think-ing Australia, where rugby traditions were not etched in stone. The great rugby-playing communities of rural New Zealand, the Natal farmland and the mining towns of South Wales just did not exist in this vast country. Despite its vintage, the game in Australia has come to fruition only in modern times.

Both Gary and Glen Ella had joined their brother in retirement by 1988. Amazingly, the three never played together in the same test match, but their marketability made the money men sit up and take notice. The introduction of the World Cup in 1987 further raised the profile of the game, particularly in Australia and New Zealand. It is a great pity that Mark Ella was not available to play then. He was only 27.

DAVID CAMPESE:
RENAISSANCE MAN

Like a malevolent goblin, David Campese had the capacity to cause mischief and mayhem both on and off the pitch. As the outstanding attacking wing and try-scorer in world rugby, he had the talent to embarrass his opponents and make them appear slow-witted. As holder of the biggest mouth in world rugby, he was always happy to have a bit of fun with the media to stir things up before or after a game. His attacks on England's style, and Will Carling in particular, taxed the headline-writers' skill during the 1991 World Cup. He became the self-appointed chief baiter of the home team, the man people loved to hate yet could not help but admire. At least he grabbed the attention, which was almost certainly his purpose. In his prime he was the most famous rugby player in the world and acknowledged to be the best. It was also an open secret that he was a professional rugby player while the game still persisted with the charade of amateurism.

Campese was fortunate to be part of the spectacular Wallabies team of the early 1980s. It was a supremely adventurous team that readily absorbed Campese's swashbuckling style. He had starred in his first test series against New Zealand in 1982 and then proceeded to weave his magic on the Grand Slam tour to the British Isles in 1984. Against Scotland, he scored one of the finest tries ever seen at Murrayfield. Australia were already comfortably ahead and Scotland were throwing everything into attack. Inside the Wallabies' 22-metre line a Scottish pass was intercepted and Mark Ella fed the ball to Campo, as he was universally called, to clear the ball to touch and run down the clock. Campo, the great entertainer, was having none of that. He counter-attacked and was off down the field, passed to number 8, Steve Tuynman, and then looped around him to receive the ball again. He sprinted fully 50 yards to the line, outpacing a desperate John Beattie. No wonder Bill McLaren describes Campese as his favourite player.

The young Campese was not a product of the Australian private school system (the equivalent of British public schools). He grew up in a small, working-class town near Canberra playing Rugby League. He represented his age group in League right up to high school, when, at 17, he tried his hand at Union. Like Mark Ella, he was able to overcome class prejudices by sheer natural talent. His unorthodoxy caught the attention of the national selectors when he was still a teenager. Just before the team was picked to tour New Zealand in 1982, they saw the young Campo score a typically outrageous try in Sydney. With just the full-back to beat and a team-mate outside him unmarked, Campese decided to kick. He chipped the ball over the full-back, ran round him and scored. He made it look so easy.

Campese, at the age of 19, had the advantage of knowing little about rugby history, so the All Blacks held no fear for him. On that tour he was up against Stuart Wilson, then thought to be the most effective wing in the game. The upstart Campese made him appear ordinary in comparison. Campese had perfected a unique feature of his game – the 'goose-step'. He would hurtle towards opponents and then begin taking exaggerated steps which gave the illusion that he was slowing, when, in fact, he was speeding up. It was like a turbo-charge and practically impossible to stop. By today's Jonah Lomu standards, Campese would be on the small side for a wing, but he made up for that with athletic ability, fitness and guile. Will Carling memorably observed in his autobiography, 'He had the balls to try things which ordinary mortals could not even conceptualize.'

That courage to try something different could end in disaster, which was part of Campese's charm. Like the peerless Ian Botham in cricket, he would look foolish if it all went wrong, but he would be back to try again. The crowds loved him for it and he was undoubtedly the biggest draw in world rugby. The most famous occasion when it all went wrong was against the British Lions in 1989. Campese still groans at the memory. He was caught in possession running the ball from his own line, and as he scrambled to get the ball away, Ieuan Evans pounced on his pass and scored the try that won the Lions the series.

Sometimes his boldness did work, magnificently so, as when the Barbarians took on the Wallabies at Cardiff during the 1988 tour. A counter-attack launched by Nick Farr Jones on the half-way line resulted in a ruck from which the ball was spun out to Campese. He beat Gavin Hastings on the outside with his famous change of pace, cut inside Matt Duncan and then bamboozled Jonathan Davies, no less, by swerving to his left and to his right. With three red-faced defenders left behind, Campo strolled over for a try between the posts. The Cardiff crowd rose as one to applaud a piece of rugby genius. As Bill McLaren observed, 'You could have been excused for thinking that Gareth Edwards had just scored a last-minute try to win a game for his beloved Wales.'

By 1984 Campese had moved to Italy to play his rugby. He was approached by an Italian coach after the Grand Slam tour of Britain. Campese recalls, 'He thought my name was Campezzi, so he came to me and said, "Do you want to come to Italy and play?" and I said, "Yeah, why not?" I always believed that if someone offers you something, go and do it. It's no good saying no and then ten years later saying, "Jeez, I wish I'd done that." I took every opportunity that came my way.'

Campese admits that the Italians looked after him very well. In the understated words of Andy Slack, everyone was pretty sure 'the players who went to Italy didn't go for the pasta'. Campo played there for ten years, honing and maintaining the skills that would keep him at the top long after many of his contemporaries had retired. During the summer months he would fly home to Sydney to link up with the Ella brothers at the famous Randwick Club. In fact, Mark Ella coached Campo for a couple of seasons in Italy, and a sprinkling of his subtle handling skills were invaluable to Campese later in his career when he had lost a yard of pace.

Campese passed the previous world record for international tries during the famous World Cup defeat at the hands of France in 1987. That was his twenty-fifth. By 1990 he

Following pages: David Campese in action – simply the greatest entertainer in modern rugby

had reached 37 tries and become Australia's most capped player when he ran out for his fifty-second international. When he retired in 1996, he had clocked up 64 tries in 101 internationals.

Campese had enormous charisma. Whether you loved him or hated him, you had to admire him. He was a born entertainer. As historian Gareth Williams observed, 'If he had been a circus performer, he would have been known as "the Great Campo".' Depending on your point of view, he was probably the last entertainer of the amateur game or the first of the professional. He combined many of the best qualities of both. He respected the traditions of a beautiful game but brought to it levels of fitness, skill and dedication that were scarcely possible in the old days of Saturday afternoon rugby. He realized that people pay good money to see rugby players, to watch in anticipation at what a Blanco or an Ella or a Campese might do next. He would never disappoint.

THE TELEVISION WAR

Television rules sport with a rod edged with gold. The astonishing success of rugby was not lost on two of the most powerful media magnates in the world, Rupert Murdoch and Kerry Packer. Before the game had woken up to the perceived threat of commercial interests, it was effectively whisked into a full professional era – an operation conducted under general anaesthetic. Murdoch and Packer, both Australian, squared up to one another to slug it out with rugby as their prize. The game in Australia had that decisive advantage over the rest of the world in that its popularity was a modern phenomenon thanks to decades of relative mediocrity. The Ellas, Gould, Farr-Jones, Campese and World Cup-winning coach Bob Dwyer had shown that Union was a game in which Australia could excel. It was entertainment and that was enough for Murdoch and Packer.

The TV tycoons were not the first Australian entrepreneurs to recognize the potential of sport. At the turn of the century the legendary Hugh D. McIntosh, who rejoiced in the nickname of 'Huge Deal', lived up to that sobriquet by graduating from selling meat pies to staging the World Heavyweight Boxing Championship bout between Jack Johnson and Tommy Burns of Canada at Rushcutters Bay, Sydney, on Boxing Day 1908. McIntosh owned the Sydney *Sunday Times*, but eventually overstretched himself when a chain of

Nick Farr-Jones steered his world champion Australian team to a comfortable 26–3 win against the re-emerging South Africa in 1992

THE SECOND WORLD CUP FINAL
ENGLAND 6 – AUSTRALIA 12
TWICKENHAM
2 NOVEMBER 1991

There's something about a World Cup. The words themselves have a magic ring. They conjure up images of schoolboy dreams, of Bobby Moore lifting the Jules Rimet Trophy in 1966 and thousands of 'if only' conversations in pubs and bars. They bring prestige, publicity and national pride to any sport. The football World Cup is now a bigger event than the Olympic Games. No wonder almost all sports boast a World Cup, trying to capture some of football's reflected glory. For rugby the new championship had proved a sensation, and the 1991 tournament in Britain created more interest in the game than it had ever enjoyed. England carried the expectations

of the nation on its shoulders. Carling's powerful XV had swept all before them in the Five Nations Championship, winning the Grand Slam earlier in the year. But they had to do well or public attention would have been lost like the air from a pricked balloon.

In all honesty, the two best teams did not contest the final. As in 1987, Australia and New Zealand should, on form, have been at Twickenham on that blustery November afternoon. Instead, Australia had dismissed their southern hemisphere rivals in the semis to set up the perfect box-office final. England, hosts and champions of the northern hemisphere, were up against the team who

Troy Coker of Australia and England's number 6, Mickey Skinner, compete for the ball during a tense struggle

could justifiably claim to be the best in the world. Now, despite being favourites, the Wallabies had to prove themselves where it really counted, at the home of the Union game.

England had been performing short of their best to reach the final. Workmanlike would be a fair description. They beat the United States, Italy, France and Scotland, but were cosily beaten by the All Blacks in a group match 18–12. By contrast, Australia were on a roll and any students of form had only to refer to a match just four months earlier in Sydney when they trounced England 40–15.
But the beauty of a Cup Final is that underdogs can win. The newspapers and television were full of it and the nation licked its lips in anticipation.

The final could not justify the build-up; very few can. The 1995 final in South Africa was an exception because of the extraordinary circumstances of the occasion. In reality, 1991 mirrored the final of four years earlier when the favourites, New Zealand, never really looked like losing. The chief decision-maker, Michael Lynagh, gave Australia the first points after England were penalized at a line-out. His thumping kick in a gusting wind from 45 yards demonstrated why he remains the world record points scorer in international rugby. With so much attacking flair on the field – the likes of Campese, Jeremy Guscott and Rory

Underwood to name but three – it was to be expected that the only try, a singularly unmemorable one, would be scored by Australian prop Tony Daly. He smuggled the ball over from a line-out a few yards from the England line. Lynagh converted.

The entertainment, typically, was provided by Campese. Seventy yards from the English line he took a pass from Tim Horan and panic set in among the England defence. A finely judged kick ahead looked sure to lead to a spectacular score but the ball bounced unkindly and as he tried to gather it, a scrambling Guscott was there to put him off. Then, to round off his afternoon, he deliberately knocked on, spoiling a very promising scoring chance for England. It was, dare one say,

Despite the support of Mickey Skinner, England wing Rory Underwood fails to break the Australian defence

261

a 'professional' foul. A nonchalant Campo cheerfully acknowledged the booing of the crowd. The referee gave a penalty and Jonathan Webb, who had struggled all afternoon, kicked three points. Many observers felt a penalty try could have been awarded because Underwood would have had a clear path to the line but for Campo's intervention. Perhaps England deserved more from a second half in which they enjoyed the greater pressure but Australia were like a heavyweight boxer, content to stay on the ropes and absorb the punches, secure in the knowledge of winning on points. The best team won and they proved the point by beating both New Zealand and South

Africa in subsequent test series.

For England there was the massive consolation of raising the public profile of the game. Carling, however, came in for a lot of criticism as captain. According to the armchair experts, England should have played a more conservative game, keeping the ball tight to the forwards instead of squandering so much good possession with poor passing and uninspired movement among the backs. They never looked likely to breach a powerful defence, except when the 'hand of Campo' intervened to deny them. As Carling himself said, they had tried that in Sydney in July and been beaten by a cricket score.

Near right: Nick Farr-Jones celebrates, holding the World Cup trophy aloft
Far right: Will Carling salutes the crowd after England's narrow defeat

milk bars in England failed badly, and he died penniless in London. He would undoubtedly have been putting together a few huge deals after the victorious World Cup team returned home in 1991 to a ticker-tape reception in downtown Sydney. Australian sport was in a boom period and the very next year the country picked up 27 medals, including seven golds at the Barcelona Olympics.

Big business was recognizing the potential of sport. Sponsorship had grown dramatically and that was inextricably linked to television coverage. The second rugby World Cup made a profit of £5½ million. The third, in South Africa, realized the astonishing figure of £22 million. This was no longer an élitist sport conducted for the amusement of a few committed fans. The audience was huge. The thirst for sport on television showed no signs whatsoever of being quenched. The players themselves were demanding a greater slice of the cake for so long denied to them. They were in demand for sponsorship and advertising but, theoretically, any commercial deals were subject to the amateur rules of the International Rugby Union.

Above: Media tycoon Rupert Murdoch watches a Super 12s game at Canterbury, New Zealand in 1999
Following pages: Australian skipper Phil Kearns barges his way through on the way to scoring an important try against New Zealand in 1994

Enter Packer and Murdoch. The two men were fierce rivals, particularly on their home turf. Murdoch had already usurped Packer's control of Rugby League when he launched the new Super League on 1 April 1995. It contained its element of surprise by organizing a flurry of signatures at midnight, sealing deals that had been set up secretly in the preceding months. Packer hit back by bankrolling a bid to take over the Union game throughout the southern hemisphere. The rugby war had begun. Former Australian internationalist and journalist Peter Fitzsimons observes, 'The rugby war started when there was a sudden realization that what everyone thought was merely a muddy pastime for a lot of funny people was actually an extremely valuable televisual product. When they realized that, there was a battle for the hearts and minds of the rugby people, particularly the players.'

The chief weapon in Packer's armoury was a huge wallet. His negotiators would travel from star player to star player effectively saying, 'You're getting nothing for playing but we think you are worth a quarter of million dollars.' Packer's outfit was called the World Rugby Corporation (WRC) and his representatives moved swiftly to sign up the leading

Dan Crowley of Australia is stopped in his tracks by All Black Justin Marshall during the 1998 tri-nations tournament

players in the world. Australia's test captain, Phil Kearns, and New Zealand's Sean Fitzpatrick were among those who were persuaded. Ross Turnbull, the chief negotiator, confirms that he signed up 300 of the world's best players within three weeks. To say that players were ready to earn a few bob from the game would be a gross understatement. They were falling over themselves in the rush.

Turnbull's greatest hurdle was not the players but the old guard (or old farts, depending on your point of view) who still exercised extraordinary control over the sport. He explains, 'They were concerned about where they would park their car, where they would sit in relation to the president, where their wives were sitting and whether they would get a ticket for the next international. They weren't thinking of the broader issues.'

Certainly, the rugby authorities seemed to have little grasp of the threat that Murdoch's Super League posed to the amateur game. His men were travelling around the world signing up players, which would have a devastating effect. The race was on for players' signatures on mouth-watering contracts, and for the most part Packer's Paratroopers, moving with stealth and speed, were beating Murdoch's Marauders. Crucially, though, they did not have the backing of the International Rugby Union. Considering how little Rugby Union had changed in the 20th century, momentous events were now happening at breakneck speed.

The conflict produced gaping wounds of jealousy and lost friendships as the scramble for ownership of the Union game continued. The game was up when the newspapers in Australia revealed that most of the Wallabies had already signed for Packer. Murdoch, meanwhile, stung into reaction, had been negotiating a secret deal for television rights with the international unions. It was a masterly stroke, but it would require sufficient player backing to succeed. The crucial battleground was South Africa. They had just been crowned World Champions. Peter Fitzsimons explains, 'It was very clear to everybody that whoever controlled the South Africans really controlled world rugby.' On one side was Packer's professional circus and on the other a game funded by Murdoch but still under the control of the individual unions of the rugby-playing countries. Everything hinged on which of the two would receive the backing of François Pienaar and his victorious Springboks. Fitzsimons remarked, 'Pienaar's mobile phone must have been on meltdown.' Pienaar, it was acknowledged, could deliver the players. And he delivered them full square behind Luis Luyt and the South African Football Union. Without South Africa, the WRC was doomed. It would be like having an English premier football league without Manchester United.

Pienaar reportedly received a very generous 'commission' for his efforts.

Meanwhile, in New Zealand, a campaign to get the backing of provincial players for a deal with Murdoch was proving successful. The WRC was top-heavy with leading players, but it was becoming increasingly apparent that rugby was bigger than just a handful of sportsmen. Packer withdrew his financial support and the whole enterprise collapsed, despite attempts to raise money from other sources. Murdoch, if nothing else, could deliver money in wheelbarrows. SANZA, the company that represented the rugby interests of South Africa, New Zealand and Australia, signed a deal with Murdoch for televised rights to a provincial competition, the Super 12s, between the three countries and for the now-famous Tri-Nations annual international tournament. The purchase price was $564 million for ten years, which Peter Fitzsimons, for one, thinks was pretty cheap.

The WRC did a great service to rugby players because their involvement guaranteed that they would receive the lion's share of the television revenue. The top players could look forward to pay cheques on a par with professional footballers. That is not necessarily a good thing, as those not involved in the VIP group have been left struggling. At a meeting in Tokyo in September 1995 the International Rugby Union passed a resolution declaring the game to be 'open' – both amateur and professional. They had been able to offer the players one precious commodity, as well as the prospect of riches, and that was the wearing of an international shirt. The Wallabies, the Springboks and the All Blacks still existed and the World Rugby Corporation ultimately could not compete with 100 years of history.

TWO MODERN PROFESSIONALS:
JONAH LOMU AND JONNY WILKINSON

Rugby in the new professional age became awash with money and with it came the unquenchable thirst for young heroes who could justify the investment of sponsors and television. Two such men were Jonah Lomu and Jonny Wilkinson.

In Jonah Lomu's neighbourhood of south Auckland you had to know how to fight. If you didn't, there would always be someone ready to give you a good hiding. It was a violent culture. Both his uncle and his cousin were stabbed to death in a racially motivated revenge attack. The young Lomu, already oversized for his age, could more than look after himself,

The incomparable Jonah Lomu powers over the line during the All Black thrashing of England in the 1995 World Cup

but even he admits to introducing his fists first and asking questions later. He recalls, 'It reached a point where if anyone looked threateningly at me, I would whack them.' It was very different from his early life on the idyllic, electricity-free Tongan island of Ha'apai, where his parents had moved from Auckland when he was a year old. The young Jonah spent his days on the beach shinning up palm trees to grab coconuts. If he was hungry, there was always a chicken running around to roast over an open fire. On his return to Auckland, Lomu showed every prospect of going off the rails. His devoutly religious parents, worried that he might suffer the same fate as his uncle, packed him off at the age of 13 to Wesley College, a well-known Methodist boarding school near the town of Pukekohe. Within two hours, he was up before the headmaster after 'beating the crap' out of another boy who had called him an insulting name.

From the time he took up rugby, however, Lomu became a radiant example of its ethos which had survived since Victorian times in public-school England, where it was used to channel the energies of aggressive and rowdy schoolboys and turn them into men. Lomu observes, 'Sport is a great way of releasing tension. It's a safety valve. I found mine in rugby. It has given me friends and a lifestyle that I could never have dreamed of as a boy.'

Lomu is not the first rugby star to benefit from having a renowned Rugby Union coach on the teaching staff of his school. The deputy head, Chris Grinter, had coached the New Zealand Secondary Schools team on a tour to success in Japan in 1988. It was an awesome side, containing such future All Blacks as Va'aiga Tuigamala, Craig Innes, John Timu and Walter Little. Grinter quickly spotted the potential of the young giant. Lomu recalls, 'I was playing basketball in the school hall. I was the only one hanging off the basketball hoop and I got into trouble for ripping them off. The next thing I know I was walking out of chapel when Chris Grinter asks me if I fancy a trial for the first XV. I was 13 but I said I'd give it a go, even though I had never played Rugby Union in my life.' Lomu had played Rugby League and that boyhood experience of the rival code served him well. He made the team after just one trial, the youngest ever to do so. At this point in his career, the scourge of England was a prop forward and subsequently a mobile number 8.

By the time he was 18, Lomu was playing in the final of the Hong Kong Sevens in an All Black jersey against the World Champions, Australia. A wild whim from the coach put Lomu out on the wing against the then greatest name in world rugby, David Campese. Lomu, ball clamped to his chest, charged towards the Wallabies' line with just the great

Campo between him and his breakthrough into the big time. He ran over the Australian like a Sherman tank rolling a vintage Mercedes out of the road. Jonah Lomu had arrived. By the time of the third rugby World Cup in 1995, Lomu had made an impact as a formidable sevens player, but in terms of international rugby, he had yet to make a name for himself. After two poor début matches against France in 1994 at the age of 19, he had been dropped and sent back home to learn his trade as a winger. With commercial interests about to ambush the game, Lomu would end the tournament the most famous rugby player in the world. He was a new face and a blank canvas for the world's media. He was different, a man mountain who looked like he could pull a steam train and should have been buried in the pack, yet here he was on the wing. He was coloured, a piquant addition to the first major sporting event in the new democracy of South Africa. Most of all, he made the crowd gasp every time he took the ball.

If one game can make a career, then the World Cup semi-final against England made Jonah Lomu. It guaranteed him untold riches whatever happened in the final. England fans of a sensitive nature will not need reminding. Within 25 minutes, the All Blacks had scored four tries. In the first, Lomu went outside opposing wing Tony Underwood, ignored Will Carling snapping at his ankles and ran straight over Mike Catt on the line. Poor Underwood looked like Gulliver in the land of the Brobdingnag. A battered Carling remarked ruefully, 'Superman on a steamroller would have come off second best.' It was humiliating stuff.

The final was not such a happy affair for the new king of world rugby. South Africa knew he was coming and their superior defensive qualities snuffed out the challenge. The New Zealanders afterwards claimed that they had all been laid low by food poisoning. There's always something. It was a lesson that Lomu would learn again in the future. As an unknown quantity, he was devastating, but when teams realized his capabilities, they could plan to make him less effective. The legacy of his success in the World Cup is that practically every team immediately tried to find wings who could double as front-row forwards.

Lomu himself left South Africa with lucrative deals from Reebok and McDonalds in the back pocket of his manager and partner Phil Kingsley-Jones. Lomu is now a corporate sportsman in the manner of Tiger Woods or Linford Christie. Financially, he is the most successful rugby player of all time. But already his career has been threatened by serious illness, which kept him out of the game in 1997 and allowed him time to sort out his priorities: 'I just wanted to get back playing the game that I loved and to pull on an All Blacks jersey again.'

WALES 32 – ENGLAND 31
WEMBLEY
11 APRIL 1999

*Any second now the referee would blow
the final whistle. England, six points up,
had the Grand Slam in their pockets. Tim
Rodber, who had played another colossal
physical match from second row, conceded
a penalty inside the Welsh half for a
marginally high challenge. A useful touch-
kick from Neil Jenkins saw Wales up to
the England 22, nothing particularly
promising as the Welsh midfield had not
had much success during an afternoon
when only the prodigious boot of Jenkins
had kept them in the hunt. The ball was
spun quickly into the centre where the
powerhouse Scott Gibbs tried one last
lunge at enemy lines. This time he had on*

*his dancing shoes and, to the utter aston-
ishment of England, waltzed past four
defenders to claim a try that will be
talked about in the pubs and clubs of
South Wales for generations to come.*

*It was the third minute of injury time
and England were now just one point
ahead, with a precious two resting on the
conversion attempt from the superlative
Jenkins, who had not missed in seven
previous kicks at goal. But nothing could
match the tension and importance of this
conversion, an easy kick compared to his
earlier touch-line penalty from all of 40
yards into a swirling wind, yet the most
difficult one of the gingertop from*

Welsh centre Scott Gibbs scores the decisive try in the dying seconds to thwart England's Grand Slam

Pontypridd's life. How could anyone watch? He wasted no time. Three steps to the back and one to the side, a well-rehearsed last look at the target and straight through the posts.

Wembley had not witnessed such scenes of pandemonium since Geoff Hurst made sure it was all over in 1966. The soon-to-be-demolished stadium, filling in while Cardiff Arms Park was rebuilt as the Millennium Stadium, became a little piece of Wales that early spring afternoon. Two further gut-wrenching minutes of injury time elapsed before England's misery was complete and Laurence Dallaglio's men slumped on to the hallowed turf, barely able to believe that defeat had been plucked from the jaws of victory. They knew that they should have won comfortably. Despite all their endeavours, Wales were playing catch-up all afternoon. England started the game like a greyhound out of the traps, running in three tries in a frenetic first half which saw them leading 25–18 at half-time. Amazingly, Jonny Wilkinson missed one conversion, but little did the England fans realize then how important that was to become.

After the interval, Wales cut the deficit again thanks to their first try of the game. The normally reliable England flanker Neil Back committed the cardinal sin of an unforced knock-on deep in his own 22. The resulting scrum gave the

Welsh promising ball, and Jenkins' long pass found unmarked full-back Shane Howarth wide on the right. He sprinted over for the score. Jenkins cut the gap to one point with the conversion.
A cautious England surely but steadily pulled away again, thanks to two

Neil Jenkins is a Welsh hero as he kicks the winning points in injury time

The Millennium Stadium in Cardiff, venue for the 1999 Rugby World Cup

penalties from wonderboy Wilkinson, and were grinding out the win. With ten minutes left, Wales conceded a penalty within Wilkinson's range and the Welsh supporters in the crowd groaned, only to breathe a sigh of relief when England captain Dallaglio inexplicably decided not to go for goal. Instead, Mike Catt kicked for touch towards the corner. Later, observers blamed Dallaglio for a crucial tactical error. 'I was surprised,' said Scott Gibbs afterwards. 'We would have needed a converted try and a penalty with time running out. I wouldn't have fancied our chances.' Instead, England left the door ajar and Gibbs thundered through it. To be fair to Dallaglio, it was a stroke of rugby genius which is not seen too often.

England would disagree, but the game of rugby probably derived huge benefit from the Welsh victory. Critics of professional rugby carp that it has taken some of the excitement and unpredictability out of the game. They could have no complaints about this encounter, probably the most exciting match ever between the two great rugby rivals. It gave an enormous boost to the hosts of the fourth World Cup, as well as allowing Scotland just reward for playing the best and most exciting running rugby seen for many a year by claiming the Five Nations trophy. And England? Perhaps they are just too 'professional'.

The name Jonny Wilkinson is a marketing dream. Jonny with no 'h' must be the lead singer of a Brit-pop band. Wilkinson is a gift for headline-writers. 'Wilkinson the Sword' screamed the papers after the 19-year-old sensation had kicked seven out of seven against France at Twickenham in March 1999 as England won easily 21–10. It mattered little that England had managed not one single try against a team that had been leaking them all season. The media, desperate for a new icon since the departure of Will Carling from the rugby pages to the gossip columns and women's magazines, seized on the Newcastle teenager, determined to create a sporting superstar. The formula had worked for Michael Owen in soccer, so why should it not succeed with the equally youthful rugby player?

Wilkinson is the first superstar of the game to be entirely a product of the new professional era. When the game cast off its amateur shackles in 1995, he was a 15-year-old schoolboy at Lord Wandsworth College in Hampshire. By the time he was ready to swap his schoolbooks for the big world, Newcastle were there to groom him for stardom. The club had quickly realized his potential, so much in evidence on the 1997 schools' tour to Australia, where he scored 94 points in five games. It had helped that the Newcastle coach, Steve Bates, was at one time a master at Wilkinson's school. The young man was put into the team alongside the vastly experienced Rob Andrew, one of the great driving forces of professional rugby and player-manager of the club that had been first out of the blocks to sign up big names for big money. After just 58 minutes of senior rugby, he was called up to the England replacements bench for the 1998 game against Scotland.

When Newcastle, backed by the millions of Sir John Hall, rocketed to the top of the rugby tree in England by winning the premiership, Wilkinson was at Andrew's shoulder, learning the tactical side of the game from the master. He wanted to be the play-maker and control the game at fly-half, but even in the age of dominant youth, it is not easy to dislodge one of the greatest players in the game, especially when he's your boss. Wilkinson is

Jonny Wilkinson holds the future of English rugby in his boots

275

not a flashy player, making dazzling breaks like Jeremy Guscott or Gregor Townsend who keep the crowd on the edge of their seats. Instead, his game is founded on a rock-hard defence and intelligent positional play. He is stocky, well balanced and quick off the mark but is never going to outstrip a defence by speed alone. He is also an outstanding goal-kicker and was able to fit comfortably into Andrew's kicking boots when England's most capped fly-half decided he wanted to pass that responsibility on to the younger man.

Under Andrew's direction, Newcastle have become leaders of the professional game in England. His philosophy is very simple: 'This is a professional rugby club.' That principle has cleared away the debris of the old amateur Gosforth club and streamlined a new enterprise clearly aimed at building a successful future. The social 'ten-pints-a-night' sides were the first to go, and the junior teams followed. They can, says Andrew, play that rugby at other clubs. Those other, still amateur, clubs will act as the nursery for the number one club in the area – the Newcastle Falcons. That policy, in terms of rugby, is paying off, with, Andrew says, very successful under-17, under-19 and under-21 sides producing players on the fringes of the first team. He maintains, 'We are interested in getting the very young players to come and see if they can be professional rugby players, but we are doing things differently. We have various cup competitions for schools and clubs and we are spreading the word in a different way.' He helps to arrange training sessions where aspiring youngsters can take part alongside Wilkinson and the fearsome Va'aiga Tuigamala. Other clubs in the area, he believes, can operate the old social side of rugby and then, he hopes, support the area's professional team when they play.

The essential ingredient for the Newcastle strategy is a very large cheque-book. Already they are having to dig deep into their reserves to keep Wilkinson happy. After the French game, his father, who, fortuitously, is a financial consultant, received a flood of offers from potential sponsors hungry to find an English superstar for the flourishing game of television-friendly Rugby Union. Wilkinson is just different enough to fit the bill. He might not have the charisma of Michael Owen, but he is the same age, wears a headband when he plays and, most crucially, kicks left-footed. The last feature may appear a minor consideration, but it makes him stand out in a crowd. His smooth, unruffled method has made the tensest part of the game seem like a picnic. But, like all professionals who make a game seem easy, Wilkinson achieves his success through hours and hours of practice. While his schoolfriends were donning rucksacks to travel the world before starting university, he was out on the pitch slotting home kicks from every angle. It is practice that gives him the peace of mind to assume his on-field responsibilities in such a relaxed and confident manner. He explains, 'For some guys it might take five minutes, but my conscience takes more time to satisfy.'

Wilkinson takes being a professional rugby player very seriously. He confessed to hardly sleeping for three nights before the French game. He is a thinker. The next move will be to fly-half, the position he wants to play both at club and international level. Andrew, mindful of the interest in his protégé from other premiership clubs, has already indicated that he is ready to vacate the number 10 jersey at Newcastle. Wilkinson has the world at his feet, but he is still a young man whose new superstar status could yet go off the rails if England fail to live up to expectations. A cricket score of 58 points in the Five Nations Championship was not enough. The shuddering defeat against Wales in the final match of the 1999 Five Nations tournament shows just how fickle fame can be. Wilkinson missed one kick out of seven and England lost by one point. 'The Wilkinson Sword' was blunted and the next day the papers had eyes only for the Welsh number 10, Neil Jenkins, who kicked eight.

POST-MORTEM

The Union game? Throughout its history rugby has, in reality, been a breeding ground for conflict and division. Now money, as ever, is causing the greatest strife. All the weeping and wailing for the death of the amateur game cuts little ice with those who believe that it is right and just for a man to be paid for the thing he does best in the world. The respected journalist Stephen Jones of the *Sunday Times* observes, 'I think a lot of people who propounded amateurism were delighted to do so on salaries of £100,000 a year.' Jones is right. It's easy being an amateur if you're already rich. Unfortunately, the question of money is only one element of being amateur. Respected voices in the game are worried that the community spirit that rugby has so often helped to foster will be lost in a professional age. It will be truly ironic if the most élitist of games continues its exclusivity into the 21st

Previous pages: The awesome Va-aiga Tuigamala scythes through the St Helens defence in his Rugby League days with Wigan, prior to his return to Newcastle and the Union game

Scotland take time out in front of the Lloyds Bank/TSB logo – the sponsors of the Five Nations Championship

century not on the basis of class, education and tradition, but on the basis of money. The lesson is clear in the example of Association Football. Success equals money, equals best players, equals more success, equals more money... recurring. Manchester United and Arsenal are the living proof. The most successful professional rugby clubs in England will play in the European Cup competition and so get a share of a huge pool, perhaps as much as £1 million, which will enable them to pull away from the pack. Clubs, such as Saracens and Newcastle, are reaping the consequence of this characteristic of modern sport, where other famous clubs, such as Bristol and Moseley, are going to the wall. The great Gosforth has been confined to the scrap-heap by the new Newcastle Falcons, a name with all the allure of a second-rate ice hockey outfit.

As journalist and commentator Chris Rea observes, 'When money comes into the equation it is inevitable that the top of the game tends to become divorced from the bottom.' Already the number of rugby players in England has dropped by 20 per cent since the advent of professionalism. Former Wallaby Peter Fitzsimons fears that rugby's unique quality as a sport for everyone may be lost. 'The great thing about rugby is that it will give you a game if you are fat, if you are thin, if you are ugly, if you are good-looking, if you are fast, if you are slow. Rugby has always said, "Come and play because we have got a game for you." Anybody can play. If you never get your knees dirty, you can play on the wing.'

The Union game has reacted to professionalism by spending like an over-enthusiastic lottery winner. Players have been overpaid by money men anxious to secure early advantage. The leading players are on more than £200,000 a year. It is all very different from the days when Bill McLaren played for Hawick and the players considered it their lucky day if there was carbolic soap for the post-match bath.

Rugby is now a global multi-million pound sport. It is a product to be picked up, paid for and consumed as if on display in a supermarket. Although the southern hemisphere countries, with their more enlightened attitude to change and the market forces that dictate modern sport than their northern counterparts, have been better prepared, there is no reason why the game universally should not go from strength to strength when the euphoria of becoming a million-pound business has worn off and the cold reality of proper organization and book-balancing comes into effect. At the end of the day, rugby is not the possession of Rupert Murdoch or any other tycoons who now run the premier clubs. Nor has it been sold to the players. The deeds of ownership have passed to the public and they will decide its future. If they do not go and watch the game in its stadiums, if they don't turn on their television sets to watch the Super 12s or the new Six Nations Championship, the sport will die. The public have made a huge investment in rugby and it is up to the game itself to bring a satisfactory return on that investment by continuing to be a great and entertaining sport.

Is there anything worth saving from the amateur carcass? The sense of national pride that rugby has brought to countries like New Zealand, Wales and South Africa will continue whether the game is amateur or professional. The famous jerseys will not change, although these days supporters might have to get used to seeing the name of Vodafone or Reebok next to the national emblem. But just look at tennis players, golfers, skiers, Grand Prix racing drivers and footballers. This is the way it is and it hardly spoils enjoyment. There's no need for team spirit and camaraderie to disappear. Players do not have to go out and sink ten pints of bitter to play for each other and want to win. With luck, the leading players of today's generation will not have to drop everything to go war.

That leaves community spirit and this is where rugby must fight tooth and nail to retain some of the amateur values. Throughout rugby's history, it has brought communities together. How can that continue if clubs are playing in different countries or at stadiums miles away from the communities whose name they still bear? The Saturday culture which made the Union Game the focus of a community's life in New Zealand in the 1950s has inevitably been lost forever. Television will have won if dads prefer to settle down and watch a meaningless game on the telly instead of going down to their local town's pitch, standing frozen to the bone to cheer on their team. It would be a disaster for rugby if a meaningless game of Australian Sevens became more important in the life of the Welsh valleys than the local derby game between Blaengarw and Nantymoel.

BIBLIOGRAPHY AND SOURCES

Television scripts by Dai Smith. Additional work by Phil George, Daffyd Llŷr James, John Jenkins and Gareth Williams.

1. THE CLASS GAME

Barnes, Stuart, *Smelling of Roses*, Mainstream, 1994

Carling, Will, *Captain's Diary*, Chatto & Windus, 1991

Carling, Will, *My Autobiography*, Hodder & Stoughton, 1998

Esbeck, Edmund van, *The Story of Irish Rugby*, Stanley Paul, 1986

Golesworthy, Maurice, *Encyclopedia of Rugby Union*, Robert Hale, 1976

Holt, Richard, *Sport and the British: A Modern History*, Oxford University Press, 1989

Keating, Frank, *Up and Under*, Hodder & Stoughton, 1983

Macrory, Jennifer, *Running with the Ball – The Birth of Rugby Football*, Collins Willow, 1991

McLaren, Bill, *Talking of Rugby*, Stanley Paul, 1991

Morgan, Cliff, with Nicholson, Geoffrey, *Beyond the Fields of Play*, Hodder & Stoughton 1996

Owen, O.L., *The History of the Rugby Football Union*, Playfair, 1955

Quinn, Keith, *Encyclopedia of World Rugby*, Lochar Publishing, 1991

Reason, John, 'Wales Make Sure of Grand Slam', the *Sunday Telegraph*, 28 March 1971

Reason, John, 'Scotland Find Crowning Glory', the *Sunday Telegraph*, 18 March 1990

Smith, Dai, and Williams, Gareth, *Fields of Praise*, University of Wales Press, 1980

Tuck, Jason, 'Patriots, Barbarians, Gentlemen and Players: Rugby Union and National Identity in Britain since 1945', from *One Day in Leicester*, Chris Hart (ed.), 2nd Journal Sports Historians, 1996

Williams, Gareth, *1905 and All That*, Gomer Press, 1991

Williams, Gareth, 'Rugby Union' from *Sport in Britain: A Social History*, Tony Mason (ed.), Cambridge University Press, 1989

Television interviews

John, Barry, *In Conversation with Dai Smith*, BBC Wales, 1999

Chandler, Tim, School of Exercise, Leisure and Sport, Kent State University, USA

Collini, Stefan, Clare College, Cambridge

Collins, Tony, International Centre for Sports History and Culture, De Montfort University, Leicester

Holt, Richard, International Centre for Sports History and Culture, De Montfort University, Leicester

Macrory, Jennifer, former librarian and archivist, Rugby School Museum

McLaren, Bill, broadcaster

O'Leary, Paul, University of Wales, Aberystwyth

Smith, Dai, head of broadcasting (English Language), BBC Wales

Sugden, John, Chelsea School, University of Brighton

Williams, Gareth, University of Wales, Aberystwyth

2. THE EMPIRE GAME

Carling, Will, *My Autobiography*, Hodder & Stoughton, 1998

Howitt, Bob, *New Zealand Rugby Greats*, Hodder Moa Beckett, 1997

Jones, Stephen, 'One Team, One Nation, One Kick', *The Sunday Times*, 25 June 1995

Macdonald, Finlay, *The Game of Our Lives*, Penguin New Zealand, 1996

Mason, John, 'Kirk Faces New Missions', the *Sunday Telegraph*, 21 June 1987

McIlvanney, Hugh, 'South Africa Heals the Scars', *The Sunday Times*, 25 June 1995

McLean, T.P., *The All Blacks*, Sidgwick & Jackson, 1991

Nauright, John, *Sport, Cultures and Identities in South Africa*, Leicester University Press, 1997

Nauright, John, and Chandler, Timothy J.L., *Making Men*, Frank Cass, 1996

Parker, A.C., *The Springboks 1891–1970*, Cassell, 1970

Reason, John, 'All Blacks Take Prize in Last Kick Lottery', the *Sunday Telegraph*, 13 September 1981

Stent, R.K., *Green and Gold*, Longman, Green and Co., 1954

Television interviews

Bedford, Tommy, South Africa, 1963–71

Dobson, Paul, historian, author and former referee

Jabaar, Cassiem, South African Rugby Union (SARU)

Kirkpatrick, Ian, South Africa, 1953–61

Laidlaw, Chris, New Zealand, 1964–70

Lange, David, prime minister of New Zealand, 1984–9

Lochore, Brian, New Zealand, 1964–71

Lomu, Jonah, New Zealand, 1994–

Meads, Colin, New Zealand, 1957–71

Mourie, Graham, New Zealand 1977–82

Nauright, John, Department of Human Movement Studies, Queensland University

Odendaal, Andre, curator, Robben Island Museum, South Africa, years?

Phillips, Jock, chief historian, New Zealand Department of Internal Affairs

Plessis, Morne du, South Africa, 1970–80

QeQe, Dan, former Kwazakele representative

Richards, Trevor, founder member, Halt All Racist Tours (HART)
Starke, James, South Africa, 1956
Tobias, Errol, South Africa, 1981–4
Tshwete, Steve, minister for sport, South Africa, 1994–9, minister for safety and security 1999–
Watson, Cheeky, former player, Junior Springboks, and Kwazakele Rugby Union (KWARU) representative
Williams, Bryan, New Zealand, 1970–78

3. THE ADOPTED GAME

Dine, Philip, *Money, Identity and Conflict: Rugby League in France*, British Society of Sports History, 1996
Herd, Michael, 'French Football United in Hate', the London *Evening Standard*, 15 April 1999
Holt, Richard, 'Sport, the French and the Third Republic', *Journal of Modern and Contemporary France*, August 1988
Mason, John, 'French Champagne Puts World Cup on the Road', the *Daily Telegraph*, 15 June 1987
Terret, Thierry, *Learning to Be a Man: French Rugby and Masculinity at the Beginning of the Century*, translated by Karen Tucker

Television interviews

Albaladejo, Pierre, France, 1954–64
Benazzi, Abdelatif, France, 1990–97
Blanco, Serge, France, 1980–91
Bodis, Jean-Pierre, University of Pau
Boniface, André, France, 1954–66
Celaya, Michel, France, 1953–61
Dine, Phil, Department of European Studies, Loughborough University
Fassolette, Robert, Rugby League historian
Ferasse, Albert, president, French Rugby Union

Fouroux, Jacques, France, 1972–7
Holt, Richard, International Centre for Sports History and Culture, De Montfort University, Leicester
Lanfranchi, Pierre, Department of History, De Montfort University, Leicester
Prat, Jean, France, 1945–55
Spanghero, Walter, France, 1964–73

4. THE NEW GAME

Adair, Daryl, and Vamplew, Wray, *Sport in Australian History*, Oxford University Press, 1997
Armstrong, Robert, 'England Stunned as Jenkins Snatches Last-gasp Victory, the *Guardian*, 12 April 1999
Jackson, Peter, 'Andrew Will Give up His Fly-half Role', the *Daily Mail*, 24 March 1999
Jackson, Peter, 'Dallaglio Blunder Cost You the Lot, Clive', the *Daily Mail*, 13 April 1999
Keating, Frank, 'Jenkins Lands a Fitting and Final Blow, the *Guardian*, 12 April 1999
Norrie, David, 'Hero Jonny Puts Boot In', the *News of the World*, 21 March 1999
Phillips, Murray G., 'Rugby', from Vamplew, Wray, and Stoddart, Brian, *Sport in Australia: A Social History*, Cambridge University Press 1994
Pienaar, François, 'All-round General Needs Pivotal Role', the *Sunday Telegraph*, 21 March 1999
Reason, John, 'Solid Yellow Brick Wall', the *Sunday Telegraph*, 3 November 1991
Slot, Owen, 'Wilkinson Ready to Call the Shots', the *Sunday Telegraph*, 28 March 1999

Television interviews

Andrew, Rob, England, 1985–95
Burns, Gill, England captain, Women's Rugby World Cup, 1999
Burton, Mike, England, 1972–8
Campese, David, Australia, 1982–95
Catchpole, Ken, Australia, 1961–8
Ella, Mark, Australia, 1980–84
Fitzsimons, Peter, Australia, 1984–90
Griffith, Edward, chief executive, South African Rugby Union (SARFU), 1994–6
Hickey, Tom, rugby historian
Hobbs, Jock, New Zealand, 1983–86
Jameson, Neil, Gosforth Rugby Football Club
Jones, Stephen, *The Sunday Times*
Kearns, Phil, Australia, 1989–
Lewis, Wally, Australia (Rugby League), 1981–91
McMillan, Russell, chief executive, M-Net Television
O'Reilly, Tony, Ireland, 1955–70
Phillips, Murray, University of South Australia
Pugh, Vernon, chairman, International Rugby Board
Rea, Chris, journalist and broadcaster
Short, John, Gosforth Rugby Football Club
Slack, Andy, Australia, 1978–87
Smith, Simon, chairman, Gosforth Rugby Football Club
Thorburn, Brian, marketing executive, Australian Rugby Union
Turnbull, Ross, Australia, 1968, and former agent, World Rugby Corporation
Watkins, David, Wales, 1963–7
Williams, J.P.R., Wales, 1969–81

INDEX